A HANDBOOK

OF

SUGGESTIVE THERAPEUTICS, APPLIED HYPNOTISM, PSYCHIC SCIENCE.

BY

HENRY S. MUNRO, M. D.

AMERICUS, GEORGIA.

SECOND EDITION.

C. V. MOSBY
Medical Book and Publishing Company,

ST. LOUIS.

1908.

PRESS OF
SECURITY PRINTING CO.
OF ST. LOUIS

SUGGESTIVE THERAPEUTICS
APPLIED HYPNOTISM
PSYCHIC SCIENCE

To the Memory of My Mother

whose beautiful example and most frequent
suggestion, "Be sure you are right and then go
ahead," has given to my life whatever
dynamic quality characterizes this book.

PREFACE.

I **bring to** the consideration of the medical profession not merely the facts of personal experience and clinical evidence as proof of the value of suggestive therapeutics in the general practice of medicine, but also a **detailed explanation of how to apply suggestion efficaciously,** both with and without hypnotism as a therapeutic adjunct. I give in explanation of those facts, experience and clinical tests as interpreted in the light of modern scientific knowledge.

Many volumes have been written upon this subject by neurologists, scientists, and phsychotherapeutists of note, but in most cases they lack the practicability so essential to its successful employment by the general practitioner. My aim is to emphasize the value of suggestive therapeutics in a field of work that comes within his domain, which has not heretofore been pointed out by the authors of other works of this character. The presentation also embodies what I have assimilated and found practical from a careful study of the investigations of leading authorities on this subject. To make this book practical and easy of assimilation has been my constant aim. And here it may fitly be pointed out, with a view to forestalling criticism, that this book is not intended principally, or even mainly, for neurologists and psychotherapeutists, to whom the constant repetition of what to them are well known facts must inevitably prove wearisome. It is intended rather to instill into the vast mass of the profession to whom this entire field is as yet *terra incognita,* those basic principles of physiological psychology upon which the scientific therapeutic application of suggestion in all its forms necessarily depends. With that end in view, principles of all pervading importance are iterated and reiterated as often as their application comes under consideration, in order that they may become so fully absorbed and assimilated as to be almost axiomatic to the reader.

To hundreds of American physicians I am indebted for many kindly criticisms and valuable suggestions concerning my lectures and demonstrations, which have been of invaluable aid in laying the foundation for this work. I also desire to acknowledge the valuable assistance rendered by Dr. K. W. Millican of Chicago and Dr. C. R. Lightner of St. Louis in the review of the manuscript for the press, etc.

HENRY S. MUNRO.

AMERICUS, GEORGIA.

PREFACE TO SECOND EDITION.

The author is profoundly grateful to the Medical Profession for the kindly reception accorded the first edition of this book. The exhaustion of a large edition since its appearance nine months ago attests its popularity.

The practability and efficacy of Suggestive Therapeutics, as an adjunct in the treatment of disease, is no longer questioned by physicians who have personally tested the methods herein advocated.

The present edition has a more complete index and has been brought up to date by the addition of new material on those phases of the subject upon which advancement has been made during the past year.

H. S. MUNRO.

ELLAVILLE, GA.

CONTENTS.

———————◆———————

[2]

INTRODUCTION.

It would be superfluous here to do more than briefly allude to the conditions under which this book was written. **The problems of Psychotherapy** are forcing themselves so strongly upon the attention of the medical profession that I do not think that any experience that may throw light upon them should be withheld. About fifteen years ago, while a general practitioner of medicine, I became impressed with the great importance of properly directing the **psychic factor in therapeutics,** and for several years groped in the dark in search of ideas, with such aids as could be gained from the older writers on hypnotism and allied subjects.

Quite an impetus to my efforts was received during a three months' stay in New York twelve years ago, in the personalities of well-known men in the schools of postgraduate instruction in that city, but the far-reaching influence of suggestion or the **personal influence of the physician** as a therapeutic aid in the general practice of medicine was not even faintly appreciated by the profession at that time.

About seven years ago I became convinced that the general profession should have a better understanding of the theory and efficacy of suggestive therapeutics and a knowledge of the practical methods of its administration; and being fully satisfied that the methods which I had **successfully employed in general practice** for several years would be of practical value to all physicians, as an addition to their therapeutic armamentarium, and believing also that this knowledge would be a means by which they could successfully combat the enormous increase in all the forms of quackery which were at that time springing up as the natural offspring of the rapid evolution in psychological development, I began going from city to city, giving a lecture on suggestive therapeutics, applied hypnotism, and physhic science, limiting my classes exclusively to the medical profession.

The cordial reception and appreciation accorded me in this self-chosen field of endeavor by the more representative portion of the medical profession was beyond my most sanguine expectations, and in all places that I visited the physicians taking my lesson insisted that it be put into a permanent form, to be used by them for future reference.

I was **not yet ready to commit myself** to writing upon this much mooted and misunderstood subject. Within the last seven years, however, the attitude taken by the larger part of the medical profession in regard to the influence of the mind over the body has considerably changed. **The study of psychology** with laboratory instruments and methods has demonstrated the relation between thought and matter in a most convincing manner.

Monism, a philosophy which amalgamates or unifies the two entities called mind and matter, is becoming more popular. **Physiology, psychology** and **biology** are on friendly terms, and harmoniously laboring to solve the problems that are being forced upon all thinking people, as well as physicians.

In contemplating my venture of seven years ago, I now fully appreciate the trite saying of Pope, that "Fools rush in where angels fear to tread." **Be that as it may,** I have been in association with those of the profession who have studied Psychotherapeutics **in all parts of the world,** and they have made no hesitancy in saying that I had boiled down and crystallized the subject into a readily assimilable and excellent form for practical clinical use. So now, after enjoying the confidence and appreciation of the medical profession as a student and teacher of Psychotherapy, I should deem myself reprehensible and cowardly did I not give my "mite" to help those who need strengthening on this line of advanced professional equipment.

The strong prejudice and open opposition to the free investigation and employment of Psychotherapeutics has exerted an overmastering **influence upon the minds** of many of the members of the medical profession, and many there are who lack the courage and moral stamina to enter this field and employ its truths for the relief of countless thousands of individuals who do not need medicine or surgery, yet are vainly crying to us for help. **While this state of apathy exists** in the ranks of the medical profession, the popular "ists" and "paths" and other disguises are standing with open arms beckoning these discontented and unfortunate ones to come into their ranks and get their Psychotherapy in a placebo capsule of religious dogma or bonepath massage.

I am also fully aware that it is not good policy for one seeking popularity to speak out frankly and honestly upon this subject and tell the truth. Even physicians in many instances who admit that they have made no effort to comprehend the principles of Psychotherapy and apply them as a therapeutic adjunct, feel that any theory or conception or method that does not conform to their preconceived ideas, however worn out, moth-eaten and useless, is an insult to their intelligence. Yet, in spite of my **well grounded and justifiable** apprehensions, I now dare to offer this little volume containing ideas, impressions and opinions, based upon conscientious observation, demonstration, tests, and clinical evidence, on the one hand and upheld by the more enlightened element of the medical profession in the leading cities that I have visited, on the other, **perfectly willing** to be ridiculed by those desiring to do so. If I succeed in convincing some part of the profession of the justice of the cause which I defend, and at the same time give others the opportunity of discussing it **with a thorough knowledge of the facts** upon which it is based, this alone will justify me in having undertaken the preparation of this little handbook.

It is not my desire to oppose any system of therapeutics, but to emphasize the importance **of the mental factor** in health and disease, and to point out practical methods that can be applied by the general practitioner as an adjunct to his therapeutic resources.

I fully realize that the ideas herein expressed will be of value only to those who find in themselves that inexplicable psychic response, which amounts to a conviction as regards the truth of the principles elucidated, sufficient to dispel the general unconcerned apathy or half-hearted uncertainty toward the practicability of these methods.

It has been my privilege to get in close touch with my colleagues in towns and cities, in private practice and in hospitals. Here I have studied their problems and been uplifted and inspired by their courage and devotion to their work, and have learned to honor and reverence character, manifested in the personality of a physician, as second to nothing in life. In their homes, in their conveyances, in the sick room, and in their private office work, as well as in hospitals and medical societies and colleges, I have been given a cordial welcome, and here I desire to **express again my profound gratitude** for such attentions by turning this little book over to them as a grateful reminder of bygone pleasant relations.

CHAPTER I.

HYPNOTISM OR SUGGESTION?

Hypnotism is the art of persuading an individual to **act upon or execute an idea or a series of ideas,** either consciously or subconsciously. The condition is brought about by suggestion. Thus defined and regarded in the light of present day knowledge, the term has a **significance entirely different** from that generally believed by investigators of twenty years ago.

The hypnotic or suggestive condition is induced with the consent and co-operation of the subject brought under any person's influence, or it is accomplished by playing upon his or her ignorant credulity. **The educational methods in vogue** at the present time in our schools and colleges are bringing to bear upon the minds of our youth the same methods that are adopted when we hypnotize an individual, having first secured his intelligent attention and active co-operation.

The more intelligent person always makes the best subject, just as the best minds take an education—another form of suggestion—more readily. **In both education and moral teaching** the individual is induced or instructed **to act upon or execute an idea or series of ideas,** in order that his life and conduct may be brought under their influence. **All knowledge** on any line is the result of assimilated ideas, and its value is in direct ratio to the extent to which these ideas are acted upon or executed. **The orator or actor** who sways his audience with emotion from tears to laughter is in the truest sense using hypnotism or suggestion. **The mob leader,** blood-thirsty and murder bent, carries his crowd at the point of emotion in the same way.

From this more modern conception of the meaning of hypnotism, **we all use it unconsciously** every day of our lives, both upon ourselves and upon others. The successful men in every community are those who are persuading others **to act upon or execute their ideas.** This is true of men in all professions and all occupations and branches of trade or commerce. Physicians are no longer afraid to enter the field of physiological psychology and appropriate its truths as therapeutic aids. The possibilities and advantages to be derived from a knowledge of Psychotherapy are appreciated today as never before in the world's history.

In the following pages I expect to lead the reader to see this subject as I see it, and to be persuaded **to act upon a series of ideas and execute them** in relation to his patients in a way that will assist him to help them to get well.

By the use of suggestive therapeutics, results can be obtained where drugs, surgery and other methods of treatment are inadequate. The reading of this book alone by many of your patients will give them all the suggestion needed to relieve certain psychopathic conditions. Our more intelligent patients **have a right** to be taken into our confidence. Many of them are assuming that right and desire to know, aye, they demand that you tell them, why you are adopting a special method of treatment. They want to know what you are giving them and what is to be expected from such measures.

In numerous instances after getting well *en rapport* with my patients, I have educated them into the principles of psycho-therapy and turned them away from my care **stronger men or women,** feeling that they no longer need rely upon a physician. Through getting possession of him I have put him in possession of himself. We cannot do our best for our patients without taking into consideration the **higher evolutionary elements of human personality,** call them psychic, mental, intellectual, moral, or spiritual, as you choose.

We are on the threshold of a great awakening to a conscious realization of **a higher conception of our duty** toward our patients and our privileges as physicians. By degrees, step by step, slowly but surely, are we getting away from the superstition that has so long darkened our conception of life. From the time **the little** *amoeba* began to develop by sucking into its jelly self nutriment from the water around it; from the time its little jelly cousin, **the** *moneron,* put out his first pseudopodium, there began the journey toward and the feeling out after a higher conception of life. Long and tedious has been the way, slow and painful has been the ascent from darkness to light. **The law of evolution** in even the lower realm or sphere of life has never mocked an *amoeba* or a *moneron.* The faculties back of the *amoeba* and *moneron* realm whereby they found what they reached out after were no more natural than those that move us to seek a higher conception of life. **The infant** reaches out hand and mouth for food; it is there. The real man, the higher self which is here in a material nursery, **is in the infant stage of** existence—it seeks to manifest itself in a truer sense. If the little *amoeba* was not mocked, shall he be?

I am a confirmed optimist, it is true, but **in the light of present day knowledge** we are warranted in having a high degree of optimism in regard to the laws of heredity and training. Where there was once an overpowering sense of the infallibility, inexorableness and certainty, of what was called law—of the absolute dependence of phenomena of all sorts, including the supreme one of will, upon visible, tangible, **material elements in the physical body** and its activities—there is now a growing consciousness of self-activity and freedom. **Pessimism as a philosophy** has not the sway that it had yesterday, and we are dwelling more and more upon the will and its privileges as a basis of character and health. We now realize that the mind helps the body as much as the body helps the mind, that both mind and body constitute a manifestation of **the real self in action,** and that every human being has within him an inherent quality of force that he can use for his welfare and happiness.

It may be that the light upon the landscape of the future is but a reflection from the luminous regions of my own hopes, but if we take into consideration **the broader and higher course of human events,** such as the work done by the medical profession in problems of social vice, intemperance, hygiene, dietetics and preventive medicine, sanitation, pure food, etc., we can but feel that we are at last coming to a conscious realization of **a lofty ideal of the brotherhood of man,** and that the day is not remote when the physicians will be found doing all within their power to help their patients to help themselves.

It is now believed by advanced thinkers who have gotten over the stunned and stunning stages of **the light that evolution has shed upon us,** that some individuals of all races have not reached the point of development where the self-conscious ego is capable of taking their lives into their own hands. It is quite likely that this is true. Such people will be helpless dependents upon others to think and do for them as long as they live. There can be **no higher function of a physician** than that of getting such patients to act upon an idea or series of ideas and execute them consciously or subconsciously, in order that their lives may be brought under its influence, and health and happiness be maintained.

The following pages will serve **to illustrate and explain** the position I have taken. I could easily fill this volume with the reports of cases furnishing clinical evidence of the value of Psychotherapy in the routine work of the general practitioner and specialist, but I am fully aware that, after I have elucidated principles and described technique and methods of application, each reader must adapt these principles to **his own personality.**

CHAPTER II.

NOMENCLATURE DEFINED.

By Suggestive Therapeutics, or Psychotherapy, is meant mental influences in the treatment of disease, as applied both with or without hypnotism, with the definite understanding that **any influences** brought to bear upon the mind of the patient, e. g., the impressiveness of the modern static electric machine, the crudest device of the charlatan, including all such methods as are employed by christian scientists, osteopaths, magnetic healers, and divine healers, as well as the influence **exerted in any way** by the personality of the physician in words of encouragement, reasoning, persuasion, advice, etc., **all come under the broad domain** of Suggestive Therapeutics.

Any mode of influence exerted by a human being by any means whatsoever for therapeutic purposes conforms to the same general law. When we understand Suggestive Therapeutics we know the why of all the cures brought about by all so-called mysterious methods in both ancient and modern times. **The miracle of the past** is the fact of today, and what was regarded in ancient times as a miracle was a result of the employment of some law at that time, and perhaps even now, not understood.

Suggestive Therapeutics is the only form of mental therapeutics that is **based upon scientific principles,** and is not in open opposition to other rational therapeutic measures. It is regarded simply as **a therapeutic resource** and not as a complete system of medicine, though with it cures can often be brought about **where other methods have failed** and even when used alone, other therapeutic measures will frequently be unnecessary.

In Suggestive Therapeutics, or Psychotherapy, we make use of hypnotism. By the aid of hypnotism it is possible to exert a greater influence upon the mind of the patient than can be done through any other agency. But suggestion is of great value in the treatment of disease without the aid of the deeper suggestive condition called the hypnotic state, By suggestion in that state, or in that suggestible condition known as the hypnotic state, however, results can be obtained that cannot be obtained by suggestion without that condition. I have demonstrated and proved that proposition to **several thousand American physicians,** and I confidently expect the facts set forth and demonstrated here to remove the least shadow of doubt from the reader's mind upon this question. Simple suggestion, however, will be used ten times in the practice of medicine for each occasion on which it will be necessary to resort to actual hypnotism. Yet I insist that it is the **same treatment in kind,** with a difference only in degree as regards results. By the aid of hypnotic suggestion results are obtainable that cannot be obtained in the general practice of medicine in any other way.

H y p n o t i s m D e f i n e d .—**Hypnotism,** as we saw in the last chapter, is nothing more than the getting an individual to **act upon or execute an idea or a series of ideas,** either consciously or subconsciously. Whenever an individual can be induced **to act upon a suggestion** in any department of life in that sense, then he is, strictly speaking, hypnotized; but for our **present purposes,** let us regard hypnotism as being the induction of a mental and physical condition in which the subject is **more amenable or susceptible** to suggestion at the hands of another, and possesses an increased ability to carry out that suggestion. In this condition **a greater influence** can be exerted over the mind and body of the patient. It is the induction of a suggestible condition. By suggestion in the hypnotic state, powers and potentialities lying dormant and unused in the patient can be brought into play. A consciousness of those potentialities can be awakened in him. He is thus introduced to a new element in his own life, be it physical, mental or intellectual, or moral, and that can be accomplished by suggestion for the patient which cannot be done by any other means.

The cases reported by Dubois, which he describes in high-sounding, neurological phraseology, are just such cases as compose nine-tenths of the work of every general practitioner in the United States; and there are thousands and thousands of American physicians who have not one-fourth the verbosity wherewith to describe it who are using their own individual methods of Psychotherapy in this class of cases with equally good success. We all use suggestive therapeutics every day of our lives, either consciously or unconsciously.

I desire to introduce you to **a higher conception of this subject,** one that is distinctly American, one that has **struck a responsive chord** in the character of the more enlightened element of the American profession, hundreds and hundreds of whom have studied this subject in Europe and have witnessed European methods of applying suggestive therapeutics.

Suggestion Defined.—You have no doubt observed that I use the terms "hypnotism" and "suggestion" **as synonymous terms.** Any idea or hint or intelligence or impression made upon the mind of an individual is a suggestion. Usually, however, when we use the term suggestion, we mean an **oral** suggestion. So to make myself clear I will define suggestion to mean **what you say** to your patient, and **the way in which you say it.** It embraces everything in the personality of the physician and his conduct in the sick room.

Suggestive Therapeutics, then, is the **sum total of the influence** exerted by the physician on his patient to help him toward recovery, or for the relief of any mental or physical symptoms of whatever kind; and, as we shall see later, this is always accomplished through the **normal physiological processes.**

Pardon me for being so explicit, almost prolix, in the definition of terms, but I desire thus to make plain my point of view of this subject at the outset, and at the same time to utter a protest against **the lack of moral courage** that some individuals have assumed toward hypnotism and suggestion, while attempting to hypnotize or suggest the profession into believing that they use an entirely different method and employ neither hypnotism nor suggestion!

It is the duty of every physician who is true to his Hippocratic oath to adopt and use every measure that will alleviate human suffering. A little deception in one sense is used as a therapeutic measure **by all physicians,** and anyone who denies this is yet in the embryonic stage of his appreciation of the psychological factor in therapeutics. But it should be expected

[3]

of medical men, in discussing means to secure an end for the greatest good of their patients, **to be absolutely honest with each other,** as becomes men who are members of a high and noble profession.

"**Psychotherapy** is **suggestive therapeutics,** and it is applied in many different ways according to the requirements of each individual case," as Forel concisely remarks.

Pre-Hypnotic Suggestion.—Prehypnotic **suggestion** is the mental preparation of the patient to be hypnotized.

So much which would have the effect of **prejudicing the lay mind against its employment** has been done and said and written upon hypnotism in the evolution of this subject, through the ignorance and superstition of the last one hundred years, that you will find that the best results will be obtained when you conceal from the patient the fact that you are using hypnotism or suggestive measures, until after you have obtained therapeutic results. **Then you may explain** what you are doing and why, and the patient will appreciate your efforts. In some cases I make no explanation because the patient is incapable of understanding it. **There is a prejudice, a fear, an antipathy,** a skepticism, toward the use of hypnotism in the minds of some of the laity to such an extent that you will succeed with suggestive measures just in proportion as you cover them up with some other name or theory, **as is done by the christian scientist, the osteopath, the magnetic healer, the religious revivalist, the patent medicine vendor and the health food manufacturer.**

CHAPTER III.

HYPNOTISM DEMONSTRATED.

I will describe to you now a method which I have used in connection with my class work with physicians on **nearly four thousand subjects,** with the result that practically every one who gave his consent and co-operation was hypnotized, without failure, I am sure, in one per cent of the cases.

Instead of appearing to use hypnotism in the presence of the physicians on the individuals brought in for demonstrations, we use a medicine in a bottle, one of the local antiseptic solutions, and call this medicine **"Somno-Analgesic Compound."** We ascribe to this medicine whatever value or therapeutic property we desire it to possess, and **picture on the mind** of the individual what effect it will have, and getting his consent for us to use the medicine, we secure all the co-operation necessary on the part of the subject to put him into that suggestible condition which **is produced by suggestion** and known as the hypnotic state—the most unfortunate term, so far as the successful application of suggestive therapeutics is concerned, that could ever have been devised.

Some people will let a "medicine" put them to sleep, quiet them, influence them, relieve their pain, even though it be only **a little bottle of pure water** that we call "Somno-Analgesic Compound," but they are alarmed at the bare idea of hypnotism or suggestion. **They will stand for Dubois** to use his "moral orthopaedia," "reasoning," "persuasion," etc., while he unconsciously hypnotizes them into **acting upon an idea or series of ideas,** and executing them both consciously and subconsciously, as his reports show. People who will not stand to have the truth explained when one attempts to show them that **all forms of mental therapeutics** are based on sound, sensible, rational principles of physiology and psychology, will allow **the christian science teaching** to hypnotize them into an attitude of denial of pain, sickness, and death, on the one hand, and into a mental attitude of affirmation, iteration and expectancy of health and happiness on the other. **A very excellent form of suggestion** they have, based on a theory that is one-half truth only, but with that one-half truth they get results.

If you were to ask me **how to make a suggestion,** I would say, "In a perfectly natural way of talking, with the least affectation possible." If you in the least doubt your ability to use the method which will be explained to you here, **be actor enough** to speak and act as if you had not the slightest doubt about the results to be obtained. **Talk as if you meant it,** talk calmly, earnestly and kindly. Use a monotone voice. Look at your patient while you are talking to him. Look right into his eyes and get him to look at you.

The following demonstrations and explanations were stenographically reported showing in detail my method of demonstrating hypnotism in my class work among the physicians. There were **present several well-known physicians** who took part in the demonstration described, who will vouch for the correctness of the incidents here reported.

When we were ready for material for the demonstrations of hypnotism, **two of the physicians** present were requested to **go out on the street** and bring in two or three men who were absolute strangers to us all.

The method here described demonstrates a simple, practical, efficacious method of inducing the hypnotic state to the extent that anaesthesia can be produced, and **each one of the several physicians** present demonstrated his own ability to do so, using an entirely new subject, brought in from the street, whom we had never seen before. **The physicians bringing in the men** obtained for demonstration purposes were requested to seat them in the ante-room. One of them was brought into the room at a time, to be hypnotized, and as he walked in at the door I addressed him as follows: (Take note that the medicine used upon this occasion was only a small vial of water.)

A Pre-Hypnotic Suggestion Given.—"Take **this chair, please.** Now, I will explain to you what I am doing and what I wanted with you. Do you see this little bottle of medicine? This is a sample of a preparation that I am introducing to the physicians, known as "Somno-Analgesic Compound." "Somno" means sleep producing, and "analgesic" means pain relieving; so, then, this is sleep-producing and pain-relieving medicine. It is used by rubbing it on the forehead just as you see me rub it on mine. You notice it does not harm me and it will not harm you. Now, I have explained to the physicians here that, in order for this remedy to have its effect, it must be applied in a certain way, and that **it is the way that we get our patient to do and be** while the medicine is applied,

Fig. 1.

A Condition of Voluntary Receptivity.

Before beginning suggestions to induce hypnosis, after giving pre-hypnotic suggestions, have your patient relax every muscle, close his eyes lightly and breath through his mouth, as illustrated in the above cut.

that determines its effect. I want you to take a seat in this chair, lean your head back against the wall, relax every muscle, close your eyes lightly, and breathe through your mouth, just as if you were going to sleep. Then, as I apply the remedy, you will soon get quiet all over, then get drowsy and sleepy, and go to sleep, and awake feeling better. Now, see here, my man, **don't resist the effect of the medicine; just sit here and let it have its effect."**

Suggestions to Induce Hypnosis.—"All right, take this seat. Lean your head back against the wall. **Close your eyes lightly and breathe through your mouth and think of going to sleep.** Now, as I apply this remedy you will soon become quiet all over and get drowsy and sleepy, and go to sleep, and awake feeling better.

"I will talk to you to help you to concentrate your mind. Now, as I apply this remedy, you will get sleepy, sleepy, sleepy, so-o-o-o sleepy. Now, go to sleep, sleep, sleep, sleep.

"Now, you feel quiet all over. Your muscles are relaxed. Everything is dark to you. You do not hear anything but my voice. You are drowsy and sleepy, so-o-o-o sleepy. You feel the sleep coming over you. You are going to sleep. Sleep, sleep, sleep.

"By the time I count ten you will be **fast asleep.** One, two, three, four, five, six, seven, eight, nine, ten, and you are asleep, fast asleep, sound asleep.

"By the time I count **five more** you will be **sound and dead asleep,** just as you are in the dead of night when sleeping soundly in your own bed. One, two, three, four, five, and you are asleep, fast asleep, sound asleep, **dead asleep.** Don't awake now until I tell you.

"Every second your sleep will become **sounder and sounder** and deeper and deeper. Sleep on quietly until I awake you.

"Now, you will not feel anything or hear anything or know anything except what I tell you. Sleep on quietly until I awaken you."

"Now, gentlemen, this subject is **in a suggestible condition,** which I will proceed to demonstrate. I raise his arm.

Suggestions to the Subject Hypnotized.— **"Sleep on quietly.** When I count three this arm will be stiff, so stiff that you can't take it down. One, two, three; your arm is stiff, and you can't take it down until I tell you. Now, **when I rub this medicine on your arm** three times it will be dead and have no feeling in it. **Now, I pinch this arm"** (thrusting a pin through a fold of the skin), "but you do not feel it; there is no feeling here at all; this arm is perfectly dead."

"Gentlemen, **no one minds being pinched,** at least with your finger nails, so I give the easiest suggestion to accept, to accomplish an end. For the same reason I say to a patient, 'I will **examine this tooth,'** while in reality I apply the forceps and extract it. This makes it easier for the patient to accept the suggestion."

"Now, sleep on, and when I count three, stand up. Put your heels together, and when I say "stiff," **be as stiff as iron, so stiff I can lay you across two chairs and you will not bend.** One, two, three. Now, stand up! Get stiff, stiff as iron."

"Place his heels in the other chair, please, doctor." (The man is placed with his head on one chair and his heels on another.) "Now, hold strong, be stiff." (Standing upon his body.) He sustains my weight of two hundred pounds easily. "Now, relax, limber, sit down and sleep on."

"Now, my man, when I count three you will open your eyes and be wide awake. **You will be feeling good all over.** You will remember nothing that has been said or done, and will find that you **never felt better in your life,** and will always be glad that you came up here. One, two, three, and you are awake."

"**Have a good nap?**"

"Yes, sir."

"**What do you remember** since coming into this room?"

"Nothing at all but sitting in that chair and going to sleep."

"**You are sure that nothing has hurt you** since sitting there?"

"No, sir, nothing has hurt me."

Now, **the talk that I gave that man** about my selling the medicine, and how it was used, and what it was used for, etc., was **the prehypnotic suggestion.** In that way I got his **voluntary consent** to sit in this chair and let the medicine have its effect. In doing that, he was letting me put him in that suggestive condition unfortunately named the hypnotic state. Notice again, **I had that man relax every muscle, close his eyes lightly, and breathe through his mouth.** He was then in a condition of **voluntary receptivity.** The very fact that he agrees to relax, close his eyes, and breathe through his mouth, indicates that he is a hypnotic subject, **because it signifies his willingness.**

As to who is a hypnotic subject, it is the individual that does not know that he is to be hypnotized, whose confidence I can secure sufficiently to get him to conform to the conditions, just as we have demonstrated. I always **secure the voluntary co-operation of the individual** and get that supreme factor in human consciousness, the will, to assist me in accomplishing the result. I get the co-operation of the **voluntary waking consciousness** to act upon or execute an idea or series of ideas, either consciously or subconsciously. In getting an individual to go into **that sleep-like condition** known as the hypnotic state, I am simply getting the real ego to **act upon or execute an idea through intelligent co-operation.** That is the way by which that subconscious condition known as the hypnotic state is produced. Then, **after the subject is hypnotized,** I get him to act upon or execute an idea subconsciously.

In over four thousand instances in which I have used men of all nationalities for demonstration in my class work, I have yet to see the **first unpleasant result.** In all cases pins were stuck through their faces or arms and their bodies put across chairs and one or more men stood upon them. I have used **lawyers, preachers, doctors, dentists, merchants, mechanics** and people of all trades and classes. As regards nationalities, Germans, French and English, Italians and Chinamen, Japs, Indians and negroes, have been my subjects. They have all proved about equally susceptible as regards race.

The more intelligent individuals of all races made the best subjects.

Everyone that left the room went out with a pleasant smile on his face, and most of them thanked me for the experience. I treated them all kindly and acted in a way to secure the co-operation of a high element of human consciousness.

One exception should be mentioned where we had a little variety. In Colorado Springs a man came in drinking and I suggested that he was getting sick, **suggestion without hypnotism,** and that he was going to vomit, and he did vomit, copiously. In giving him a suggestion to relieve him of this condition, after suggesting that he was feeling easy and comfortable all over, and that his nerves were steady and quiet and strong, I suggested that he was feeling fine, and would go out **feeling like a fighting cock.** I walked out behind him into a dimly lighted hallway to tell the man securing men for demonstration purposes not to bring in another drinking man, when this ruffian, a miner weighing about one hundred and ninety pounds, both tough and strong, began to **exhibit his fighting cock qualities on me.** After flooring him, which was necessary for self-defense, I got him into the room, but secured his release from arrest by exacting from him a promise **never to hit an old man or a little boy** when he wanted to fight, but to always hit a man just like me. This he promised, and with my arm around him I led him to the door with the injunction to be good and quit drinking.

In this case we had a demonstration of the efficacy of **simple suggestion** on the one hand, and of **"forced suggestion"** on the other. I suppose Dubois would have styled that **"moral orthopaedia."** Many men, when drinking, are **very amenable to suggestion** without hypnotism, and so is a drinking woman, but you can never get an individual to accept a suggestion that **is not in accord with his character. Self suggestion** is always stronger than the suggestion of another, and the home training, moral conviction, religious influences, etc., all go to form a self-suggestion in the individual **which is the basis of character,** so that the individual will never accept a suggestion not in accord with, or that antagonizes, his own autosuggestions.

People have faith in medicine, and when we proceed as if using a medicine, we utilize the faith or confidence that is reposed in this material agency, inert though it is as to physiological effect, which proves a **most powerful factor** in producing that condition known as the hypnotic state, on the one hand, and getting results by suggestion applied as a therapeutic measure, on the other.

This was illustrated for me once, when a woman brought a seven-year-old child to my office in a great hurry to get something done very promptly that would prevent a small silver coin that he had swallowed from killing him. She had frightened the child badly. After drawing the attention of the child away from itself by showing some curios in my office, I said to the little fellow, **"Now you feel all right, don't you?"** "Yes, I am all right," was his reply. I then turned to the mother and set out to assuage her fears by telling her that there would be no danger to the child from swallowing the coin, that I had swallowed a coin when a small boy and it did not hurt me. That I had repeatedly had children brought to me who had swallowed a coin and it never did any of them any harm at all. That her child needed no castor oil, which she was about to give it, or anything else but to be let alone. When I arose to turn her out of my office, she exclaimed in a most emphatic manner, **"Why, doctor, are you not going to give him any medicine?"** I saw at once that it was impossible to reason with that woman, so I said, "Yes," and forthwith prescribed one ounce of compound rhubarb and soda mixture, and handing it to her, directed that she **give ten drops of this every two hours,** and that I would guarantee that inside of a week he would expel that coin all right and never suffer the slightest inconvenience. She received more satisfaction **in two minutes** from that prescription than from a ten-minute conversation in which I had reassured her all that I could.

Our therapeutic measures must be **in accordance with an individual's preconceived beliefs.** I notice more patients in the office of a physician who uses medicine as a means of satisfying the mind of his patient, as well as persuasion, reasoning, advice and other forms of suggestion, in conjunction with the placebo prescription, in one day than I do in a week in the office of a physician who entirely relies upon **"therapeutic conversation."**

In another similar case, the mother was perfectly satisfied when I advised that her child eat a baked potato with his meals three times a day, stating that this would conduct the coin to a safe delivery without the slightest harm to the child.

Our therapeutic measures must be **adapted to the individuality of the patient** with whom we are dealing.

Demonstration No. 2.—"Now, Doctor Blank, I want you to hypnotize the next man. I want you to **convince yourself that your suggestions** are just as efficacious as mine.

"See, I have **tacked these printed suggestions upon the wall,** over the chair that the man will occupy here. I will give him the pre-hypnotic suggestion for you. By this I convert him into a hypnotic subject. **I talk him into willingness** to sit in that chair and **let the medicine** have its effect, while you carry him, by reading those suggestions on that wall, into a deeper state of suggestibility. Bring in another man, please." (Another subject is brought in.)

A Pre-Hypnotic Suggestion Given.—"Take **that seat** and I will explain to you what I am doing and what I want with you. Do you see this little bottle of medicine? I am introducing to the physicians here a remedy to cure headache, quiet nervousness, relieve pain, etc. It is applied by rubbing it on the forehead just as you see me do here. It must be applied in a certain way to get results. The physician here knows how to apply it. I have explained to him that it is important **to get his patient to conform to certain conditions** in order that the medicine will produce results that are expected. That is what I will show you. I want you to sit in this chair and let the doctor apply this to you just as if you had a headache and he were going to relieve it for you. Now, look at me. I want you to sit in this chair as you see me, **relax every muscle, close your eyes lightly** and **breathe through your mouth.** Then when the physician here applies this remedy, you will soon get quiet all over and get drowsy and sleepy and go to sleep, and awake feeling better. Now, I want to ask you, **don't resist it,** just sit here and allow the medicine to have its effect. Take this seat." "**Proceed to apply the medicine,** doctor." (Rubbing "the medicine" on his head on either side, the physician read the following suggestions in a **conversational tone, with a low monotone, affirmative voice**):

Suggestions to Induce Hypnosis.—"You close your eyes lightly. Breathe through your mouth. Think of going to sleep. As I apply this remedy you will soon get quiet all over, and get drowsy and sleepy and go to sleep and awake feeling better.

"I will talk to you to help you concentrate your mind.

"Now, as I rub this on your head you will get sleepy, sleepy, sleepy, so-o-o-o sleepy. Now go to sleep, sleep, sleep, sleep. Now you feel quiet all over. Your muscles are relaxed. Everything is dark to you. You do not hear anything but my voice. You are feeling quiet from your head clear down to your feet. You feel a torpor all over your body. Your arms and limbs are so-o-o-o heavy. You are drowsy and sleepy, so-o-o-o sleepy. You feel the sleep coming over you; you are going to sleep. Sleep, sleep, sleep, sleep.

"By the time I count ten you will be fast asleep. One, two, three, four, five, six, seven, eight, nine, ten—and you are asleep, fast asleep, sound asleep.

"By the time I count five more you will be sound asleep and dead asleep, just as you are in the dead of night, when you are at home on your bed,—one two, three, four, five—and you are asleep, fast asleep, sound asleep, **dead asleep. Don't awake, now, until I tell you.**

"Every second you sleep will become sounder and sounder and deeper and deeper. You now see what a quiet, sweet experience you are having. You are having a quiet, refreshing sleep. **Sleep perfectly quiet until I awake you.**

"Now you will not feel anything or hear anything or know anything except what I tell you. Sleep, sleep, sleep, quiet, refreshing sleep. Sleep perfectly quiet until I awake you. Every second you sleep will become sounder and sounder, deeper and deeper. **Sleep on quietly until I awake you."**

I then proceeded: "Now, doctor, hold up this man's arm and suggest to him that when you count three it will be stiff, so stiff that he cannot take it down." (The arm staying there as suggested **indicated that the individual was in a suggestible condition.**) "Now, take hold of his wrist, doctor, and say to him, 'Your arm will come down now.'

"You notice that arm came down with **a wax-like resistance,** no volition exercised by him at all. When I feel that **wax-like resistance** as I make the 'arm test,' I am quite sure that **I can produce anaesthesia** by suggestion.

"Doctor, suggest to him that his arm will be dead when you rub the medicine on it three times, that it will **be perfectly dead** and **have no feeling in it** at all. You see, gentlemen, after that suggestion I am able to thrust a pin through his arm without the slightest evidence of pain."

(Doctor Blank asks if **any other part of the body** can be rendered anaesthetic by suggestion, and if it is not a fact that the back of the arm is neither very sensitive nor vascular.) "All right, rub some of this medicine **on his lower lip** and suggest that when you rub it three times it will be dead and have no feeling in it. Notice this, please, gentlemen." (Thrusting a pin through his lower lip from outside to inside an inch through the lip.) **"You see it does not bleed,** even on the inner surface of his lip."

No place except the eye is more sensitive than the lip and no place in the body is **more vascular.** As to why this does not bleed, I will refer later on in my lecture. It is supposed to be the influence exerted by suggestion upon the co-aptation of the neurons.

Upon one occasion in the presence of the faculty of Tulane University, and of at least one hundred physicians and three hundred medical students, I thrust a steel hatpin through **the cheeks of three hypnotized subjects.** Then I requested a noted surgeon there **to name one man's face** that should bleed, and bleed more than just a few drops, and that I would remove the pin from the faces of the other two men **without bleeding,** while this man's face would bleed. The experiment was a perfect success. I made the same experiment in Mobile, in the presence of the Medical Society there.

The method of **getting the part to bleed** is to suggest pain in the part, and the control over the blood supply to the part through **the influence of the higher centers** over the vaso-motor neuro-regulation of the blood supply is augmented. **To keep it from bleeding,** suggest that the part is dead, perfectly dead, and has no feeling in it. Then the higher centers seem to exert an inhibitory influence over the flow of blood in the part, with which in suggestive anaesthesia, the face pierced by a steel hatpin does not bleed, at least in nine-tenths of the cases.

"Your subject seems to be comfortable, doctor. Now, suggest to him that when you count three he will stand up, and

[4]

when you say 'stiff,' that he will be as stiff as iron from head to foot. I will lay him across the chairs for you, as there is a knack that I have acquired of lifting a man in that position that makes it easy for me.

"Put your foot there, doctor, and **we will both stand upon him.** Give me your hand. Tell him to be stiff! to hold strong! Now, come up gradually.

"You see, **he easily sustains our combined weight** of over four hundred pounds in a line in the center of his body.

"Tell him to **relax. Sit down. Sleep on.** Doctor, suggest to your subject that when you rub this medicine on his arm three times it will **be dead and have no feeling in it** as long as he is in this room. Tell him that **when he is awake** you can thrust a pin in the skin of that arm while he is looking at it and he will have no feeling in it, that his arm will be **perfectly dead** as long as he is in this room.

"Now, suggest to him that when you count three he will be wide awake, that **he will feel good all over,** that he will not remember anything that has been said or done while in the room, that nothing has hurt him, and that he will **never have felt better in his life,** that he will be glad he came up here and will always feel better. Now, count three and tell him to awake."

"All right, my man, how do you feel?"

"All right, sir."

"Has anything hurt you since you came into this room?"

"No, sir, not in the least."

"**Do you see this pin?**" The doctor put some medicine on your arm here and it has no feeling in it. I am going **to stick it with this pin.** If you feel it in the least, let me know. Now, look at it, here it goes; **do you feel that?**"

"Not a bit."

"That will never hurt you or never get sore in the least."

(The doctor asks if we ever have **any trouble in waking** a subject?) "Not in the slightest. He is in a condition of increased suggestibility, and to awaken him is only to get him **to act upon an idea or suggestion,** and this he will do easier now than ever before, provided you make the suggestion properly.

"Occasionally it is necessary to repeat again, 'Wake up.' **Rarely have I found** it necessary to thump him on the face or slap him lightly and speak more emphatically, 'Wake up!' Be calm, well poised, and self possessed. Should you ever find a subject that anyone else had hypnotized and found difficulty in awakening, either turn an **interrupted current of electricity** upon him or administer one-tenth of a grain **of apormorphine** hypodermically, and see what he will do. **I have never found this necessary.**"

What effect does hypnotism have on the subject, is asked. "Whatever effect you suggest. The effect is determined altogether by **your suggestions.** Hypnotism is but the induction of a mental condition in which your suggestions will be more effective and lasting. I will cover that question in detail in my analysis of the subject later on.

"Gentlemen, you notice those men go out of this room **with smiles on their faces.** They seem to appreciate and enjoy the experience. The higher evolutionary element of human personality has in them **been put to a test.** They have proved their mastery over the physical man. Call this intelligence, **will, or reason,** as you choose. It functions with the mind and is **a psycho-physical process.**

As these experiments are conducted here I regard our demonstrations as splendid mental gymnastics. Those men are sent out of here with a new element of selfhood having been aroused within them. **The real man, the ideal ego,** is more self conscious of his mastery and control of mind and body, his servants, than when he came into this room. I never hypnotized an individual in my life who **was not my friend after that,** all because I dealt with him kindly and he appreciated it. **The man himself, the** real self, is not weakened and dethroned by the methods that we employ, as some would have you believe.

When you rightly appeal **to the higher self,** you can take that old physical hull, his body, and stick it, stand upon it, cut it, etc., and it is all right with the master of that house, or physical body, because every step you are taking is through **the power possessed within him.**

How frequent it is that **the operator becomes hypnotized** instead of his subject, thinking that it was some power that he was exerting over the hypnotized individual, rather than the use of an inherent quality of force **within the individual himself.**

It is largely a matter of confidence in human beings. **Faith in your fellow man,** confidence in his ability to exercise inherent potentialities that are written in his blood, and chiseled in his cerebral cells, is the secret of success in this line of work, as well as **an important essential** in rendering genuine service to your fellow man in every department of life.

(**Demonstrations Nos. 3, 4, and 5** were about like those just described, and a further report of these cases is therefore unnecessary.)

"Gentlemen, with **the next subject waiting** on the outside, I will demonstrate another method of inducing the hypnotic condition by having him **fix his eyes** upon some bright object, so as to get his attention while making suggestions.

"Take this seat, my man. These are physicians and I desire to show them how I can get a man to look at this bright collar button until his eyes become tired and how he will go to sleep in a few minutes. I will put you to sleep and you will sleep not over five minutes and awake feeling better."

"But I do not care to go to sleep, doctor," says the patient.

"All right, then, we will excuse you."

A physician: "Doctor Munro, I should like to see you put that man to sleep and put him through the same test as you did the others."

"I should be glad to do so, doctor, but this man says he does not care to go to sleep and that is the end of it so far as our efforts to hypnotize him are concerned. **No one can be hypnotized against his will.** Consent and co-operation are absolutely necessary, except where auto-suggestion on the part of the patient can be brought into play through credulity or fear—conditions which would remove the experiment altogether from the realm of the justifiable.

The point that I have attempted to **drive home** upon your consciousness here is that more people will consent for **the medicine** to put them to sleep than will give their consent to be hypnotized; so by the use of the medicine you can accomplish results **that cannot be secured otherwise.** It is a means to secure an end. **There is no deception in it,** for I tell the individual what I expect **him to do,** what **will be the result,** and what I want him to do in order that the result may be obtained. **The medicine actually** is the material means through which the effect is induced. It does it by the impression it makes upon the mind, the sensory nerves, if you please, and this impression reaches and influences the higher cerebral centers. It accomplishes its work in accordance with the **normal physiological processes.**

It may seem queer to you at first glance that we can influence the physiological processes **by psychological methods.** But all medicines produce their results by their influence upon function, even when taken into the stomach or applied hypodermically. **Medicine used locally** as a means of suggestion is a powerful functional stimulant. By it we can inhibit certain brain centers and call into play an increased activity of others. We quiet nervousness, we relieve pain, we restore sleep, we encourage secretion, nutrition and excretion.

All therapeutic measures can accomplish their results only by acting in conjunction with those inherent properties and forces within **the biological element of the organism.** Our internal medication only acts upon function. **Medicine used internally or externally,** whether for its physiological or psychic effect, can through the suggestion giving it its psychological potency, stimulate the function of every organ in the body.

Every center of activity in the brain can be influenced by suggestion. Every organ in the body and all bodily functions are under the control of the nervous centers. **Every element of the organism** has its center of activity in the brain. All these we can influence by suggestion, and we can use medicine and surgery and all other therapeutic measures, **not only for the effects produced by their own physical influence** upon the organism, but also as a means of successfully combating the disturbing psychic factor through **the influence of those measures** upon the mind. Every physician uses these measures, consciously or unconsciously, every day of his life.

Do not understand by the ground that I have taken that I am a therapeutic nihilist. I am **first and last a regular physician,** anxious for any therapeutic aid by any means whatsoever that will help to alleviate human suffering and cure disease. **We can demonstrate** the physiological action of our medicinal agents upon the physical organism, even in unconscious persons and animals, as impressively and conclusively as by a slap or a kick we can demonstrate to the person who denies it our ability to use our hands and feet.

But understand, I am talking to you about the **psychic factor in therapeutics,** pointing out its value as an important therapeutic adjunct, to be used in conjunction with any measure, medicinal, surgical, or otherwise, **that will help to alleviate suffering** and cure disease, or that will put the individual in such condition that a cure may take place.

This science as applied in the practice of medicine is based upon these premises: There is **inherent in mankind** a psychic power or mental force presiding over the functions, conditions, and sensations of his body, and this inherent potentiality, **which is a property of the cells** that compose the complex mechanism of the animal physiology, can, under proper conditions, be **evoked** and **controlled at will** and applied to the alleviation of human suffering.

WHAT that inherent quality of force represented by each individual cell in the human body is, has in ages past been called by many names. It has been designated by such expressions as the "vis medicatrix nature," "the resident energy within," "neuric energy," and, in the terms of psychology, "the subconscious mind," "the subjective mind" "the subliminal consciousness," etc.

Tennyson referred to the same incomprehensible life principle when he pulled **a little flower from crannied wall** and said:

Little flower—but if I could understand
What you are, root and all, and all in all,
I should know what God and man is.

The tendency of modern science is toward **the possibility of reducing all phenomena,** physical as well as psychical, to a common cause.

Verworn remarks that "The attempt to explain the mystery that surrounds living substances, the substance that nourishes itself, breathes, moves, grows, reproduces and develops, **has exerted from the earliest times** a peculiar stimulus upon the mind of inquiring thinkers."

But while **we do not know** what that inherent quality or force as represented by the individual cell is, neither do we know **what electricity is,** nor what matter is, in any form in its ultimate analysis, **but we do know something,** not all, of the laws that govern these of Nature's forces, and by conforming to these laws we are better enabled to make our struggle for existence.

By conforming to this psychological law, we can get results in the alleviation of human suffering, and as broad minded men we want to make use of anything that will help us **to grapple with the problems of health and disease.**

Just as **steam and electricity** were governed by Nature's laws that existed forever and only required science to make use of them, **so has psychic law existed forever,** and a better understanding of, conformity to, and appropriation of this law are destined to make the same revolution in the practice of medicine as has been effected by steam and electricity in methods of **travel, manufacture and communication.**

The intelligence of our age demands that the higher evolutionary factors of human personality, call them by whatever name you will, be recognized, and **their truths be appropriated** for the welfare, health, and happiness of our patients.

CHAPTER IV.

SUGGESTION, ITS USES AND ABUSES.

This is an age of dynamics. It is a day when all minds are turned in search of laws that govern hidden forces. The intelligent comprehension and utilization of Nature's forces, through compliance with the laws that govern them, has revolutionized the external world of travel, manufacture and communication. **Step by step,** humanity is entering upon the field of finer forces. Electricity, a force unseen, through intelligent compliance with the laws that govern it, is utilized as never before for the comfort and happiness of man. **Man's progress in the scale of evolution** has been in just that degree that he has utilized forces governed by laws not understood and has appropriated them for his happiness and welfare.

We are in this world for growth, and to help raise humanity in the scale of evolution is the only worthy purpose of all human endeavor and achievement. Each individual represents just so much energy, and by his use or abuse of this inherent life force is he a factor for good or evil. **A better understanding** of the laws governing the power that we are all using, either ignorantly or intelligently, should be a means of helping each individual to use his life forces for the advancement of self and for the good of others. **The struggle for the achievement of happiness and health** is the greatest incentive to the activity of the human race.

Evil is simply the result of misdirected energy. The universe was made for man, and all the forces of Nature are **beneficent** and are placed here for his utilization. By perfect conformity to Nature's laws, health and happiness may be maintained; but for violation of, or opposition to Nature's laws, disease, impotency or premature death is the penalty.

In the study of hypnotism and the laws that govern its application we are led into the study of the laws governing and controlling the mind and its influence over the physical organism. **Suggestion,** or an idea aroused in the mind of the subject by impressions from without, or conveyed from one mind to another, is found to be the dominant factor in producing the psychological condition known as the hypnotic state. **Perhaps no one subject** has been so much abused as the subject of hypnotism by the very class of people who use the all-potent factor, suggestion, which they either ignorantly or maliciously deny, as the force by which most of their results as curative powers are obtained. I refer to **christian scientists, weltmerites, faith healers, and such like.** **To point out the danger** which attends the unconscious and ignorant use of suggestion, both with and without the aid of hypnotism, **as well as the possibility of benefit** that may accrue from its intelligent use as an adjunct in the practice of medicine, is my purpose .

Suggestion is an impression conveyed by any means of communication whatsoever from one mind to another. It has been used by every human being, profession, school of learning, sect, "ist" or "ism" that ever existed. **All education** is the result of repeated and accumulated suggestion. **All theological sermonizing, dogmas** and **religions,** make employment of suggestion upon the mind. **Our belief** upon any subject is the result of dominant suggestion. **By our use or abuse** of our powers of suggestion do we become a force for good or evil.

So receptive is the human mind to suggestion, that we become **a part of all** with which we have associated during our existence. Our beliefs or convictions upon any subject are **the sum of the suggestions** that have possessed us.

By suggestion we are enabled to **build character** in those susceptible. Its use is of inestimable value for the **correction of vice, the cure of evil habits,** and the prevention of certain forms of insanity. By it the **will power is strengthened,** latent talents are developed, and inherent capabilities of mind and body brought into activity.

By the use of suggestion **brain centers can be stimulated** and brain cells developed. **Virtue can be instilled** and vice eradicated; purity or impurity, confidence or fear, love or hate, joy or grief can be made the **dominant quality** of the mind.

By suggestion we exert personal influence which stirs human activities and is a tremendous power for good or evil in the universe. By this **all available energies** or forces of Nature are being controlled and utilized for the happiness of man.

By suggestion every center of activity in the brain can be strengthened and every organic function in the body increased or encouraged to new activity. **War and bloodshed,** theft and wreck and ruin of manhood and character, are the result of evil suggestions that have been allowed to dominate the mind of an individual or a nation.

The most sacred shrine of the soul itself is invaded, dominated and profaned by suggestions intruded upon the individual in which the ideal ego has not been awakened and evolved.

Suggestions are forces operating in the realm of cause with effects that are as sure and unfailing upon those in whom the ideal ego has not been awakened as the law of gravitation itself.

Suggestion is but disguised hypnotism. Suggestion **without the use of hypnotism,** is often malicious, but clothed in the garb of truth it is the dominant force that **rules the life of every human being,** of every nation, of the very world itself.

By its use on the part of the "Mother of Christian Science," thousands of **innocent,** but **honest** and **conscientious,** followers are being robbed of their individuality and selfhood. **By the use of suggestion** on the part of wicked and designing men, the markets are flooded with spurious wares of all kinds and honest money is given for worthless trash. Here is the stronghold of the **patent medicine vendor, the health food manufacturer** and the advertising medical quack, as they play upon the **ignorant credulity** of those who have not learned the intelligent use of their own thought powers.

Through the use of suggestion, people are made to submit on the one hand to many **useless surgical operations,** which often aggravate the functional trouble they were intended to relieve, and on the other hand they are caused to **refuse the help of** honest surgery for the relief of pathological conditions beyond the reach of any other method of treatment.

There is absolutely no difference between hypnotic suggestion and suggestion without hypnotism. It is the same in kind, the difference being only one of degree as regards its effects upon the physical organism. Suggestion without hypnotism, even when used unconsciously, may stealthily and subtly dominate the mind without the consent of the individual; while hypnotic suggestion, intelligently applied for the relief of functional ills of the physical organism, is always employed with the individual's consent.

One cannot be hypnotized without the consent of the true ego—never against his will or without his co-operation. The true ego is the real man. It is the intelligent life entity that can control all the mental faculties and use them to vitalize and energize every part of the organism. When fully awakened and evolved, the mind and body are its obedient servants. It is beyond the vision of the microscope or the range of the dissecting knife, and just in proportion as it is developed will it control the mind, and through the mind produce harmonious and healthful results in the body.

I have no wish to be visionary. Life is too short for impractical theories and suggestions; but to speak plainly, some of us have been half-doctors long enough. We have been dealing too much with effects, and have failed to consider an important etiological factor of disease.

Man is both a mental and a physical being and cannot be treated simply as if we were conducting experiments in a chemical laboratory. Heretofore all the advance made in the progress of medical science has been **on a physical plane,** and the achievements made in the branches of **surgery, bacteriology, pathology, and hygiene** challenge the admiration and applause of modern civilization. But while bacteriology and pathology can detect, and surgery remove and destroy the diseased part and hygiene lessen the conditions that occasion the infection of the organism with pathogenic germs, **the causes of many so-called functional diseases**—among them neurasthenia and certain forms of insanity— have remained obscure.

The number of inmates of the insane asylum in every state is yearly increasing far beyond the ratio of increase of population. Why so many diseased bodies and imperfect nervous organizations? **These bear a strong evidence** of the tendency for the species to degenerate rather than to grow healthier and stronger. These are burning and pertinent facts that are beginning to dawn **upon the thinking portion** of our craft.

Nor are the people satisfied; all over the world is the spirit of unrest and dissatisfaction being made manifest, as is indicated by the different "mind cure" schools and cults which attempt to carry their claims **into extravagant absurdities. The doctors themselves** realize this, and just in proportion as they are honest and educated men are they deeply troubled at their own deficiencies.

With a large acquaintance of professional men, I am prepared to say that physicians study hard and work unceasingly, and **their brain and muscles and their very heart's blood itself is** at the disposal of their patients; but still something more is needed.   Either our remedies are insufficient, or we fail to understand the great human machine upon which we are experimenting.

While we do much good, and earn sufficient gratitude to enable us to strive on, and while we can maintain enough courage to look our patient squarely in the face, the suffering **which we have not been able to relieve** and the relief and cures which we have not effected, and the universal prevalence of **diseases that have not been eradicated** have become such prominent factors in the history of our profession as seriously to humble our pride.

The time has come when psychology should be brought to the front.   I would that a chair of physiological psychology were established in all our regular medical schools.   I should like to see **every boy and girl** in our common schools, old enough to understand it, made to realize that a power resides in the mind, and how they can use it to maintain a healthy body, and how, by an abuse of this force, they increase their susceptibility to disease from whatever cause.

To say the least of it, the medical profession should better acquaint themselves with the **importance of psychic influences** as etiological factors, as well as equip themselves to make use of this therapeutic power in the cure of disease.   When the members of the medical profession become **leaders and teachers** in this important branch, the practice of medicine will be elevated to a higher plane.   Then will the breach between that portion of intelligent laymen who feel that physicians are not doing their duty be bridged over.

The **indifference of science** has always been the mainstay of charlatanism.   When the intelligent scientific application of any therapeutic measure is adopted by the medical profession, charlatanism is robbed of its power. **That these people effect cures** of certain forms of functional ills right before our eyes, ills that had not been amenable to cure by our ordinary methods of treatment, is self-evident. **In every city, town and hamlet,** the followers of the different cults and "isms" are gaining in number, and thousands of dollars are reaped by them that should go into the pockets of the medical profession; while on the other hand, thousands of innocent lives are sacrificed on account of the **neglect of scientific medical treatment.**

With the intelligent **recognition** and **application** of suggestive therapeutics **as an aid** in the practice of medicine, conditions and symptoms can be relieved that cannot be reached by any other remedy, and it is cases of this very class that are **going from physicians** and seeking aid from other sources.

The effect of **the mind upon metabolism** is now well established. Emotional conditions of a hopeful, optimistic and cheerful kind, encourage **anabolism** or constructive metamorphosis. On the other hand depressing emotional conditions that conduce to fear and despondency and the like, encourage **catabolism,** or destructive metamorphosis. By suggestion we can produce such **mental impressions** as will increase the **potential energy inherent in the cells** of the organism and thus render them less vulnerable to pathogenic germs and other etiological factors of disease. **This is an effectual means** of conserving energy and increasing the resistive powers of the individual and lessening his susceptibility to disease.

[5]

Since the observation of Beaumont upon Alex. St. Martin, the Canadian who had a fistulous opening in the stomach sufficiently large for him to watch the physiological processes of digestion, the effect of certain emotions upon the functions of digestion has been clearly recognized. Beaumont observed **that mental conditions, such as fear and anger,** diminished and sometimes entirely suppressed the secretion of gastric juice by the stomach. At times, under these conditions, the **mucous membrane became red and dry,** and at others it **was pale and moist,** showing the effect of mental impressions upon the vasomotor neuro-regulation of the blood supply to the stomach through the involuntary nervous system. Under the conditions mentioned fluids were immediately absorbed, but food remained undigested for from twenty-four to forty-eight hours.

More recent discoveries by Prof. Elmer Gates, of Washington, D. C., have shown that bad and **unpleasant feelings create harmful chemical products** in the body called catabolins, which are physically injurious. On the other hand, good, pleasant benevolent and cheerful feelings create chemical products called anabolins which are physically helpful.

Quite frequently neurasthenic patients maintain a condition of auto-toxemia on account of **morbid emotional conditions** that dominate their minds, giving rise to headaches, **preventing sleep, conducing to insanity** and proving destructive to all physiological processes. In this class of cases, suggestion **both with or without hypnotism** is our most reliable therapeutic aid.

From the earliest periods in the history of mankind down to the present time, there is **abundant and sufficient proof,** undoubted and acknowledged, going to show that in innumerable instances cures of manifold diseases and ills of the physical organism have been wrought by influences brought to bear upon the mind of the person afflicted. You are too familiar with the history of these cases for me to make further mention of them here. **One well demonstrated fact,** the result of honest investigation, is worth a thousand opinions prompted by prejudice. Having witnessed the efficacious application of suggestive therapeutics, both with and without hypnotism, **in hundreds of instances,** I should still feel confident of the inestimable value of this important therapeutic adjunct, if every other physician in the world doubted its efficacy.

You must face the facts as they are: Exact science has proved to us the correctness of the claim of the efficacy of this method of treatment as a therapeutic agent. **The people who make use of it in disguised form are here;** and the proposition that confronts us is, Shall we appropriate the laws that govern the influence of the mind to the intelligent and scientific treatment of disease and make use of them as therapeutic measures, or shall we leave these laws to them?

My observation is that the members of the medical profession are ever ready and anxious to avail themselves of any therapeutic resource that will help to alleviate human suffering. **All that is needed** is a more thorough understanding on the part of the general profession of the theory and efficacy of suggestive therapeutics, and a better understanding of the technique and practical methods of its application.

The idea has been emphasized that only functional and neuropathic conditions are benefited by this treatment. But be it remembered, that **a functional disturbance or disease, if** neglected long enough, may lead into an organic condition, and that the timely administration of suggestive therapeutics to correct or cure the functional disorder may prevent its resulting in an organic issue.

Furthermore, suggestive therapeutics **should be applied with an understanding** and comprehension of the anatomical and physiological relations of the organism, as well as **of the pathological conditions** to be alleviated. It is not to be used to the exclusion of other therapeutic resources, but can always be used with them, **for it is not antagonistic to or incompatible** with **any** remedy which helps to cure disease.

It is evident that some physicians are afraid that if they should adopt this method of therapeutics, they would be counted as allies of the quacks and charlatans who misuse these methods. **It is the duty of every medical man** who is true to his Hippocratic oath, to adopt and use every measure that will help to alleviate human suffering. This science, **in the hands of a conscientious physician,** is capable of curing diseases, and reaching conditions that no other remedy can reach.

CHAPTER V.

THEORETICAL CONSIDERATIONS.

For our present discussion, let us regard man as being a living, thinking entity; a functioning organism that nourishes himself, breathes, moves, grows and reproduces, adapting himself to his environment, **both acting and reacting** under the influence of innumerable internal and external stimuli.

His body, with its structures, organs and parts, is composed of millions on millions of cells, each one of which, however much it may differ in structure and function from those belonging to other organs and tissues than its own, is a lineal descendant from a single primordial cell. **Just how the mind** of man is related to the brain and nervous system is as yet far from being clear, but we do know that **as the brain is, so is the mind,** and that a healthy, well developed mind corresponds to a healthy, well trained, well developed, and well nourished nervous system.

In the use of such expressions as **soul** and **spirit** in this discussion, it is with the same meaning as **the word mind,** and to suggest that the **mind has emotion, feeling and will,** as well as intellect.

Emotion and will are frequently regarded as spiritual, intellect as mental, and sensation as physical, but they are all **qualities of the same individual mind, soul, or spirit.** So in the sense that I use the term "mind," let it be held to embrace or include

the whole of man's psychic or mental activities, conscious and subconscious, voluntary and involuntary.

Let us think of the human mind as being manifested by or through **the sum total of the functions of every cell** in the body, expressed in thought, feeling, volition, action, motion, perception, conception, memory, etc.

When I say **action and motion,** think not only of objective, conscious, external action and motion, such as feeling, seeing, hearing, reading, talking, walking, etc., **but also of subjective, unconscious, internal action** and motion, including even the action of the lowest cell in the body, in its ability to take in new matter, fix it, change it, and throw it off.

In one sense, each cell seems to have a mind of its own, for it goes on performing its special functions, be it brain cell, or gland, muscle, bone or skin cell. Yet no one of these microscopic organisms is capable of independent existence. **Each has its duty to perform,** but each in turn is dependent, at least in a very large degree, for its own existence upon the activity of other cells of the body, the functioning of which constitutes the complex mechanism of the animal physiology.

Conscious Mind.—Man, as an entity, has conscious psychic or mental activities, which correspond to the functions of the motor area of the brain, the gray matter, the higher centers, the voluntary processes. **The functioning of these** we designate as the conscious mind. These centers respond to stimuli that reach them through the five special senses: sight, hearing, feeling, taste, and smell; and through these **all the lower functions can be**

reached and influenced. Here is the seat of all voluntary action, the home of reason and the higher intellectual faculties.

So far as we know our higher mental functions seem to have their immediate seats in the cortex of the brain and of these mental functions the anterior frontal lobes appear to have the power of inhibition. This is as near as we can come to absolute localization of the mental faculties.

Articulation is a motor act and, in common with other motor functions, is governed by groups of cells in Brocars convolutions; but the mind which is symbolized by language, giving expression to our thoughts, desires, ideas, aspirations and volitions, is a phychic phenomenon dependent upon the entire brain and nervous system. All forms of life that have ideas, however crude they may be, have the power of symbolizing them. Language is but the symbolization of ideas and even the lower forms of life have a language of their own, however elementary and primitive they may be.

The failure of memory, as we know, is dependent upon the disolution of the entire nervous system. The latest acquired and consequently the least organized mental attributes disappearing first indicates that the mind as exhibited by speech, through the combined effort of feeling, memory, desire and will, is an acquirement dependent upon environment and quality and mode of neuron organization.

Our conscious mind, then, seems to be an outgrowth of education and experience, resulting from the conditions that environ us during our struggle for existence from the cradle to the grave. This is the mind that we use in our normal, waking consciousness, as we go in the smooth, even tenor of our ways, attending to our respective vocations in life, not dominated by fear or anger or emotion, but controlled by reason and will. This, I say, is **the conscious mind** and **represents the higher brain centers in action.**

Hypnotism is the process or method of using suggestion to influence the action of the conscious mind. By suggestion the functions of the motor area of the brain can be soothed, quieted, made still, passive, inactive, at rest, or placed in abeyance. As an individual the subject ceases to use these brain centers and **consents to allow you to use them for him,** and through them to reach and influence the vegetative brain and nervous system, which presides over the physiological processes of the body.

Hypnotism, in one sense, is induced sleep. The only difference between induced sleep and natural sleep is that in natural sleep you are completely oblivious to the outside world, while in induced, or hypnotic, sleep, the subject is, as it were, asleep to every one except the person who induced the sleep. **This is always the result of suggestion.** He is *en rapport* with the operator, in relation with him. He hears and acts upon the operator's suggestions, but appears to pay no attention to anyone else except the person who induced the condition. **This is also the result of suggestion.**

When the conscious mind is rendered passive, as when an individual is hypnotized, then we can better reach and influence all those **psychic activities which lie below the threshold of consciousness,** the study of which throws much light upon the subject at hand.

Subconscious Mind—All those psychic activities which are found below the threshold of consciousness correspond to the functions of all **the involuntary physiological processes**—the functions of the involuntary nervous system, including the functions of the ganglionic and sympathetic nervous systems and the functions of the lowest cell in the body in its ability to **play its part in the game of the life** of the entire physical organism. These functions we designate the subconscious mind.

Moreover, the subconscious mind, which corresponds to the functions of the vegetative brain and nervous system, perceives by intuition; it is the storehouse of subjective memory, and the seat of the emotions. It presides over the functions, conditions, and sensations of the body; over all the vegetative or nutritive processes; over digestion, secretion, excretion, nutrition, waste, respiration, calorification; in short, over all cell life function and development.

When the conscious mind is inhibited or soothed into passivity, as in the hypnotic state, this subconscious mind is amenable to influence by suggestion. **It can be influenced by suggestion without hypnotism,** but in the hypnotic state there is an increased amenability or susceptibility of the subconscious mind to suggestion, and also **an increase in its power to execute an idea** or **suggestion** through its control over the physiological processes of the body.

In the hypnotic state we can influence and make such impressions upon the subconscious mind as will be fully carried out in its influence over the physical organism. And the fact that the subconscious mind does preside over the functions, con-

ditions, and sensations of the body, and is more amenable to
suggestion when the conscious mind is inhibited, **gives us in a
nutshell** the reason why the results are obtained from hypnotic
suggestion or suggestion in the hypnotic state.

How do we prove that the subconscious mind is amenable
to suggestion? For upon the truthfulness of this proposition is
based the entire structure of the science of suggestive therapeutics.

First, we **use suggestion upon the conscious mind.** This we
do when we hypnotize a man, as was demonstrated in a previous
chapter. Then, by suggestion in the hypnotic state we can
better reach and influence the deeper thresholds of consciousness.

After an individual is hypnotized, you will remember that
we held up his arm and suggested to him that when we counted
three that arm would be stiff and that he could not take it down.
We challenged him, "You can't take it down." The arm remained stiff, showing **that voluntary function** was here influenced
or inhibited by suggestion; that the **conscious mind** which presided over this motor function was amenable to our suggestion.

Then it was suggested that after the **medicine had been applied to his arm** it would be dead and would have no feeling in
it; and a pin was thrust into his arm **without the slightest evidence of pain,** showing that the subconscious mind, which presides over the sensations of the body, was also amenable to
suggestion.

Then that both the conscious and subconscious minds were
amenable to suggestion, was proved by suggesting to him that
when he stood up and we counted three, he would be stiff, so

stiff that we could lay him across two chairs and he would not bend. We then caused him so sustain the weight of **from two to four hundred pounds** without the slightest inconvenience.

A further demonstration that the subconscious mind presides over sensation and is amenable to suggestion was given when we suggested to the individual **that his lip was dead** and had no feeling in it, and a pin was thrust through his lip, not only without the slightest evidence of pain, **but without producing bleeding.**

So we see that the mind of man, both conscious and subconscious, both voluntary and involuntary, is amenable to suggestion, and that suggestion to the voluntary waking consciousness is as much hypnotism as is suggestion in that increased condition of suggestibility usually referred to as the hypnotic state; that any influence brought to bear upon the mind of any individual by any means whatsoever is hypnotism; that the individual is hypnotized by suggestion, and that an individual with his eyes wide open, thinking he is in possession of all his conscious faculties, is frequently as much amenable to suggestion as is the subject in that sleeplike condition usually referred to as the hypnotic state.

The conscious mind presides over the voluntary functions; it corresponds to the functions of the gray matter, the motor area of the brain, the higher intellectual faculties; but in the presence of a stronger personality, be it an attorney at law, a minister, a teacher, a salesman or physician, it is amenable to influence and controlled by suggestion.

The hypnotic state, when induced by the method that we employ with the medicine, is always induced with the consent of the voluntary waking consciousness. We always get the **consent and co-operation of the will** of the individual to be hypnotized; but by suggestion without a sleeplike condition, as is used by all classes of individuals, the conscious mind may **be stealthily and subtly dominated.** Hypnotic suggestion, however employed by the medicine method which we have demonstrated and described, is always used with the individual's consent.

The subconscious mind presides not only over the involuntary functions, but over all cell life function and development. I have frequently **produced copious emesis** by suggesting to an individual that he had taken ipecac, thus showing the effect of suggestion upon the involuntary physiological processes. In a number of instances I have had physicians accomplish this result in my class work by suggestions made by them **to the subject that they had hypnotized.**

I say by suggestion we **can influence cell life.** In not less than one hundred instances have I taken a hatpin from a lady's hat and **without sterilization** thrust it through a large fold of the cheek of a person without the slightest ill results following. **In several hundred instances** have I thrust a smaller pin without sterilization through the face or an arm of an individual without the least untoward results.

We certainly cannot influence the bacteria upon the pin; then we must increase the resistive power of the cells in the face in some way. Whether it is done by encouraging leucocytosis or the migration of phagocytes, or whether we increase the resistive power of protoplasm direct, has never been explained. **Theorize upon that proposition as you will;** its meaning has a far deeper import than appears at first upon the surface. To me it indicates that we can increase the resistive power, life, strength and energy, **of every cell in the body** by suggestion, both with and without hypnotism; so that in the fight between the etiological factors of disease, which is ever being made by the cells of the body, we can help these cells in their struggle against pathogenic germs or other etiological factors of disease.

Physiologists have ever endowed the brain centers with a peculiar form of energy of their own, indefinitely referred to by such expressions as **neuric energy, nerve force,** and the like. These higher centers occupy a relation to the general cells comprising the physical body similar to that occupied by a dynamo to a piece of machinery. By suggestion we can **convert potential energy into dynamic energy,** latent energy into moving energy, and in this way increase the resistive power of every cell in the body.

I am aware that some physicians will shrug their shoulders and raise their hands to heaven in protest against the foregoing statement. It goes against the grain to present an idea so completely at variance with their preconceived opinions. But **if they will reflect and verify,** they will be forced to bow down before the evidence of facts.

I do not mean to say that an instrument previously **infected with a culture of** *anthrax bacilli* can be thrust with impunity into the flesh of a hypnotized subject, neither do I mean to give license for any failure to observe the strictest rules of asepsis, which has been the means of the brilliant achievements that have crowned the efforts of modern surgery; **but let the facts in the case speak for themselves.** Let us hew close to the line of truth, let the chips fall where they may.

I have in **at least five hundred instances** taken a pin that has not been previously sterilized and thrust it through a fold of the skin in the face or arm and with **but one single exception** have never observed **the least unpleasant results.** Even the exception in this case only goes to prove the efficacy and power of suggesttion in the accomplishment or support of the position that I have taken.

In one instance I used a **small blade of my pocket knife** and jabbed it under a fold of the skin for an inch without soreness resulting. **The antiseptic property of the blood** is not to be discredited in making allowance for the result, nor elimination by bleeding, but in this case the arm bled only a few drops. **On an average** where a pin was used, the arm did not bleed one time in fifty. Nor do I forget the **natural resistive power** of the cells themselves in a healthy individual, and this, in my opinion, can by suggestion **be strengthened** to a wonderful extent.

The one exception where the arm became sore **was in the case of a physician** for whom I gave a treatment by hypnotic suggestion and relieved him of a **tinnitus aurium of twelve years' standing.** He was an extremely neurotic individual and when I awoke him after the treatment for his tinnitus and asked if anything had hurt him in the least, he replied, "No."

"**Did you know** that I had thrust a pin into the flesh of your arm?"

"No, you did not or I should have felt it," said he.

"Do you feel it now?" I asked. "No, not in the least," said he. "You did not stick me really, did you?"

"Yes," I replied, "And here it is now," and I pushed back his cuff and let him see the pin yet through the fold of the skin.

"**Take that out,**" said he, in a most excited manner.

His tinnitus was relieved, and after one year when I last heard from him, had not returned. Yet he seemed hurt with me that I, a physician, should have taken such a risk as to thrust an unclean instrument in his flesh.

In the afternoon he had a **red, painful arm,** with a general temperature of 103° F. and he asked that I hypnotize him again and get rid of that condition! I hypnotized him and gave him appropriate suggestions to relieve his pain, quiet his nervousness, and give him a good night's sleep. After awakening him, I assured him that his temperature was **due to malaria.** He took twenty-five grains of quinine that evening and was all right the next morning.

This, I say, was **the only case** that I have ever experienced where there was the slightest unpleasant symptom after sticking a pin without sterilization into the flesh, and I am quite sure that I have made that experiment **not less than five hundred times.**

It has been reported that a physician jabbed a dull lead pencil into the flesh of a hypnotized subject and produced an infection. Such a procedure would destroy the cells in that part and is **not at all a parallel case** to where a sharp instrument is used and proper suggestions given to influence the result.

These facts have led me to conclude that through the influences **exerted by the higher centers of the brain,** over the vasomotor neuro-regulation of the blood supply to the part, **increased leucocytosis results,** and that the theory of **phagocytic resistance,** as advanced by Metchnikoff, is an important and constant factor in natural immunity. **According to this author,** leucocytes having arrived at the spot where the intruders are found, **seize them after the manner of the amoeba** and with their bodies subject them to intracellular digestion.

The facts mentioned in regard to the case of the physician, whose auto-suggestions were adverse and most unfavorable, as **against at least five hundred cases** where suggestions were given in the hypnotic state that would possibly favor this **natural physiological process of immunity,** lead me to conclude that cell activity is increased or retarded in **even a local area by suggestion. We know that every cell** in the body through the complex mechanism of animal physiology is influenced by centers of activity in the brain. These centers can be stimulated and encouraged into action by suggestion. **We can convert potential energy** into dynamic energy, latent energy into moving energy, and in this way all the physiological processes can be increased or encouraged, and by suggestion both with and without hypnotism, we can aid the cells of the body in the fight **against the etiological factors** of disease, whether due to pathogenic germs or other causes.

The physician, then, in the light of such indisputable facts is a **factor** either **for good or harm** in the sick room. How often is it the case that his training in the pathological laboratory so fills him subconsciously with **fear** of pathogenic germs that it completely offsets his confidence in the **natural resistive powers of his patient;** like a dog frightened and cowed, he goes into the fight with a drooped head and his tail tucked in, exercising a most depressing influence upon his patient, rather than with a sufficient faith in the **potentialities inherent in the living cells** that comprise the physical organism, to encourage them into action!

Has it not often been your experience to see a patient very sick, so that from the pathological condition there existing, reason would cause you to doubt the possibility of his recovery? But he had **faith in you,** expected to get well, was hopeful and optimistic, and that encouraged you both to encourage him and to do your best for him. Later on, when he was safely on the road to recovery, when he was thanking you for what you had done for him, you gratefully reminded him that he was getting well on account of his **courage and bravery,** and that had it not been for his will power and determination he never would have recovered. You really felt that **your services played a small part** in his recovery.

On the other hand, you have had patients who were not at all seriously sick, so far as their **apparent pathological conditions** would indicate, yet from the very first visit you realized that you had failed to get *en rapport* with them. You realized that you "did not make good", and upon your return the next morning you found that he was nervous and had not slept well that night; there was an increase in pulse rate, his respirations were quickened, and he was over anxious about himself,

[6]

and from this condition he continued to go on from bad to worse until, finally, upon your last visit, when you realized that he would not recover, chagrined, humiliated and mortified you could not but feel that he had **failed to recover on account of the morbid mental attitude** taken towards his condition in its incipiency. He died for the lack of the will to get well.

The experience of hundreds and hundreds of physicians coincides with the cases just cited. Why is it that the mental attitude of an individual plays such an important part either toward recovery or non-recovery? For this reason: Everybody's subconscious mind is constantly amenable to the influence, suggestion, and control by his conscious mind, and when you fully comprehend this proposition, you see very plainly that every one is treating himself by self-suggestion all the time, whether he realizes it or not. Your own thoughts, your own beliefs, your own predominating mental characteristics, whether you will it or not, whether you believe it or not, whether you know it or not, are the suggestions that are ever influencing your subconscious mind either for good or harm.

So much so is that true, that you can put it down as a safe proposition that the individual who is hopeful, optimistic, and cheerful, constantly looking on the bright side of life, carrying sunshine and cheer into the lives of others—that such an individual by his mental attitude conduces to the health and strength and well being of his own physical organism as well.

On the other hand, the individual who is pessimistic, despondent, and blue, having morbid fears about his own physical condition, worrying over the affairs of life, unduly emotional, pining and complaining; such an individual, by his mental attitude has a wrecking, weakening, ruinous effect, not only upon his own physical organization, but upon that of others.

As we pointed out in a previous chapter, emotional conditions of a hopeful, optimistic, and cheerful kind encourage anabolism, or constructive metamorphosis, a building up of the cells of the body; while depressing emotional conditions, worry, fear, envy, anger, jealousy and such like, encourage catabolism, or destructive metamorphosis, a tearing down of the cells of the body.

In the study of **the etiology of neurasthenia** and allied conditions, including all functional disturbances—and their name is legion— **self-suggestion** enters into these cases **as a causative factor** that is of a far deeper import than is generally recognized; and in treating this class of cases, as well as for the nervous element of any disease, acute or chronic, surgical or otherwise, it is our duty as physicians to make such impressions upon the conscious minds of our patients in our daily association with them as would indirectly influence the subconscious mind, **through autosuggestion.** At least we must make the patient feel that we understand his case; that we are especially interested in him; that we are giving him due consideration, and as far as possible we should hold out a strong belief or expectancy that he will get well. Just in proportion as we keep him cheerful, hopeful, and optimistic, **just so far shall we help him on the road to recovery.**

Think of these two minds as two sets of men upon a war vessel. **The men upon the upper deck** give their attention to the fleet over yonder. They give their attention to the objective world. These are performing the function of the conscious mind.

The men below deck give their attention to the **internal machinery of the ship,** paying no attention whatever to the outside world. They represent the subconscious mind. Their respective duties are entirely separate and independent, yet the men below stand ever ready to obey the dictates or orders or signals from the men above.

Every human being is giving orders that will encourage the performance of every organic function every minute and hour of his life; or he is giving orders that will inhibit, retard, and weaken the involuntary psychic activities or nervous functions. So you see that suggestion is used both with and without hypnotism, and that any influence brought to bear **upon the conscious mind** of your patient indirectly reaches his subconscious mind. We are using it every day of our lives for the good or harm of ourselves and for the good or harm of our patients.

To show you the influence of the mind upon the bodily functions, I will cite one illustration. I was once talking to a physician about hypnotism or suggestion when **a band stopped in front of his office** and began to play. In a jocular way he remarked, "I should like to see you hypnotize that band and stop them from playing." "All right," said I, "come and watch the procedure." **I procured three lemons** and gave a half of each to as many little boys on the street, instructing them to walk round and round the band, **sucking the lemons and making faces** at the musicians. The result was such an increase in the secretion of their salivary glands that the men were compelled to stop and swallow or empty their instruments of saliva. They were **unable to continue** their music and the little boys were put to flight.

An individual with **a large "bay window"** is usually a man who gives full appreciation to the thought of the dinner hour, the breakfast hour, the lunch hour. This pleasurable anticipation of the approaching meal time encourages the free flow of blood to his gastric mucous membrane, with a result that he has a plentiful supply of gastric juice, a good appetite, a good digestion and a healthy physique.

On the other hand, **our cadaverous looking brother** usually approaches his meal hours with pessimistic forebodings and goes to his home at meal time more as a matter of duty than otherwise; thus he unfortunately fails to encourage this passive organ sufficiently to enable it to secrete sufficient gastric juice to give him an appetite or to secure a perfectly digested meal.

By suggestion we **can influence man's conscious and subconscious psychic activities** and thus every organ and every cell in the body can be stimulated. **The daily visit of the physician** to his patient is one of the most important therapeutic factors at his command through the very influence of his own personality.

Before going into the practical application of the theories of hypnotic or therapeutic suggestion, I desire briefly to call your attention to other phases of this subject, which, though they may not appear to you perfectly scientific, have a bearing upon the subject at hand of such importance that it cannot be ignored.

We remarked in the outset that the subconscious mind perceived by intuition, that it was the storehouse of memory, the seat of the emotions, and presided over the functions, conditions, and sensations of the body. So far, we have been elaborating the influence of the subconscious mind over the functions, conditions, and sensations of the body, having made it clear that **when the conscious mind was inhibited,** the subconscious mind was more amenable or susceptible to suggestion, and that suggestions given in the hypnotic state were **more effective and lasting** in certain selected cases than suggestions without hypnotism. We also made it plain that the **conscious mind** of every individual was amenable to influence by suggestion, and that **any influence brought to bear upon the mind** of an individual by any means whatsoever, came under the broad domain of suggestive therapeutics.

The Subconscious Mind Perceives by Intuition.—It is now **considered that thought transference,** or telepathy, is rendered possible on account of the ability of the subconscious mind of one individual to be impressed or influenced by another mind b**y** some means apart from the generally recognized modes of communication. **It may be** that this is based on sympathy existing between two persons concerned and deals with something in which they are mutually interested. Be that as it may, that there should be such a relation between two individuals of congenial habits of thought and action seems to me to be no more unreasonable than that **two mechanical instruments** delicately and harmoniously attuned the one to the other should receive electrical vibrations through air and earth and water thousands of miles apart by which our wonderful system of wireless telegraphy has been perfected.

In connection with this phase of the subject I am **at present an agnostic,** but I am ever ready to stand by facts as I find them, hoping that some day, perhaps not far distant, some of the problems that have so perplexed honest investigators on this line will be explained by the discovery and control of a **natural law** that has been in operation forever and, like all other natural laws, only required the intelligence of man to appropriate and use it for his welfare and happiness.

I have had some **demonstrations** and **observations** of certain phases of this subject presented to me which have led me to certain conclusions that I desire to bring to your attention, without which it would be impossible intelligently to practise suggestive therapeutics.

I once **took a young man** whom I had frequently hypnotized, and, while in the hypnotic state, blindfolded him. I wrote upon a piece of paper the following suggestion: "Go to the mantelpiece and get the baby's photograph and bring it to me." My wife, who was also present at the time, read the suggestion. **Not a word was spoken** more than to tell him that, when I counted "three," I wanted him to go and do what was written upon the piece of paper; that I would not indicate what I wished him to do by look or gesture or word, but would constantly think of it.

I then removed the blindfold, told him to open his eyes and do what was ordered on the piece of paper. He at once went to the mantelpiece, put his hand upon the first photograph nearest to him, which was the wrong one, but put that down; then to another which he also put down; then to another which he also put down; and lastly he took the Baby's photograph indicated, held it in his hand and turned around with a blank expression on his face and handed it to me. "Good," said I. "Be seated and sleep on."

At this juncture my wife threw a **winter coat over his face** and I wrote on another piece of paper, that he would go to a washstand, thrust his hand in the water pitcher, and wash his hands, which he did. I again wrote on another piece of paper that he would take a stool upon the floor and turn it bottom side upwards and take a seat in the bottom. This being done, I wrote that he would go to a lounge in the room, lie flat down upon his face, cover his head up with a pillow, and go to sleep.

Take notice that all these suggestions were written, not one word being spoken. Each suggestion was carried out precisely as written upon the piece of paper. When I awoke him and asked what he had been doing, he replied "Nothing." When I told him what he had done **he denied it.** When I presented the written suggestions and assured him positively that he had carried out every suggestion given in writing, and that not a word had been spoken to indicate what we wanted him to do, **he laughed aloud** and said that we had played a great joke upon him.

Since that one demonstration I have never doubted that man has a means of conveying an idea or impression to another individual which lies outside the domain of the five special senses. It is by this that thought transference or telepathy is made possible. **As to whether the reader believes** in thought transference or telepathy or not, is a matter for him to decide. It is recognized as a fact by some of our ablest scientists and psychologists of the present day. It affords an explanation of a **great mass of unexplained phenomena** that have been hitherto relegated to the realm of mysticism. If there be any truth in it, it has its practical bearing upon our subject at hand in this way. The more faith one has in his ability to hypnotize a subject **or to use suggestion both with and without hypnotism,**the greater will be his success. The more faith we have in any therapeutic measure the better will be the results from its administration. **The more faith we have in that inherent quality of resistive power** within our patient, call it by whatever name we please, the better are the chances of our patient to recover.

The physicians who have the **most confidence** in suggestive therapeutics always secure the best results in its application. A **doubtful mental suggestion** may outweigh a positive oral suggestion, if it be possible to give a positive suggestion orally when one is in doubt, and a physician may fail to get results for the lack of confidence in the procedure.

Furthermore, we, as physicians, should cultivate a spirit of optimism and self-confidence in our demeanor with our patients. The physician who goes into the sick room with an air of self-sufficiency, which is based upon professional qualifications and an understanding of human nature, will always inspire his patients with confidence and secure that mental attitude on the part of the patient that is desirable. **Such a man usually possesses tact** sufficient, not only to influence the mental attitude of his patient in regard to his own condition, but to drop a suggestion here and there upon the minds of those around him which will secure the proper psychological environment under which the best results may be obtained.

Many men succeed in the practice of medicine far beyond their professional qualifications, because they possess tact and self confidence sufficient properly to impress and inspire confidence in those with whom they associate.

On the other hand, we often see a well qualified physician fail to succeed, on account of his lack of ability to carry that suggestive influence which is so essential to the personality of the successful physician. **A lack of faith in self,** however much one may try to conceal the fact from observation, repels that confidence that others would have in one.

I am frequently asked how to acquire confidence in our ability to succeed in accomplishing what we have undertaken in life, and I usually answer: **"By going the route; by making the fight, by hard work, concentration and study, and the acquirement of self-confidence which can only come through knowledge and experience."** That indefinable quality of personality called "personal magnetism" is comprehended here. The man who goes down the stream of life day after day **self reliant,** optimistic and cheerful, with a pleasant greeting for his friends, glad that everything is as well with him today as it is, glad of the privilege **to work** and **to study** and **to learn** and **to be of use in the world,** is always the one that is looking out for a better tomorrow, and unconsciously attracts to him the elements that go to make up success in life.

With the physician this is indicated by **his library, his postgraduate diplomas, his office equipment,** and the interest that he takes not only in his profession, but in all questions that contribute to the welfare, happiness, and onward development of the human race. **The world has no use for human inertness.** We must keep in line with the progress of our age, or step aside.

The individual who is pessimistic, despondent, and gloomy, and so **morbidly self-conscious of his own life's battles** that he has no time to speak to his friends, who is continually speaking disparagingly of life and its opportunities, brooding over his own troubles, whining and complaining, will drive away those elements that go to make life worth while.

This intuitive faculty of the subconscious mind often forces itself upon the recognition of the physician in his routine work. You have frequently called to see a patient who was not properly within your clientele. You perhaps wondered why you received this call. On returning the next day to make your second visit the minute you entered the sick room you could tell whether your patient **was better or worse, and who** among the environment was for you or against you, and you have at times observed that the patient would be progressing very satisfactorily but for the **antagonistic suggestive influence** of some influential member of the family or friend who favored the patronage of another physician.

Properly to get *en rapport* with all those who collectively go to make up the environmental influence brought to bear upon your patient constitutes tact, and is one of the greatest elements of success in the practice of medicine.

The Subconscious Mind is the Storehouse of Memory.— **Memory** seems but to be the impress made by previous experiences in life upon the entire brain and nervous system. Aside from conscious objective memory **every experience in your life** has left its indellible impress upon your subconscious mind. This is what gives rise to a great many **subjective impressions and sensations** which haunt the lives of neurotic individuals.

All education and instruction and experience of any kind is retained by the subconscious mind. These ideas or impressions here lie dormant until ready to be brought out by the association of ideas. You would say that some of your best prescriptions have been extemporaneously devised upon the spur of the moment; but the **skilled surgeon finds every previous experience** in the dissecting and operating room and pathological laboratory instinctively forcing itself upon the domain of consciousness as an impelling guidance or impulse to every step of the procedure.

By suggestion in the hypnotic state we **can obliterate old impressions and memories** which are the result of unpleasant experiences in life and plant new impressions and ideas that will influence the future life and conduct of an individual both consciously and unconsciously.

The physician who has the happy faculty of getting the confidence of his patients and keeping them feeling good is always a successful therapist. **At every visit** he lifts his patient out of a morbid self-consciousness of despondency and gloom and impresses him with his own strength, optimism, and cheerfulness. Dignity and self-poise should at all times be maintained to obtain the best results.

That the subconscious mind is the store house of memory explains why you can give a patient a **suggestion in the hypnotic state at nine o'clock** this morning that will give him a good night's sleep, beginning at a specified time, the **following evening** and **every night afterward.** I have frequently broken up nervous, wakeful habits of neurotic individuals in a single treatment by suggestion in the hypnotic state.

The nervous element of an acute disease may be aggravated or a neurasthenic condition maintained on account of some morbid emotional condition resulting from an unpleasant experience in the previous life of the individual, rendering the patient nervous, preventing sleep, and proving destructive to all physiological processes.

By the use of hypnotic suggestion we **can modify the sense impressions causing these** depressing emotional disturbances; give such people more plentiful and refreshing sleep, and plant upon the subconscious mind such impressions as will make them more hopeful, more optimistic, more cheerful, and happier in many ways, resulting in a good appetite, good digestion, improved nutrition, and a complete restoration to health. **By suggestions properly given** in the hypnotic state we can change the individual's point of view in regard to experiences which upset the mental and nervous equilibrium. I cite one case for example:

I once had a patient, a lady, who had a son **accidentally killed.** She was of an emotional nature, neurasthenic, and rather inclined to be on the hysterical order. Three hours after the accident which caused her son's death I was called. The large bed-room was full of friends who had come to express their sympathy. These people had **unconsciously used suggestion** to make her feel worse. Her minister had been on the scene to express his sympathy, and unconsciously used suggestion to make her **more self-conscious of her bereavement.**

As I walked in the door I began to ask each of those present to leave me alone with my patient. By the time I had reached the bed, the room was cleared of all present except her husband. I attempted bravely to talk her into being quiet, but my very presence seemed to have been a signal for an outburst of this emotional condition. **At every attempt to reason** with her or to soothe and console her, she would cry vehemently and answer, "Oh, you don't know, you don't know."

Seeing that I was making no headway, I prescribed chloral-hydrate, 15 grains, and potassium bromide, 30 grains, to each dose, four doses, repeated every two hours. I directed that no company be allowed to come into the room and instructed her husband to sit by her bedside and place a cold towel upon her forehead, changing it every ten minutes. This was in August and the weather was extremely warm.

After the fourth dose of the prescription just mentioned had been taken, I prescribed 15 grains of trional to the dose to be given every two hours for four doses. Three hours after the last dose of this was taken I administered a **hypodermic injection** of morphine sulphate, one fourth of a grain, with hyoscyne hydro-bromide, 1/100th.

Three hours afterward she had still been unable to sleep, was very nervous, had a terrific headache, and I felt that it would be unsafe to administer more medicine. **At that juncture I hypnotized her.** The medicine previously given apparently had a cumulative effect as she was very easily hypnotized.

I then suggested that she **would sleep soundly all night;** that her sleep would be quiet and refreshing; that while she slept a perfect spirit of **resignation** would come over her and she would wake in the morning feeling perfectly resigned to the accident and bereavement; that she would sleep soundly until eight o'clock the next morning, at which time her husband should awaken her, by placing his hand upon her forehead and commanding her to wake up; that she would be **feeling perfectly resigned** to the accident, and would eat her breakfast and give her attention to her domestic relations and feel proud that she had ever been permitted to be the mother of so worthy a son.

On my return the next morning I found that she had slept soundly all night, and she at once began to tell me that she had decided—giving me the very ideas that I had suggested to her the night previous.

I feel quite sure that a greater change in her mental and nervous condition had taken place during this one night's sleep, together with the influence of the suggestions given, than would have resulted under normal conditions after a period of several months had elapsed.

I am furthermore convinced that **there is much insanity, the etiology of which is obscure,** where, in many cases, if the timely administration of hypnotic suggestion had been used to give those people good sound sleep, to change their mental attitude toward the conditions that were worrying them, to **make new impressions upon their cerebral cells and substitute more wholesome mental states,** a large proportion of these cases could have been prevented, upon the principle that an ounce of prevention is worth a pound of cure.

The proof that all insanity is dependent upon diseased states of the brain has never yet been rendered in its entirety. **Organic pathological changes** are found in paresis, senile dementia, alcoholism, and probably in epilepsy, dementia praecox and climacteric insanity and this leaves out of consideration the condition of a large proportion of those adjudged as insane. **The correlation between mental symptoms and pathological anatomy** is as yet largely to be determined, at least in a considerable part of the acknowledged field of insanity.

Many people are incapable of thinking and reasoning for themselves, as the result of false training, education and environment. **You can give them advice** and make all the appeal to reason within your power, and yet they seem **unable to execute your ideas.** The physician who has that spirit of altruism sufficient to enable him to appropriate these methods can here apply hypnotic suggestion and obtain results that cannot be obtained in any other way. **He gets control of his patient** and **puts him in control of himself.** He educates the individual in the art of controlling and directing **his conscious and subconscious psychic** or **mental activities.**

There are others upon whom the **cares of life** have borne heavily, whose involuntary nervous system has received many a hard blow; it has been shocked and wrought upon by cruel impressions or experiences which take possession of a patient and torment his life. **These are found among all classes,** from the highest bred college graduate to the most ignorant working class.

They have not yet learned to control these involuntary impressions. By suggestion in the hypnotic state you plant within them a new consciousness, a consciousness that is power.

When they are sick there is no time for re-educating and re-training them. Like miners buried in a deep, dark hole in the earth, where huge piles of shale and debris had caved in upon them, they need help. Like a man in jail, they want to get out. **They expect you to do something for them.** To give them narcotics and sedatives but temporarily benumbs their psychic activities, interferes with all functional processes, weakens their powers of resistance, interferes with elimination, and is **actually destructive** and **weakening** to both mind and body. The judicious, intelligent application of suggestion, both with and without hypnotism, in this class of cases, is a boon to these unfortunate sufferers who rely upon us for help.

The Subconscious Mind Is the Seat of the Emotions.—Whatever impulse dominates the individual— whether fear, worry or anxiety, envy, anger, jealousy, love or the purely animal passions—makes its appeal to and impress on the subconscious mind, which corresponds to the functions of the involuntary nervous system.

We all have noticed that the functions of the different organs of the body are greatly disturbed through emotional influences; sorrow brings tears to the eyes; prolonged grief interferes with the secretion of gastric juice by the stomach. Of all emotional conditions which are most detrimental, however, **fear, which is the opposite emotion to self-reliance** and self-confidence, is the worst. Fear is the **natural accompaniment** of **weakness,**

[7]

ignorance and disease. Fear has a wonderful inhibitory influence upon both the motor and voluntary, as well as the involuntary, functions of the body. Fear of sickness, fear of death, fear of failure—fear of anything of any kind, of any nature—is detrimental to all physiological processes. We invite what we fear. **Fear weakens our resistive powers to disease.** It is the frequent experience of physicians to have pneumonia and enteric fever patients who die of fear and not on account of the pathological condition existing. This has been observed by physicians everywhere.

In the **Century** for December, 1899, R. R. Bowker gives the following translation of an Arabic legend:

The Spirit of the Plague entered the gate.

One watching, asked, "How many wilt thou slay?"

"A thousand," spake the Spirit, "is my quest."

The Plague made end. The Spirit left the gate.

The watcher cried, "Ten thousand didst thou slay!"

"Nay, one," the Spirit said, "Fear killed the rest."

At the very onset of illness the patient **becomes afraid,** gets nervous, does not sleep, and manifests a lack of confidence in the ability of his physician and doubts his own ability to recover. **He thus has a psycho-neurotic condition** complicating his disease. His resistive powers are thus lessened, all physiological processes are disturbed, and death results from fear and not on account of the pathological condition, which would run its course and go on to recovery but for the psycho-neurotic element.

We should distinguish here **between conscious and subconscious fear.** Tuberculous patients are noted for their apparent optimism, hopefulness and cheerfulness, which is frequently only on the surface. Yet as a result of this very optimism, as has been observed by all physicians, even in the presence of **such a gross pathological condition,** the resistive powers of many tuberculous patients are augmented to an astonishing degree. We frequently see others, however, who are so **subconsciously dominated by fear** that all involuntary nervous functions are disturbed, on account of impressions gathered from experiences which have come to them through their own observation of the disastrous consequences of this disease. **In this class of cases** suggestion, both with and without hypnotism, is particularly beneficial. We quiet an irritable, involuntary nervous system; we get them to **breathe deeper;** we give them suggestions which produce **more plentiful** and **refreshing sleep** and plant subconscious impressions which result in the re-establishment of **the normal functions of every healthy cell** in the body as far as this is possible. The result is an **increase in the patient's resistive powers,** a conservation of his protoplasmic energy, and he is in condition more successfully to combat the pathogenic germs which are making their ravages upon him. **The etiological factors of disease,** whether due to pathogenic germs or other causes, **are powerless** in the presence of cells of an organism with a **degree of resistive power** sufficient to render them invulnerable.

All that contributes to the health of an individual in the way of nourishment, medicine, climatic conditions, exercise, etc. of course should be appropriated.

The etiological factors of disease are here, and they are here to stay, in spite of our modern methods of disinfection and improved sanitary conditions, which have practically abolished yellow fever, small pox, cholera, and other diseases regarded as inevitable curses of the human race.

We as physicians have studied the dead body too much and the **living organism not enough.** We have underrated the self-healing processes of Nature, and the physical effects of psychologic influences. This has frequently given charlatans who make use of these methods in disguised form, an opportunity to give us a black eye. We are now, however, giving more attention than ever before to **social and mental and hygienic causes** of health and disease and are placing the practice of medicine upon a more rational basis. We are giving more attention to **the prevention of disease:** and to methods of maintaining the health of the individual.

Suggestion is used both **upon the conscious and subconscious mind,** and whatever we do in the way of teaching our patients how to keep well by **conforming** to the **conditions under which health can be maintained,** comes within the broad domain of suggestive therapeutics. It is the purpose of suggestive therapeutics to help our patients to help themselves by better control and direction of their conscious and subconscious psychic activities.

It is important to remember that the subconscious mind of every individual is **amendable to the influence,** control, or suggestion of his own conscious mind. His own thoughts, his beliefs, his predominating mental characteristics, **as the result of education and environment,** are the suggestions by which he is continually influencing his subconscious mind.

So much so is this true, that we judge character by the expression of the faces of people that we see every day. **The strong face** and the weak face, the honest face and the villainous face; the face which indicates a high order of individuality and self-reliance, selfishness or servitude, all are in evidence. **The fact is,** the body is a perfectly negative element, existing according to the laws of heredity, environment and education. **Thought is a great factor** of change and growth, and thought means that brain cells are functioning **in response to internal and external stimuli.** **The will power** is a positive part which can guide and regulate our thinking, **provided it has once been evolved** sufficiently to set up a new line of mental reaction, **through memory and experience.** We are all using our thought forces or self-suggestions, then, as either creative or destructive agencies, in accordance with this natural, physiological law.

In order to think for one's self, however, the individual must be equipped. He must have a well trained and well developed mind and nervous system which can come only by conforming to the laws of health and by familiarity with the facts that are demonstrated by science, and not through the influence of the modern metaphysical theories of the present time, which act as temporary narcotics, lulling the intellectual faculties into passivity. **Yet, to cultivate habits of cheerfulness,** optimism and self-reliance conduce to health and strength of the physical organism, on account of the influences of such mental states upon the involuntary physiological processes. **Such states of consciousness** as give rise to pessimism, despondency, jealousy, anger, worry, envy and discontent, exert a wrecking, weakening, ruinous effect upon all the involuntary functions. The system becomes loaded with **metabolic toxines,** which in turn render the individual more miserable and morbidly self-conscious.

People frequently say they are miserable on account of their physical condition, and they are, but they are often **reaping in full measure** the conclusion of their own mental action. The mind governs both the conscious and subconscious actions of the human body. **The condition of the body** is largely the result of what an individual has thought and believed, and thought and belief are **determined by his education and other experiences in life.** The influence of education upon the expression of the face and physique has been observed by us all and furnishes a fitting illustration of the influence of the mind over the body.

CHAPTER VI.

OTHER PHASES OF PERSONALITY.

The tendency of the logical mind of today is toward the acceptance of a philosophy that seeks for unity of body, mind and spirit. These are qualities of the individual, but, scientifically speaking, they are one and the same thing. Thus, **monistic philosophy,** or monism, recognizes that mind, spirit and matter, soul and body, God and the world, are abstractions and not things in themselves, but are incomprehensibly bound together in their inseparable oneness. **Call this philosophy** "Monism" or "Monotheism," to suit yourself, but you cannot get away from the stupendous fact, even though our half-trained understandings and narrow experiences are unprepared to comprehend it, that the whole universe **is animated by a single principle of life,** and mode of energy, and that such expressions as **body, mind,** and **spirit** are **qualities** of this one principle, thing or substance. But since it is impossible to think of any **quality** or thing except **by comparison with something else,** each one of these qualities should be held in equal appreciation.

Knowledge is but an apprehension of facts based on **a representation** or description of those facts in terms that can be comprehended by human intelligence.

So, then, in our analysis of the qualities of personality, we can with consistency, in the light of these premises, say that each individual **becomes self-conscious** of his existence upon one of three planes respectively, physical, mental or intellectual, and moral or spiritual, **all qualities** of the same individual.

For instance, **the atom of hydrogen gas,** considered for so long a time to be the smallest subdivision of material substance, is now known to be itself composed of from twelve hundred to three thousand "**ions,**" **or charges of electricity,** or elemental units of force; and it is now recognized that there is in the universe but this one element. Every other element or combination of elements is composed of **this one elementary substance** coming together in different degrees of density. So that the space a thousand feet above our heads is composed of precisely the **same elementary substance** as is the earth beneath our feet.

Furthermore, **the cosmos,** with its countless planetary systems and planets, some of which are millions of times larger than this little earth upon which we live, together with the spaces between them, is all composed of **this one elementary substance, call it physical, mental or spiritual, as you please.**

The only logical conclusion, then, is that **the entire cosmos is an organism,** pulsating, throbbing, vibrating, living, in which we live, and move and have our existence.

And as is the cosmos, so is man. He is an organism, pulsating, vibrating, living. **And as is man, so is each individual cell** in his body with inherent potentialities and powers that are constantly being manifested, functioning in its own way, as it plays its part in the game of life **according to heredity and environment.**

Yet life is a fact, and all forms of life from the first *unicellular moneron* down through the millions and millions of years in which the evolutionary development of man has passed, are all sharers of that one ever-present life, with numberless varieties of expression, infinite and limitless.

In the **evolutionary development** of the human race and of the human intellect and character, each individual seems to become **self-conscious of life** upon one or the other of these three respective planes before mentioned, **physical, intellectual,** and **moral or spiritual,** each of which is the result of training, **education** and **environment,** so far as their manifestations **in his life are concerned.**

Heredity plays an all-important part in the growth and development of body, mind, and character. So much so, that a single fertilized cell contains **all the psychic qualities,** dispositions and traits of personality, physically, mentally and morally, of ancestors for ages past. **All the potentialities are transmitted** in this microscopic, fertilized cell.

The great majority of people are **conscious of life** only upon the **physical plane.** They have scarcely any higher conception of existence and its meaning, other than what appeals to the appetites, eating, drinking, and sensual indulgences. Like two-legged animals they live in many instances upon a plane **even lower than the brute,** as is indicated by expression of face, physique, **character of speech, habits and conduct.**

Others there are who **in self-consciousness reach** the next higher plane and seem to go no further. There are people that we all know, concerning whom, though they may have an intellectuality so cold and pulseless that it glitters as the stars, and be strong enough mentally to make wonderful achievements in the fields of politics and commerce, etc., it is nevertheless easy to discover that there is an **element in their personality** that is lacking. It is lacking in expression of face, in handshake, in tone and quality of voice and speech, and especially in their conduct and demeanor with their fellow man. In the presence of such an individual one feels more as if one were face to face with **a stone or an iceberg,** rather than in the presence of a human being.

As to what conscious existence upon the higher plane of selfhood indicated implies, it is hard to define, yet it consists in the evolving and developing of **those higher elements of human character** regarded as the ethical and aesthetic and moral sense. **We see it manifested** in its influence upon human life in magnanimity, generosity, altruism, kindness, bravery, and all other **distinctly human faculties.** It is the higher functioning of **the true ego,** the real man, call it **body, mind, spirit, life or soul.** It is manifested in man or woman by the exhibition of those inner qualities **of moral and spiritual dignity,** in the determination to do only **that which is conceived** to be good and right, **not** in the outer esteem of their fellows or in the **worthless praise of a conventional society,** but in their own inner consciousness. "Unfortunately," says Ernest Haeckel, "we have to admit that in this respect we are still largely ruled by the foolish views of a lower civilization, if not of crude barbarians."

This animating life principle that functions in human beings defies analysis, evades our comprehension, and transports our thoughts beyond what is finite and terrestrial. **But it is in man** because man is, and if it were not, he would not be. Haeckel says, "Why trouble about this enigmatical 'thing in itself' when we have no means of investigating it?"

This unexplained, undefined and **incomprehensible** element in man is **the real ego.** It is consciousness of life itself. **It is the power** that manifests itself on the physical, mental, or spiritual plane, in its voluntary human expression according to **knowledge, education** and **environment.** It is the **intelligent life entity** which, when fully awakened and evolved in the consciousness of the individual, makes him strong, independent, capable and free.

To discover this element of selfhood is to **discover the real self.** It is to find yourself out.

It is the privilege and duty of every individual to manifest the highest expression and meaning of life upon each of these planes, **physical, mental** and **moral;** to develop harmoniously **as an athlete,** in body, mind and character.

When this highest element of selfhood is evolved in self-consciousness, then **do mind and body** become man's obedient servants. Then do we discover the meaning of Emerson's expression, that "Every man is a divinity in disguise, a God acting a fool."

Strange talk this may appear to be giving to medical men, but it is the most essential truth in connection with our subject.

In the application of suggestive therapeutics we must regard man as a **thing of life, of force, of intelligence, of will and reason,** that emanates from, and is a part of, the central source of all life, with millions and millions of cells in his organism that are ready to respond to stimuli in the form of human personality, therapeutically the **personality of the physician.**

In all events in the light of this monistic philosophy that is accepted by **every prominent man of science** at the present time, let us as physicians recognize that this inherent potentiality or quality or element is **latent in every human being,** whether recognized by him or not, and let us make use of this animating life principle in therapeutics, using it as **one of Nature's forces** by conforming to the law that governs it.

The intimate relation between **neuron structure and mental activity** is now fully appreciated by both physiologists and psychologists. We are taught that the morphological structure of nerve elements bears a most important and intimate relation to mental activity. That the mode of neuron structure is regarded as mirroring the mode of organization of the psychic life.

But it must also be remembered that every psychical phenomenon has its physical concomitant; which is but to say that every mental state has its influence upon the body. The changes which appear in neuron structure are, then, **the result of education** and **experience** which promotes its growth and development. **Faculty proceeds function.** Inherent in every human organism are latent faculties or potentialities which can be developed through the influence of **environment and education—other names for suggestion.**

Step by step it is dawning upon us that **humanity is an organism** and that "the satisfaction and requirement and functioning life activity are impossible without social co-operation, and it is only then that the individual becomes **freed from the bonds of blood relationship."** "In other words," say Sidis and Goodhart, "with the growth and development of social organization, **organic bondage** is replaced by functional relationship."

The lives of human beings are thus so interrelated that personality is but the outgrowth of experience. The life of each individual is constantly influencing the growth and development of **brain** and **mind** and **character** of other individuals by whom **he is also** influenced.

Morality, the functioning of the highest element or quality of selfhood, conforms to the law of evolution, and like organic evolution, **this psychic evolution** is but the adaptation of individuals to conditions of existence. The law of psychic evolution, as of evolution in general, is **from structure to function, from bondage to freedom** of the individual elements.

In the light of the foregoing pages, then, you, reader, are a being, **body, mind** or **spirit,** animated by the one principle of life from which you come, **in common with all human beings** and all forms of life. You have a mind and a body such as you have made it for yourself, modified, of course, by the **laws of heredity and environment. You physically** are the obedient servant, or should be, to the controlling force or life entity within. Your face and physique have been formed, shaped and moulded, by your **use or abuse** of this inherent life force within you.

This inherent life force, question of all questions, what is that? Who are you? In the light of modern knowledge of **the cosmic process of evolution** we are constrained to answer that you are a part of the universal source of all life, which you see manifested wherever you see anything, from the dead earth upon which you walk, to the eyes of those that you love, flowers, trees, clouds, moon, sun and stars, even the stars so far away that a ray of light, going at the rate of one hundred and ninety-five thousand miles per second, beginning at the time that it was **formerly believed** that the world was thrown out into space **by special creation,** could not have yet reached this planet, infinite and limitless. **It is referred to by scientists** as "force." Herbert Spencer says, "The eternal energy behind and within all things." The idealists or religionists say, "The God in whom we live, move and have our being."

Think of this power, of which you are, how it converts bread and meat, fruit and vegetables into bone and muscle, brain and blood, and how you are endowed with, or have evolved, will and reason and other faculties of mind and character, and then dare to **exercise these inherent potentialities** as a co-worker with infinity. Divine molecules are we with the privilege **to think, reason, will,** and **do for ourselves.**

It is utterly impossible to hypnotize anyone without getting the consent and co-operation of **the self-conscious ego**—unless it be one in whom this self-conscious ego has not been evolved. See how we get the consent and cooperation of this, the real man, when an individual consents **to relax, close his eyes, with lips slightly apart,** to secure thorough relaxation, as if to say, "All right, doctor, **mind and body** submit I unto you, I step aside, the door is open."

At this juncture and while your patient is in this condition, by your better educated and better equipped personality you pour some of **your own psychic life** in the form of suggestion, **into his.** You thus renew and stimulate latent, dormant, psychic activities, encourage the functions of his body, and you **put life and health** and **strength** where there was weakness, **in conformity with a natural law.**

It is estimated that the normal individual has from **eight hundred million** to thirteen hundred million cells of gray matter in his brain and that the average individual uses but **about one-tenth** of this entire number. By the influence of personality upon personality, then, we convert latent energy into moving energy, **potential energy into dynamic energy,** and thus stimulate and encourage the functions of every cell in the human body.

Every time you come into the presence of a patient, it is your privilege and duty to get the consent and co-operation of **the ego, that highest element of the self-conscious individual,** and appeal to this higher psychic quality, **the man himself,** the organized, intelligent life entity, that has simply thrown this physical cloak around him, and encourage it to vitalize and energize all life processes **upon the physical plane.**

We, as physicians, have studied dead eyes that do not see, dead tongues that do not talk, dead ears that do not hear. We all know that the **mind, soul,** or **spirit,** or **life,** name it as you choose, is the real man, and yet this ever present entity has been an unconsidered element in our consideration of human beings.

I am aware of the sneers that occasionally come from a few individuals who disregard this quality of human personality.

They are usually those in which **this higher self-consciousness** has not been evolved.   They have not discovered themselves; we stand upon different planes and they deserve our pity.

There are other individuals who are so hide-bound in religious orthodoxy that they are themselves hypnotized by creed or dominated by the power of suggestion until they are not open to the consideration of this subject in its broader aspects. **There is no phase of philosophy** or religious theory or question or problem of life, educational, ethical, moral or political that a conscientious truth seeker is not likely to jar in the discussion of this subject.   **They are under the sway of precedent** and prejudice, and it seems to them a species of disloyalty to question the hoary old beliefs which have become as much a matter of family inheritance to them as the color of the eyes or hair or shape of the features.

But times and manners change.   Skepticism is the natural fruit of growing intelligence and increasing experience.   It is simply the **unwillingness of the truth seeker** to be satisfied with anything less than the truth.

The great majority of mankind are practically untouched by the progress of present day knowledge.   The tremendous task of teaching men and women to think for themselves and learn the great lesson of **self-reliance** has scarcely begun. All but our most intelligent people are creatures of a school of thought or belong to some intellectual herd.   **Never was there a time** that so demanded fearless, independent, tolerant, logical thinking.

Reason is mankind's greatest, highest and noblest faculty, and as such should be the supreme court of the mind, and all other impulses that flitter and dance and play in the stream of human consciousness, either intellectual or emotional in character, should be subject to its rulings.

Will, the executor of reason and judgment, should be loyal enough to follow their dictates. It is upon this condition only that sanity is maintained. Will and reason, however, are in keeping with the law of evolution, psychic qualities that are developed by education, knowledge and experience.

Consciousness, the most fundamental faculty of the human soul, is a stream of endless psychic states, resulting from previous experiences, incessantly changing as the restless, white capped tides of ocean, that can exist only by virtue of its endless unceasing motion; and this continuous change is what makes conscious life.

Conscious life itself, then, is a stream of varying psychical states, which quickly follow one another in perpetual motion, rolling, rising and sinking, ebbing and flowing, with never an instant of rest. The elementary psychic states which lie below consciousness constitute the subconscious realm. Here is a great ocean of memories, sensations, imaginations, emotions and impulses, desires and aspirations, hopes and ambitions, fears and disappointments, successes and failures, which are past impressions or memory pictures that linger in the human brain. These rise to the realm of consciousness and are interpreted in thoughts and feelings from which there is no escaping, and these thoughts or feelings in turn constitute mental states

[8]

which exert an influence upon **all involuntary physiological processes.**

The power of attention fixes the mind on such ideas and sensations or memory pictures as are most worth while to the individual, and **by constant assertion and iteration,** reasoning and persuasion, suggesting and impressing, we substitute such impressions as will bring the individual **under their influence,** both consciously and subconsciously.

By suggestion we can drive back these subconscious impressions or memory pictures, and if we but have personality and self-hood to dare to make an **appeal to the highest element of character** within those of our patients who need thus arousing, we have rendered the greatest service that one human being can possibly render a fellow man. **Arouse the higher intellectual faculties,** the higher brain centers, and the highest moral ideal into action, and you truly put life into your patient.

In every great battle that has been fought in both ancient and modern times, brave leadership by a strong appeal made through patriotism and pride has so **aroused the psychic element** in soldiers in battle that men have been frequently known to stand and fight through heat and cold, day and night, with hunger and thirst, for days and days at a time and conquer by **unwavering will and determination.** They have thus exhibited a degree of resistive power in many notable instances that has been **beyond human conception.** In all instances in battle the soldiers on the **victorious side easily recover** from serious wounds and mutilations, while, on the other hand, those upon the side that is defeated, die of mere trivial inflictions.

In all heroic achievements of men, reserve, **subconscious power,** has been brought into action, stimulated or evoked by the conditions of the moment, that enables individuals to accomplish which seemed absolutely impossible in proportion to their recognized capacity.

These are facts that every observing individual has frequently recognized and that are **acknowledged by us all.** If human beings have within them that **psychic element** which can be evoked under extraordinary conditions to so increase the normal resistive powers and capabilities of both mind and body, why should we as physicians not in a sense, **be generals or leaders** in our association with our patients, and in our daily relations with them **evoke latent energy** and heighten their normal resistive powers to the ravages of any disease, acute or chronic, organic or "psycho-neuro-pathic."

The successful men in every profession, in all trades and departments of life, are enthusiasts, whether it be a Martin Luther, a Savonarola, a Bismarck, a Napoleon, a Joe Wheeler, or a physician. Men have in innumerable instances been known to **stir their fellow men to action.** The simple country maiden, Joan of Arc, by her enthusiasm and unwavering self-confidence, headed the French army **in the face of defeat** and led her stalwart troops to victory.

What are we as the medical profession doing as leaders for the people? As guardians of the public health are we doing all within our power in the way of teaching people how to keep well and healthy and strong, without relying upon us to administer to their **physical necessities** or upon priest or clergy to control their **psychic activities?**

In directing an individual how to control his or her psychic activities and **steer them into channels of useful thought and conduct,** the entire man, physical and psychical, body and mind, or soul and spirit, if you choose, must be taken into consideration. **Body, mind, and spirit** must be considered as qualities of the individual, one and inseparable; their inter-dependence must be recognized.

At this time, when those possessing abnormal powers of imagination, with unlimited emotion and little reasoning, are being led by every absurd theory and metaphysical dogma that is presented under the pretense of an especially commissioned divine guidance, we should be prepared to rise to the occasion and acquit ourselves as men in the highest sense. The great need of the world today is **education, knowledge and guidance,** other names for honest, conscientious, truthful suggestion.

The problems of health are the problems of life, problems of education and economic considerations which involve the questions of **work, food, clothing, homes,** and all other essentials that make for human happiness. **Manhood is only in the making.** We are yet evolving, growing and developing. The process of evolution is as active today as it was a million years ago, and **it points to the evolution of the mind as well as the body, of the God in man, and not the triumphant brute.** All those who in any way by ideas, provision of means, or achievement contribute to the evolution of the human race, are the world's true benefactors.

Life consists in the free exercise of our faculties and happiness in the successful performance of duty and achievement. "The law of natural selection" and "The survival of the fittest" will go on forever.

The self-conscious ego can and does function on the physical plane, making a tyrant or a beast of man; or on the mental or intellectual plane, making him capable of reasoning and thinking for himself; or on the ethical or moral plane, making him a reasonable, useful human being, dependent on education and environment. The optimism of scientific minds consists in the belief that upon these three planes of life mankind must be strong, capable, and free, and that we shall not dwindle into physical weaklings, intellectual nonentities, or spiritual slaves or fanatics.

The fight made by the medical profession against parasitic germs in the fields of pathology, surgery, medicine, and hygiene, has been crowded with glorious achievement, but a greater work is still before us. Our battle is only half begun.

Since the days of Vesalius, Harvey and Jenner, down to the present time, every step of advance made by medical science has been boldly contested and fought by ignorance, fanaticism and misdirected zeal. The warfare of science must go on forever. Nature has surrendered to science her most valued treasures. We have subdued steam and electricity, harnessed the waterfalls, tunnelled the mountains, rendered the bosom of the ocean amenable to the great service of mankind, and demanded from the bowels of the earth her most sacred treasures.

Those who regard humanity as a finished product, now standing at the mercy of an anthropo-morphic deity, are in the truest sense retarding the evolution, growth, and development of the **highest psychic qualities** of man and womanhood.

Science has no fight to make against **true religion**; its struggle is with ignorance and intolerant dogmatism. She demands a religion that **appeals to the brain as well as to the emotions;** to **reason** and **not to ignorance,** one that will develop the entire individual to the fullness of perfect manhood and womanhood. Life is a struggle. Every idea that seeks to be embodied demands a conflict. In order to live, we must dare to be, to declare our own individuality.

Physicians have done much for the protection of the human body, but what are they doing to prevent the **parasitic infection of absurd beliefs and dogmas** and theories that at the present time infect the human mind with their **blighting, weakening influence** upon the development of body, mind and character?

Science and everyday experience agree that Nature cares nothing for individuals. What the people of our time need is plain living, clear thinking, and right action, to develop potentialities of both mind and body.

The psychical correlation of religious emotion and the sexual instincts is such that any sect that starts with extravagant sentiments of love to all men will fascinate and take hold of an easily impressible type of unscientific and unthinking people. Yet minds that have been stored with nothing more substantial than historical fiction and **agitated so long by unreasonable dogmas** of a capricious deity from which they naturally shrink, are easily captured and held in subjection by any mind-soothing theory under the guise of religion that has a romantic or mystical flavor. **A lack of contact with the world** and an unfamiliarity with the facts of science have left these credulous people with no more powers of reflection than a child, and they naturally have, in consequence, abnormally deveolped imaginations and emotions, and are easily captured by absurd and illogical metaphysical vagaries.

In my travels among the physicians I have talked with **many men of scientific attainments,** and in the ranks of both the clergy and the medical profession they deplore the fact that theologians of the present day have been so slow to accept and utilize the message of science, and that so many have lacked the moral stamina to shake off the worn out and useless doctrines of an ignorant and superstitious age; **yet among the clergy** are many who teach and preach better than their creed. They have **no fight to make against science,** but look upon science as the handmaiden of true religion. **The majority, however,** have been held in the coils of creed and fettered by dogma and thus coerced into a beaten path at the sacrifice of reason and judgment. **The more enlightened clergymen** realize this, and just in proportion as they are educated and scientific men, are they boldly getting away from the absurd dogmas and shaking off useless external formalities that have fettered the aspiring spirit, progress and growth of humanity so long.

In their slowness to interpret life and its meaning in the light of present day knowledge, no wonder that we see an article in one of our leading periodicals headed "Is the Pulpit a Coward's Castle?" **And yet there was never** in the world's history a greater need for strong, fearless, unblemished and unfettered men willing to devote their lives to the help of their fellow men.

Do you ask what this discussion has to do with suggestive therapeutics? It has at the present day a most important bearing. The present status of this subject is so related to those influences **of an educational nature** that furnish food stuffs to the minds of the people, that I should feel that I had dodged the issue, **the most important issue,** did I not boldly face these problems, which I know are agitating the minds of scientific medical men everywhere, and give them the consideration that they so pre-eminently deserve.

Religious beliefs and health and disease stand in precisely the same relation as does mind and body. It is simply a question of those influences that dominate and control an individual's **psychic life.** To do another's thinking for him is to regulate his actions and control his life. It is a question of the factors that are **obscuring** and **obstructing** the **path** of social and intellectual progress in opposition to those influences that elevate thought and action among living men and women.

No intelligent physician would think of overlooking the question of dietetics in the treatment of a case of chronic indigestion, especially when unwholesome food was largely responsible for this physical malady. **It is of equal importance,** if not more important, to take into consideration those elements that are harmful or healthful in the growth and development and stability and maintenance of mind and character. **The physician who ignores the psychic element** in the consideration of sickness and disease is as one-sided as the Christian Scientists who refuse to recognize the needs of the body. The consideration of the maintenance of the health of an individual involves those factors that **maintain and sustain health and strength of both mind and body.**

How many thousands of people have died before men found out which were poisons and which were foods? **To teach by killing that others may learn** to use their faculties has been the method of the cosmic process in the evolution and development of the human being. **Even today the greater part of sickness** and disease is but Nature's protest against human beings for violating her laws, physical, hygienic, dietetic, psychical, etc. In the consideration of those factors that contribute to human health and happiness, all these elements must be considered.

Every step taken by the scientific men of the medical profession to abolish cholera, smallpox, and yellow fever, has been opposed by mystics and sentimentalists. But though thousands of lives have been saved by improved sanitation, hygiene, dietetics, disinfection and asepsis in the physical realm, there is a field of **no less importance in the psychological realm** that needs to be fumigated, disinfected, drained and cleared of parasites that live and thrive upon the ignorance and superstition of weakness and innocence. Modern science is turning the **great searchlight of truth** into every dark corner where these poisonous microbes may be found lurking.

The universal acceptance of the doctrine of evolution by all the important non-sectarian universities in our country and by **the more enlightened theological schools** has sounded the death knell of the old formulated creeds and dogmas based upon the ideas of special creation that has fettered the aspiring spirit of humanity so long. **To say that you believe in the doctrine of evolution** is but to say that you believe in God's way of doing things, and of all classes of people who ought to be ready to accept this important truth and give the people the benefit of the light it sheds upon human life and conduct, the men of the learned professions should be the first.

Fear, an emotion which is the result of an analysis of consequences, has been so instilled in the human mind by the teachers and preachers of anthropo-morphic theism, until the great masses of people who are not sufficiently educated to think for themselves, have been unconsciously dominated and development of body, mind and character suppressed.

The revelations made by scientific investigators do not take God out of the world, but render us more intimately self-conscious of his all pervading presence. Moreover, they only add new luster to the matchless character whose simple teaching of faith, hope and love has for two thousand years stirred the noblest impulses of the human soul, and proved to be the greatest factor in the evolution of the ethical and moral element of the human race, in spite of the war and bloodshed and destruction of human lives that have been perpetrated by **religious sects pretending to be his followers.**

The great need of the world today is men to interpret life **in the light of present day knowledge** and to tell the people the truth as the more enlightened individuals see it, and who will not falter and be cowardly on account of the ignorance and superstition of ages past and gone that is still exercising its demoralizing influence upon our present civilization. **All the modern creeds and cults, "ists" and "isms"** of the present day are but an evidence of the recoil of the people from the dogmatism and intolerance of medicine and theology.

With the present conception and theory of the origin and destiny of man, the individual has made a wonderful discovery. He has learned that he is **no longer a serf,** but that he, too, has creative power, and he dares to give it manifest expression in his life and conduct. **With this changed mental attitude** toward the universe and its process of development, he has been made self-conscious of the God in his own soul, and life has a zest and meaning which is equivalent to having put him into a new world. It has altered his conception of himself and his relation to all forms of life, and he realizes as never before his **intimate relation and responsibility and duty to his fellow man.** He no longer considers himself **a stranger and an exile in a foreign country,** but **here** and **now** he is at home, securely abiding in the great, living, throbbing, pulsating heart of Nature. **Side by side with his fellow man** is he permitted to work and in his own way to contribute his best efforts to the furtherance of human happiness.

No class of human beings have done so much for their brethren as the members of the medical profession. In dens of poverty, fields of pestilence, or amid the heat of shot and shell in war, they are ever conspicuous for their presence. **Day and night, through heat and cold,** sunshine or rain, they are found anywhere, from the lowest brothels to gilded palaces, in laboratories and hospitals, amid contagious diseases or with the insane, laboring to promote'the comfort, health and happiness of their fellows.

Ignorant mankind has been **so long preached the worm of the dust** theory and been taught to call himself weak, humble, powerless and worthless, until many have become so on account of their own thinking. **Let them once get a glimpse** of their divine origin, in the light of modern evolutionary knowledge, and dare to exercise their faculties and inherent capabilities of body and mind on lines of useful endeavor, **and seek health by conforming to the conditions of health,** and dare to claim and exercise the ability **to think, will, reason, and do for themselves,** and many there are in this world who, like Pygmalion's statue Galatea, will be transformed into beings of life.

We are beginning to look at ourselves with new eyes. The old religions, which condemn the body as vile and sinful and advocate a locality of everlasting punishment, are passing away. We now realize **that the mind helps the body** as much as the body helps the mind, that mind, body and spirit **are qualities of the one individual** and that within every human being lies the power through intelligent living, acting and thinking, to develop both mind and body into a high degree of perfection.

The human will, **guided by reason,** is the positive part of our mental equipment and the body is the negative, responsive to its rulings and dictates. **Intelligent, logical thinking** as the result of education and experience, effort and determination, are **the great factors of growth** and the most powerful forces in the universe. It is force itself in its voluntary human expression. **By these all other forces** of Nature are controlled and utilized for the happiness of man.

We have nothing to fear from the modern unlicensed systems of healing which have arisen out of the development of a better appreciation of **the psychic qualities of man** within the past twenty years. **The fittest will survive.** As among Ruskin's Lilies, the sunflowers and weeds shoot up their heads in gorgeous array and they are only giving expression to a single phase of truth. The universe is big enough to furnish a stage of action for us all, so let them do their little stunts in peace.

The coming physician, however, must of necessity be a broad-gauged and well educated man. His therapeutic armamentarium and mental equipment will be such as to enable him to avail himself of all methods of treatment, physical, mental, social, moral, ethical, that make for the health and happiness of his patient.

A large percentage of the people who are sick, ailing or complaining do not need medicine or surgery. What many of them really need, though they may not be cognizant of their need, is direction and advice, knowledge and guidance, all suggestive measures that enable them to conform to the conditions by which the wonderful recuperative powers inherent in the biological elements of the organism can have a chance to re-establish health. **Human beings are so constituted** that they cannot in this infantile stage of their development, stand alone. The great organism of **humanity must have men strong, capable, self-reliant and well educated,** to direct and influence the functions of the great mass of the people, just as the higher centers of the brain influence all the lower bodily functions.

The hunger of the body for bread and fruit, meat and vegetables, is no more real than the hunger of the human intellect for facts and principles by which life and conduct may be guided.

The charlatanism of the past twenty years has an important message for the medical profession, as it has also for theologians. In hundreds and thousands of instances have they demonstrated to us that there **are mental and physical causes of diseases,** on the one hand, and that diseases of the physical organism, not too far advanced, can be benefitted, ameliorated and oftentimes cured, by **correcting these perverted mental conditions** on the other.

Science has pointed out and discovered the mental toxemia that has been disseminated and scattered broadcast unconsciously and unintentionally by the halting, timeworn, motheaten and useless **systems of education and ecclesiasticism,** and there are thousands and thousands of individuals who need help, in the way of aid to enable them to do rational, intelligent thinking and living.

What is disease? I believe that even Virchow would agree that it is a condition wherein the **cells of the part affected** do not properly perform their functions. At first it begins as a mere so-called functional disturbance, which, though the aid of the microscope be required to detect it, **always implies a physical change.** At least, there is a lessened degree of resistive power in the cells of the organism. In this weakened condition the individual cells are more vulnerable and are unqualified to put up a strong fight against their enemies. **Now an exciting cause**

of disease comes along in the form of a pathogenic germ or other etiological factor. In the case of the bacteriological infection a fight ensues. **Brave and altruistic little men** as they are, the phagocytes throw their bodies into the combat to destroy the pathogenic enemy by intracellular digestion, or if, forsooth, they fail in this, **they pile their bodies by the thousands and millions,** to build, as it were, an impenetrable breastwork for the protection of the remaining cells of the organism, each one anxious and willing to sacrifice his own life that his fellows may be protected. Thus an organic or structural change takes place and this may then be beyond the pale of psychological methods of treatment.

But in conjunction with surgical, medicinal and other therapeutic measures, we can, by psychological methods, aid in the re-establishment of every other bodily function which may have been disturbed on account of this local, organic, or pathological condition; and so we not only help the individual in a general way, but we indirectly **aid in the healing processes of surgical procedures** and **supplement medicinal** and other therapeutic devices. We quiet nervousness, relieve pain and promote sleep. **The result is** better appetite, increased digestion and assimilation, improved nutrition, and a consequent conservation of energy throughout the entire physical organism.

So, then, it must appear to the logical mind, that there is **no class of cases, acute or chronic, surgical or otherwise,** in which the psychological factor does not play an important part in conjunction with all other methods of therapeutics.

CHAPTER VII.

SUGGESTION APPLIED WITHOUT HYPNOTISM.

It is in functional and **neuropathic conditions** that suggestive therapeutics is most applicable, yet it must be remembered that a functional disturbance weakens the resistive power of the cells of the organsim and invites bacteriological invasion, and that the speedy and timely correction of the functional disorder may prevent its resulting in an organic lesion.

There is an important psychic element in all classes of diseases and conditions, surgical, infectious, febrile, or otherwise. Physicians on the coasts, where yellow fever until only a few years ago wrought great destruction of life, quite frequently reminded me of what an important role mental influences played in helping or hindering a patient suffering with this disease.

One physician recited a case in which he had under his care a young man sick with yellow fever, whom he had led to believe himself suffering only from malarial fever, in order to avoid the harmful influence of fear of yellow fever in his case. His family had acquiesced in this scheme and the young man was doing well and no apprehensions were entertained as to his recovery, until a thoughtless friend of the patient who had himself recovered but two weeks before from yellow fever was admitted to see him. **He made it dawn on the consciousness of the sufferer** that he had yellow fever instead of malarial fever, a severe illness instead of a trivial one, and thus so wrought upon his emotional or involuntary nervous system by the fear that he had planted by his unwise suggestions that the patient at once took a change for the worse. "His stomach and bowels and kindeys literally went to pieces," and he was dead in two hours after the young man's visit.

A physician of my acquaintance related the following case: His wife, who was supposed to have reached full term of pregnancy, was taken ill with a unilateral lobar pneumonia with temperature of 104, pulse 120, the first day. **Two days afterward** she was delivered, and on the fourth day after the onset of the pneumonia and the second day after parturition, at about nine o'clock at night after using the vaginal douche, hot poultices to the chest, and ice to her head, she went to sleep with her hand gently clasped between both of his own.

He likewise dropped off to sleep, when after perhaps two hours had elapsed, she awoke startled with a muttering delirious groan which awoke him. Her pulse was 160 a minute and the tempearture was afterward observed to be 105.5 F. He quickly prepared a hypodermic injection of strychnine sulphate 1-20 grain, and just as he had pushed the water to the end of his needle to exclude all air, he looked down as if to say, "Give me your arm."

Her condition was such **before she went to sleep** two hours previously, he had entertained very great apprehensions of her ability to recover, and now he felt decidedly uneasy about her, though he made every effort to conceal his forebodings. **As her eyes met his** he felt what she afterwards admitted, she was about to say, namely, that she was going to die or that she was dying. **Quickly getting possession of himself** he spoke to her loudly and

[9]

strongly, positively asserting, "You will be better in a moment. I have seen a hundred people more sick than you are get well. Give me your arm." As he looked at her again, having withdrawn the needle, **a smile was on her face and tears trickling** down both her cheeks. Putting his face close to hers and gently caressing the other cheek, he suggested, "You were only dreaming; let me renew the poultice and ice bag and show you how good you will be feeling in a few moments." **At once a new consciousness** took possession of her, the anxious expression was gone, her pulse was slower and her voice decidedly stronger. **That proved to be the turning point** in her recovery, though the lung did not begin to clear up until the eighth day.

There are, in the experience of every general practitioner, in certain individual cases, crises **where the psychic factor** has decided the recovery or non-recovery of his patient. Had the case just related have been surrounded by an emotional, over-anxious family, who would only have **aggravated that peculiar psychic condition,** that physician's wife would probably have been dead inside of two hours.

The author has had in his own experience several incidents where he has been called into consultation to see individuals who were seriously ill, where the entire family had confidence in his judgment, which also made the patient more amenable to his suggestions, and where the attending physician had practically read the patient's death warrant by giving an unfavorable prognosis in no uncertain terms, and after making an examination, he has begun psychic treatment by the positive statement to the patient, **"You are going to get well all right."**

In one such case that happened to be turned over to me after a brief absence, where the physician in temporary charge had given a positive, unfavorable prognosis, I assured the patient in the presence of the physician at my first visit that **he was going to get well,** that the treatment that he was on was precisely the right one, that a decided change for the better would take place that very night. **The physician,** a very dear friend of mine, followed me out of the room, and in a subdued tone, addressing me by name, said, "I hate to see you fall so hard. There is no more possibility of that patient getting well than there is of your taking wings and flying."

The case in question was that of an old man seventy-eight years of age, who had been sick for ten days with la grippe and who now had an acute lobar pneumonia. The prognosis given by the physician in this case was just such as ninety-nine physicians out of a hundred, who did not fully recognize the value **of the psychic factor in therapeutics,** would have given in such a case.

"Why do you say that he will not get well?" I asked.

"It is my opinion, based upon the pathological conditions, together with his age and continued illness," was his reply.

"But my opinion is that he will get well," said I.

"Yes, but you are not doing right to **make him believe** that he is going to get well when he is so sick," said he most kindly.

"But, doctor, that is just what is going to make him get well; because **I can make him believe it,** will strengthen the bridge that is to tide him over to recovery."

After that I assumed control of the situation and allowed no one to enter that room who **did not believe** that that patient was going to recover on account of confidence sufficient in me to rely upon my judgment. **Even the physician agreed** to co-operate with my plan out of respect for my wishes in that particular case.

When he returned the next day, he said to me in the consulting room with his face lighted with a smile, "He is really better. Your presence has greatly benefited him."

It was eleven days before that lung cleared up, his temperature went down and heart beats became strong and natural for his condition, **but he recovered.**

The point that I wished to bring out has been illustrated in this case. The physician who does not fully **appreciate the psychological factor** in therapeutics is far more likely to give an unfavorable prognosis—and in many instances he might as well knock his patient on the head with a sledge hammer as use psychic influences, unconsciously though it be, **to retard rather than promote recovery.**

It is frequently the case that the physician comes into the presence of a serious pathological condition, so depressed himself by his knowledge of pathology, that he forgets to put confidence in the recuperative powers of his patient, which can be encouraged and stimulated to increase all physiological processes. **This unconscious suggestive influence** may so plant fear in the patient, accumulating with double force on account of the depressing **environmental psychologic influence** which follows as a logical sequence, that it can be stated as a scientific truth that the prognosis frequently kills the patient.

People die frequently under such conditions of purely nervous shock. **Shock** may be defined as being a **complete suspension of some** and **partial suspension of others of the functions of the nervous system.**

Fear alone, an emotion which is the result of the analysis of consequences, exercises an inhibitory influence over all the nervous functions, **both voluntary and involuntary.** Every idea that originates in the conscious mind as the result of self-analysis of subjective sensations, symptoms, and conditions, reproduces itself in the body.

Physiologists have always endowed the nerve and brain centers with a peculiar energy of their own, indefinitley expressed under such terms as neuric energy, nerve force, vis medicatrix naturae, etc. At any rate **these higher centers** stand in a similar relation to the body to that in which a dynamo stands to a great building full of intricate and complex machinery. When properly manipulated **the influx of energy** goes to every organ, cell and function of the body, **giving stored up energy** to the special functions as occasion requires.

The mental attitude of the patient to his own condition is the determining factor in the utilization of stored up reserve psychic power. **The very belief** on the part of the patient in the possible serious outcome of his illness, even when he is, as far as it is possible for a human being to be, apparently devoid of fear, disturbs and depresses him and weakens all power of resistance.

An illustration of the influence of the conscious mind upon voluntary functions is well demonstrated by concentrating the mind upon the arm held at right angles to the body and constantly iterating the suggestion that "the arm is getting stronger and stronger."

It is usually supposed that a man cannot hold up his arm for more than five or ten minutes at a time. I once took a class of **ten young ladies** bewteen twenty-two and thirty years of age, and by suggestion each one was enabled to hold her arm at right angles to her body for one hour. **During this experiment** I held my own arm at right angles and standing in front of a circle that had been formed, I requested that each one of the young ladies look at the bridge of my nose glasses and positively assured them that **as long as the eyes** did not lose sight of this object, **their arms** would remain strong.

"Mine is tired and I cannot hold out much longer," said one, after about fifteen minutes.

"Then let me touch the point of your elbow and it will be strong again," I quickly replied. Then going from one to the other who requested it, I kept that sort of thing up until the hour was up.

Each one of the young ladies thought that I had given them the strength to hold their arms out so long. In a sense I had done so, by suggestions to their subconscious selves, though they were wide awake and in no sense hypnotized, as the term is ordinarily employed; yet in **reality there was as much hypnotism** exerted as if they had been in a state of active somnambulism.

I have frequently taken a group of children, who have always been favorite associates of mine, and began with them in what

I was pleased to call "exercises." I would first begin by having all hold out one arm in a prize contest which they enjoyed immensely. **For four out of six** to hold out an arm at right angles to the body for an hour and a half after the third or fourth day's exercises, was nothing unusual.

They could also stand on one foot for more than an hour, still at times and hopping about at other times with the other foot in hand, either in front of or behind them. At any rate, I held their attention and **constantly kept up a suggestive influence** by addressing my suggestion to one and then another, expressing my confidence in his or her ability to hold up an arm or stand on one foot all day long.

In my demonstrations and lectures given to physicians, I always have had one or more physicians present take a suggestion, without the slightest attempt to induce sleep, by agreeing to co-operate with me so that I could show him how he could convey a suggestion to his own subconscious mind and get results that would surprise him. **In over five hundred instances** have I placed physicians submitting to this experiment across two chairs and jumped upon their bodies with my entire weight of two hundred pounds, and in nine-tenths of the instances they would say that I had apparently placed no more than three or four pounds upon them. **They were astonished** and frequently incredulous when I informed them that they had sustained my weight.

Anyone who believes that he can do so, can easily lie with head in one chair and heels in another and hold up one hundred and fifty or two hundred pounds. On the other hand I have frequently witnessed a physician attempt this where **he did not believe it possible** for a man to sustain even his own weight, and he always proved that what he believed about it was correct.

It is simply a question of mental attitude.

For a suggestion to be assimilated as a self-suggestion, there must be confidence that **amounts to a conviction,** before it will reach and influence the subconscious realm. The great realm of subconsciousness, which corresponds to the functioning of **at least nine-tenths of an individual's psychic powers,** is amenable to the suggestion of the conscious beliefs of the individual. **His mental attitude,** if it amounts to a conviction, evokes or calls forth latent powers or inherent psychic activities, and renders the reserve energy available or useless as he has confidence or lack of confidence.

But suggestion without hypnotism is effective in its influence not only upon the **voluntary nervous functions,** but the involuntary functions as well. **Through the influence of suggestion** upon the physiological processes of the body, **even gross structural changes** can result.

I walked up to a physician upon one occasion who was holding the hand of a little boy in both of his own, gently manipulating his hand. He was assuring the little fellow **that those warts would go away,** that they would go away when he did not know anything about it, and in two months would be gone, etc.

The physician had attended my lecture and demonstration the previous evening, and when I discovered what he was doing, I exclaimed, "Using suggestion so early, doctor?"

"Oh, this is my own method of curing warts," he replied. "I enjoy the enviable reputation here among the little boys as being **the wart cure doctor,** and I have in numerous cases dispersed them by suggestion."

A well-known physician related to me an experience of his in the case of a uterine fibroid—yes, a fibroid tumor of the uterus! Upon his last examination before an **intended surgical operation,** he found that there was much adhesion, and rather than jeopardize the life of his patient, he decided upon a plan which he executed as follows:

"Mrs. Blank," he said, "if you will co-operate with me for one year, I feel quite certain that you can get well without the operation I intended. It will all depend upon your intelligent, persistent co-operation and effort. I **wish to see you once a week** to apply a medicine to the inside of your womb for the influence that it will exert upon lessening the circulation in that tumor, and also to apply a tampon to hold up the heavy organ so that you will suffer no more pain. **Now, what I want you to do,** in dead earnest, is this: Whenever you think of your condition at all, say to yourself, 'The blood vessels that go to this tumor are drying up, shrinking up, getting smaller and smaller, my womb is getting lighter and lighter and this tumor is going away. Every day and night it is going away."

"Doctor Blank," exclaimed she, "are you a Christian Scientist? Do you mean to tell me that any such mental attitude on my part could exert an influence upon a large, hard substance like the things you showed me in those jars?"

"**No, madam, I am not** a Christian Scientist," said he, "but I do know that persistent, intelligent use of the higher brain centers exerts a wonderful influence over the vasomotor neuro-regulation of the blood supply to any part of the body upon which attention is centered, and I tell you frankly that if you will do as I advise you, I expect to avoid the necessity of this operation."

"**Doctor Blank,**" replied his patient, earnestly, "I will **persistently** and **constantly** do some of the finest thinking that any person ever did, all the time while I am awake and when I retire at night. I will affirm and iterate that this tumor is drying up and shrinking up, that the blood vessels are getting smaller and smaller and that the tumor is getting lighter and lighter and is rapidly going away, day and night it is going away."

This physician saw that patient once a week and made a simple application to her womb, but each time assured her that the congestion was being relieved, that the blood vessels were getting smaller, that her womb was getting lighter and that she was progressing nicely in every way.

He said that at the end of one year that woman's tumor was less than one-fourth of the original size. His patient at that time said, "Oh, doctor, it is such a responsibility to have to keep forcing that suggestion upon the involuntary physiological processes all the time."

"**Then dismiss it, madam,** just as I am going to dismiss you. I am positive that you will experience no more trouble and you may think of yourself as being a well woman."

It was two years since he dismissed that patient and she had experienced no more trouble.

While upon this phase of the subject, let me state here that **the sexual instinct and its development** is a far more potent factor in the production of neurotic symptoms than is commonly supposed. Nothing so disturbs the tranquility of the average mind as the belief in his or her own sexual weakness, though it is purely imaginary.

That one individual, however, has a nose that is conspicuous for its enormous convexity and another for its concavity does not prevent this organ from performing its function. **So in the case of the female uterus,** which is probably the organ that varies more than any other in position and size and the fact that in one case the fundus points to an angle of forty-five degrees forward when the individual is in the erect position or forty-five degrees backward in another individual is no ground to give rise to a diagnosis of abnormality or disease.

This organ is also from its very nature subject to a great variety of vascular changes and when a patient is morbid in the belief that she has some serious uterine affection with all the perverted mental states that accompany such a self-consciousness, **there is no field of work** in which suggestion in conjunction with some simple application or device brings such fruitful results.

Get the confidence of your patient; let her know that you are considering her case from every point of view; find out what she believes about her case and do it tactfully, and then give her a scientific analysis of her case in your own language that will harmonize with her own convictions and her symptoms, and in making a mental picture to her as to what the outcome of the treatment will be, be sure to cover every symptom.

In other words, in conjunction with your local treatment be sure to give a suggestion to meet every indication, letting your patient feel that the treatment will bring such results. While using suggestion in conjunction with your treatment, do all you can to secure the intelligent co-operation of your patient.

In all gynecological cases there is more or less functional and neuropathic disturbance, such as insomnia, nervousness, indigestion, constipation, despondency, etc., which can be successfully combated by simple suggestion given at the time the local treatment is applied. Above all send your patients away **less self-conscious of the seriousness** of their illness and more confident of a complete recovery.

A casual remark, while holding the attention of your patient, that she will be easy after this, will sleep soundly at night, have a better appetite and feel better in every way, is food stuff for the subconscious mind **that furnishes memory pictures or ideas** that will be reproduced in the body.

A patient of mine upon one occasion had worked very hard taking stock in a dry goods store and became fatigued. He had not slept the two nights previous, though he had taken fifteen or twenty grains of sulphonal. **He said when he came into my presence** that he just must have a good night's sleep or he could not undertake the heavy task before him the next day. After patiently going into his case, asking him in regard to appetite, elimination, digestion, amount of water taken during the twenty-four hours, etc., I remarked, "Well, you will sleep if you take a dose of this prescription at bedtime and follow other directions."

I advised him to go at once and drink two glasses of water and repeat this in two hours, and again at bedtime and also insisted that he take **a long walk before going to his home,** all of which I explained was necessary both to encourage elimination and to drive the blood away from an overworked brain.

I then gave the following directions: "Now, take notice, Mr. Blank, if you are not willing to go to sleep tonight, don't take this medicine, **for if you take it you are going to sleep.** Be sure to explain to your wife that you are taking something to give you a good night's rest and that your bedroom must be kept as quiet as possible.

"After preparing for bed, shake the bottle thoroughly and fill a tablespoonful of the medicine and then swallow it. Then put out your light, get in bed and turn yourself loose," (showing him how to relax). **"By slightly breathing through your mouth,** you will take into your lungs more oxygen, which greatly facilitates the action of this medicine. In less than a minute after you relax and breathe deeply, you will feel your arms and lower limbs getting heavy and experience a sensation as if you are sinking down in your bed. **This is the effect of the medicine,** don't resist it; and in less than three more minutes you will be sound asleep and sleep soundly all night and awake in the morning feeling much refreshed."

I then arose and turned to the door in a way that suggested to him to get on out.

"See here, doctor," said he, "there is no danger in this medicine?"

"It will put you to sleep, Mr. Blank, but if you had a weak
heart it would strengthen it and all bodily functions will be encouraged and you will have the best night's rest you ever had in
your life.   Be sure to **remember to relax when you get in bed
and breathe slightly through your mouth.**   Come tomorrow and
tell me how well you slept."

I had prescribed fifteen grains of trional in thirty-two doses
of carbonated water, less than one-half grain of the medicine to
the dose, when he had taken fifteen or twenty grains of sulphonal
at each dose the two nights previous and had but little sleep.

The next day he returned and asked if there was any danger
of getting in the habit of taking that medicine, reporting that
he had slept soundly all night long and stating that his wife had
said he had not slept so soundly before in thirty years.

"Some people are very susceptible to that dose, Mr. Blank,
and **I see you are one of them.**   Don't you notice what a sedative effect it has had upon you?'

"Yes," he replied, "I feel a little lazy."

"That is simply the result of **a good night's sleep** and the relief that the medicine has given to the nervous element in your
case.   You will not need another dose of that prescription
oftener than once a week.   **You will be thirsty** and drink plenty
of water after this and that encourages all functional activity.
You will eat more, digest your food, and improve in health in
every way, but you must relax at night when you retire and
breathe through your mouth, for the increased amount of oxy-

gen taken into your lungs which is secured in that way is very essential to the success of this treatment."

The fact that he did relax and breathe slightly through his mouth, with the idea having been strongly put to him that he would go to sleep, virtually amounted to getting him to hypnotize himself, or take a suggestion both consciously and subconsciously. **In five weeks he reported** that he had taken five doses of the placebo prescription, had slept well all the while, and had gained six pounds in weight.

Two years later he reminded me of the marked benefit of that prescription. "You know how I had for several years suffered with indigestion," said he; "now I can eat boiled ham, hard boiled eggs, and cheese for supper, and sleep well, all night. **I have gained thirty pounds** and am in better health than I have been in over thirty years."

I am personally acquainted with two physicians who have for some time been engaged in sanitorium work. One of these physicians **secures a good night's rest** for his patient by directing the nurse very seriously in the presence of his patient to give a "sleeping capsule" (a placebo) at nine o'clock and if his patient is not sleeping soundly by ten, to give another. "But in no event to give more than two. She will sleep soundly all night."

"In fifteen years," said he, "I do not remember that this has failed to secure a good night's rest in more than a half dozen instances."

The other physician instructs his nurse to prepare his patients for sleep by looking after all possible requirements, making the patient conscious that he is being prepared to get a dose of medicine that will make him sleep soundly all night, and then directs her to administer one drop of a solution of potassium bromide, instructing the patient that he will be asleep in five minutes and will sleep soundly all night.

Said he, "**That is the last** I ever hear from them. **They sleep all night."**

Hundreds and hundreds of physicians have reported to me that they secured a good night's sleep for their patients by giving a hypodermic injection of pure water.

A few days ago I came in to the presence of a gentleman suffering with an acute pleuritis with a rising temperature and a severe pain. He was walking the floor, holding a hot water bag to his painful side, and stated that he had been unable to lie down on account of the severe pain. **I advised that he lie down,** relax every muscle, breathe slightly through his lips, and stated that he would at once get easy and go to sleep.

He was left alone and **conformed to the conditions** and did get easy and went to sleep promptly. I assured him before trying the method **that the thorough relaxation** would allow the blood to circulate evenly throughout his entire body and thus relieve the congestion in and about the inflamed area, and that he would get easy and go to sleep. He intelligently and consciously acted upon the suggestion and got good results.

Upon one occasion I was called hurriedly to see a patient after several attempts had been made to secure my services. **She was a neurotic woman** who was reported seriously ill. I had seen that patient before, however, and picked up a bottle of Avena sativa, a sample that had been left in my office, and carried it along with me. **My patient was extremely hysterical,** almost opisthotonic and shaking convulsively, hands cold, feet cold, pulse rapid and around her was a badly frightened family and friends. As I came into her presence I expressed a regret that I had been so long delayed, and taking her hand sympathetically, expressed the hope that she had not suffered on account of my delay. Whereupon she displayed all of her symptoms with **exaggerated emphasis.**

Her husband and the chief attendant had their say in describing the severity of the attack and related the special incidents that had transpired during the past hour or so and at the proper psychological moment I said to her strongly, "Now, be patient and let me find out just what is the trouble."

I had seen that patient before and my familiarity with her case did not require any further light to correctly interpret her symptoms. However, a physician must sometimes pursue the course that will best secure the accord of the patient in order to get best results. **I took her temperature,** counted her pulse, percussed her chest, listened to her respiration, examined her lips and the lobes of her ears, etc. I then said to her, at a moment when I had her attention, "Be patient, madam, I have just what I need to relieve you in a few minutes," holding the sample of Avena sativa in my hand before her.

Turning to her husband I requested him to bring me a glass of water, an empty glass and a spoon. While waiting for this I said to her kindly, "Be patient, you will soon feel all right after you take a dose of medicine." I poured **one spoonful of the**

[10]

medicine into the glass, followed by **six spoonfuls of water,** and stirred it briskly for at least nine seconds. Then taking a spoonful of the mixture, put it to her lips and told her to swallow it down.

Handing her husband the glass I placed one hand over her eyes closing them gently, and requested her to breathe through her mouth. "Now, breathe deeply; once again; now again, away down deep;" thus getting three full respirations. **"There, now, you are relaxed perfectly all over.** Now lie still and let the medicine have its effect, and in ten minutes you will feel all right and be quiet and easy from head to foot."

She lay perfectly still and her husband with eyes as wide open as full moons exclaimed, "See here, doctor, that seems to be a very powerful medicine you are using. Is there no danger in that dose?"

"Just what she needs," I replied. "If her heart were weak that medicine would strengthen it, her nerves will become steady and quiet and strong. Her muscles will completely relax, her hands and feet get warm and her head get easy, and her nervous equilibrium will be completely re-established."

I walked out of the room and requested that he follow me and leave her quiet for ten minutes, stating that she would be completely relieved at the end of that time and that then we would give her another dose and she would go to sleep and sleep soundly all night.

At the end of ten minutes we returned to her bedside. She lay as passive and still as a lake without a ripple. Taking her wrist, I found her pulse about seventy instead of one hundred and twenty as it was upon my arrival. "Open your eyes, Mrs. Blank, **you feel good, don't you?"**

"Oh, doctor, I could feel the effects of that medicine coming over me **just as you said it would.** I never had anything make me feel so pleasant in all my life."

"It has had a delightful effect, but I never gave a dose of medicine in my life that did not have a good effect on you. You are one patient that I can just know that every dose will produce the desired result."

"Because you understand my case so well, doctor," was her suave reply.

That was all right. Throw bouquets at your patients and they will throw them back at you. Blame them and find fault with them and they will blame and find fault with you.

In the case of the patient just described I advised that another dose of the medicine be administered and for everything to be arranged to let her go to sleep, casually remarking that she would sleep soundly all night and be feeling all right in the morning. My patient remarked that she came near going to sleep anyway from that one dose, and that if she had not been afraid that I would have left her, she would have gone sound to sleep. I left instructions that **she come to my office** the next day and gave her a prescription with several names that amounted to nothing, on account of the smallness of the dose of each, instructing her to take a spoonful in water before meals and at bedtime, suggesting to her that this would keep her nervous system functioning properly; that it would make her sleep soundly at night and prevent another one of those attacks.

At least three-fourths of the adult population of the world are relying upon some therapeutic system or method. They are followers of some herd, school, or system, that offers health in the place of disease. The self-conscious intellectual ego has not been sufficiently evolved within them to enable them to rely upon themselves. **What these people really need** is education, knowledge, and guidance—other names for suggestion—to give them the will to dare to do as well as they know how.

A large percentage of these functional and neuropathic conditions would get well of their own accord if the people were only level-headed enough to do as the dog does, who lies down and gives Nature a chance to recuperate an outraged physical constitution.

Rest in a comfortable bed, deep inspiration of pure air, light, wholesome diet, copious draughts of water to encourage elimination, with unyielding faith in the powers inherent within the biological elements, would result in a cure of a large proportion of the usual ills of human beings without a drop of medicine.

Yet, suggestion begets faith, confidence, and belief, and is at the bottom of Christian Science, osteopathy, patent medicine cures, electrotherapeutic quackery, magnetic healing, divine healing, mental science, metaphysical healing, faith cures and such like. **These people are here** and their methods are applicable to a large class of functional and neuropathic conditions. They are alert and active and here to stay as long as time lasts, under some name or guise, to make use of this psychological method of treatment.

We as a profession should not lay aside one single therapeutic measure or device, but in addition to our ordinary therapeutic measures in all classes of diseases and conditions, we have an opportunity to give our patients the benefit of this most powerful therapeutic adjunct.   **Honestly and earnestly convince thinking people** of the utility of any good thing and they will endorse it and give you their hearty co-operation, it matters not how strong their prejudices may have been.

Physicians frequently make a serious mistake by discouraging their patients with an unfavorable prognosis instead of relying with more confidence upon the psychic element which would furnish them a rational basis for a more hopeful result.

A young lady of my knowledge was taken seriously ill with pneumonia and a pessimistic, brutally frank physician, at his very first visit told her family that she was going to die.

After his second visit, an aunt of the young lady went to her with the physician's prognosis and told her that she must die.   The girl had slept a good part of the previous night and a visitor at that house who had the case under observation had not felt uneasy about her, neither had she been seriously concerned in regard to her recovery.

"Won't somebody say that I can get well?" was the wail that went up from the frightened girl in reply to the cruel message delivered by her aunt.   "Oh, if somebody would say that I could get well, I would not have to die," she continued.

The stern aunt, who conscientiously believed that the girl should know that the worst must come, in order to give her time to face the problems of the great beyond, poured into her ears the poison. "The doctor says you must die. You can't get well. We want to tell you the truth and give you time to prepare to die," etc.

No human being in that condition can stand that kind of psychic influence and live. Every nervous function became disturbed. The machinery of the entire nervous system was shocked and she did not sleep any more for the next two nights and died on the third day after the physician **had read her death warrant.** All this time she begged, "Won't somebody say that I can get well?"

There are many fatalities occurring daily all over our country for the **lack of men with faith in this psychological law** and courage and moral stamina to stand out against the popular prejudice to it and apply it as a therapeutic aid.

A number of times in my life has it been my unpleasant duty, yet high privilege to have an opportunity to stand by a patient, in the face of a positively unfavorable prognosis, made by those who did not appreciate the great power of suggestion upon the subconscious, and tell him, **"You are going to get well."** I have had such patients squeeze my hand as I held theirs and say, "If you stand by me, doctor, I will get well."

All classes of illness, sickness or disease, in conjunction with other methods of treatment, need moral or psychological support. They need leadership. **We need men in the profession to do as Napoleon did,** when his men were dying by the several hundred each day on his march in the east. He visited the camp and took each one by the hand and assured him strongly and positively that **if he would be brave, he would get well.** As this one visit of his to the sick and discouraged soldiers, put an end to an epidemic where several hundred men were dying each day, so would many human lives be saved by this simple suggestion given with confidence and with conviction, in conjunction with other therapeutic measures.

The medical profession have been looking too long at the surface of things. We have dealt too much with externals, with effects, and have neglected causes.

There are three-fourths of the human race who need arousing and being shocked into a self-consciousness of strength and ability, confidence and determination. **Not only in facing the questions of health** and disease, but in all other problems of life. The man who gives such patients some of his own optimistic personality is giving them strength and life itself. They convert **countless millions and millions of brain centers,** lying dormant and unused, into action to encourage every bodily cell to increased function.

The trouble is that the majority of people have not sufficient confidence within themselves. **They do not recognize their power** and have no confidence in the latent potentialities dormant and unused within them, that can only be called into action **through faith and confidence. A new self-consciousness needs to be awakened within them.** The great majority of people are incapable of thinking and reasoning for themselves. Their minds through education and experience have not had the foodstuffs to enable them to exercise reason. **They are governed by fear and ruled by emotion.** Others go through life in a listless, dreamlike, mental condition, referred to by Jastrow as mental loafing.

The will is only capable of reproducing those impressions made upon the brain through experience and education. Whatever idea is uppermost in their minds, whatever impression is the strongest, is the one that most influences them.

The physician who is so engrossed in the pathology of the case that at each visit he recites it over and over again to his patient, assists in encouraging not the patient, but the disease. **He fastens the morbid psycho-neurotic element** of the patient stronger upon him, and thus intensifies his disease by lessening his resisting powers.

People are hypnotized by their beliefs. Belief in an idea or a theory or a creed or a drug or a man or a woman is the place where the individual relinquishes self responsibility, takes mental refuge, **and agrees to act upon the idea or series of ideas that are presented to him either consciously or subconsciously.** It is all a matter of getting the confidence of people and making suggestions.

"Get off the grass, get off the grass," is a sign that one sees everywhere in the study and application of this subject. It is before the door of the prevailing educational systems, political and economic problems, religious and therapeutic creeds, orthodox and heterodox alike, all mould and shape the actions of men by the use of suggestion in disguised form. **How sensitive** people are when we tell them the truth!

Three years ago in one of our northern cities a gentleman invited me to attend what he called a remarkable hypnotic exhibition. It was the last service of a ten-day religious revival meeting in a tent with a capacity for fully five thousand people.

The last song had been sung and the last prayer offered before the speaker appeared upon the platform.

He walked up and down before his audience **as if heaven and hell, life and death, time and eternity** were all on his shoulders.   He then struck a pose, by the side of his little stand, that itself filled his audience who were already under the influence of his suggestions, with expectant awe and fear.   **With all the intensity of a tragedian** he then began: "There are people under the sound of my voice here tonight that before this hour is over will have made a record for hell or heaven!   There are people under the sound of my voice that before another year has rolled around will have approached the judgment bar of God!"   **One strong expression after another** of this kind followed, and in less than three minutes a little woman with an unstable, nervous organization near me dropped upon her knees with the cry, "Lord help, oh Lord, save the people!" etc.

On and on went the suggestor, the pulpit orator, the speaker, the hypnotist, and one after another followed the example of the little woman until within twenty minutes pandemonium reigned. The whole tent reverberated the echoes of crying, shouting and praying.

I walked up close to the leader and noted that he went from one to another and suggested what the Lord would do and what the penitent must do.   **To one he suggested,** "Just get up and say glory hallelujah.   It's all right."   For at least forty times the poor fellow jumped up and clapped his hands and exclaimed, "Glory hallelujah, it's all right!"   Dozens of others were playing their stunts in different ways.

This was in one of the **most enlightened and cultured states in our great union,** and this was a tame affair to some experiences that the writer has witnessed **in his own southern State, both among whites and negroes.**

Any method of getting an individual to **act upon an idea or a series of ideas,** be they true or false, either consciously or subconsciously, is hypnotism or suggestion. **Suggestion,** then is a basis of all religions, creeds, dogmas, non-medical and non-surgical therapeutic systems, and all methods of education.

"Keep off the grass, keep off the grass," however, is found posted everywhere by people who live and thrive upon the ignorant credulity of their fellow men.

Suggestion is used both for the good and for the harm of human beings. It is used by everybody and the really dangerous man or woman is the individual who is unconscious of its potency as a factor in both sanity and insanity, happiness or unhappiness, education or ignorance, truth or falsehood, health or disease, character building or moral perversion.

We frequently see fanatics upon various lines, swaying and leading men and women into all kinds of incongruous paths and actions by their fanatical zeal, enthusiasm and absurd devotion to some false theory or concept. **The only protection for the individual** is knowledge and experience, education and light, and the ability to think for and protect himself.

No special tact is required by a physician to use suggestion to fix the attention of his patient on such ideas as are desirable to influence his life and conduct for therapeutic purposes. **The**

great thing to be desired is to have more regard for the welfare of your patient than for the **remuneration for your services.**

We find everywhere pseudo-conscientious men in the medical profession who "have too high a regard for the truth" to use suggestion in a legitimate therapeutic manner for the helpfulness of their patients. **Such men usually fasten a trivial functional disorder** by the injudicious use of suggestion upon the consciousness of a patient and make it a serious psycho-neurotic condition by giving his disease a name and pointing out its serious pathology and consequences, simply giving a prescription to relieve a condition which he has made in reality ten times worse.

A North Carolina physician had a patient who was morbidly self-conscious of some functional disturbance and after going to leading men in several of the larger southern cities, he finally landed in Baltimore where he secured an audience with one of the most widely known physicians in the history of the medical profession. **The patient related his difficulty** in getting relief and told how he had gone from place to place and how the physicians did not agree and how some called his disease one thing and some another. The physician stripped him, gave him a careful examination for two or three minutes, and said, "All right, sir, put on your clothes."

He seated himself to write a letter, and by the time his patient was dressed, he said, "Give me twenty dollars, please," which was promptly handed over to him. Then with one hand on his doorknob and the other on the patient's shoulder, he looked him squarely in the face and said to him, "**My friend, go

home and read only the book of St. James, call yourself a ———
fool and let doctors alone.''

The door was opened and the man was out of the physician's
office before he realized it, another patient having gone into the
consulting room.   The gentleman **reminded the office attendant**
that the doctor had forgotten to give him a prescription and he
was informed that he must now wait until all present had gone
in before he could have another audience.

Over and over did he revolve that advice, "Go home, my
friend, read only the book of St. James and call yourself a ———
fool and let doctors alone.''   **The gentleman grew too nervous**
to sit still and decided to take a walk and return an hour later,
but while walking alone on the streets of Baltimore, blind and
deaf to everything that he saw and heard, the meaning of that
advice at last dawned upon his consciousness and he began to
laugh.

He then decided it would not be necessary to return to the
physician's office, and he took the next train for his home, all
the while remembering that his family physician had told him
that his disease was more "in his head'' than otherwise.   **The
meaning of the advice** given by his family physician was now clear
to him and he realized for the first time that he did not have a
brain disease, and that what the eminent physician really meant
was that his condition was the result of an unbridled imagination, or to speak in modern psychological phraseology, **due to
a morbid self-consciousness.**

He reached his home with his head up, wearing a smile like
a headlight on a steam engine, and though three years had

elapsed, the gentleman yet laughed at how easily he had been cured by finding a man with courage and honesty sufficient to tell him that he had been acting a ———— fool and should let doctors alone. **No doubt, he also was instructed** to quit reading patent medicine advertisements, and modern mind cure theories.

Now, that is just the point. **People so often need advice,** assurance, ideas, persuasion, or shocking, other names for suggestion, and not medicine or instruction in the pathology of their disease. **The fact that a patient comes to you** is ordinarily an acknowledgment that he is willing to take your advice, that he has confidence in you and is willing to rely on your judgment.

Here I would add a word of caution. It is a great mistake to tell a patient that you can find nothing the matter with him; almost as bad as to exaggerate the seriousness of his symptoms. **An individual with a functional disorder** may not necessarily be suffering with insomnia or have sustained a loss in weight and yet be in the incipiency of a disease which, if not properly treated, may result in serious disorders of metabolism. **He comes to you with subjective sensations,** feelings and impressions which annoy and depress him. He feels incapacitated for his work. **Every problem of life is colored** by the hue of his morbid subjective state, and when you tell him that you can find no cause for his trouble you only add to his morbidness and aggravate what may be the incipiency of a grave disorder. **A good proportion** of the more serious nervous and mental diseases begin in functional disturbances. The disorders of metabolism resulting in metabolic toxemia may begin in this way. **These patients should**

be made to feel that they have your confidence and sympathy, as well as the benefit of your knowledge and skill as a physician. Then you are in position to tactfully govern their habits of thought and conduct and to help them to execute a plan of treatment that will bring about recovery.

Elimination is usually deficient and the treatment needed in such cases tests the complete resources of the physician and embodies all therapeutic measures, medicinal, dietetic, physiological and mechanical, as well as psycho-therapeutic.

Frequently work under the proper conditions, is the only means of cure, and the far reaching influence of the physician to secure the conditions necessary for the recovery of his patient is not out of place.

The proper treatment of disease is **as varied in its application** as is the wants and necessities of mankind.

I l l u s t r a t i o n .—**A physician of my acquaintance** was called to see a frail little woman who was the only support of her two fatherless children. Day and night she labored with needle and thread, vainly striving to buy food and clothing, pay rent, and provide for other life essentials. **Deprived of fresh air and sunshine** and under constant mental and physical strain, she finally succumbed, with all bodily functions disturbed and discouraged and depressed in the extreme.

The representative of a local church organization stated to the physician that they had provided a nurse, arranged for her medicine and would send her nicely prepared meals and visit her often.

"All that will only add to the severity of her psycho-neurotic condition," said he; "go and get her $25.00 to pay her house rent, fill her pantry with substantial food to meet present demands, but above all secure her a position where she can work and get exercise and sunshine and fresh air and have time to sleep at night and she will need no medicine, no nursing, or visitors."

The representative of the charitable organization left saying that she would have the society consider the matter at their next meeting, a week hence.

There was present at that interview between the physician and the representative of the local organization, a stenographer, who was the widow of a poor young physician who had died, leaving her with nó means of support, but before her marriage she had learned to "do things with her hands," and she was independent and happy. She requested the physician to meet her on the outside of the sick lady's room at 7:00 o'clock that evening, at which time she delivered to him the amount of cash requested, and had unloaded the substantials for a well filled pantry and announced that she had secured a position for the sick lady in question, all of which she had done quietly and unostentatiously during the day, requesting that the part which she had played in the matter never be disclosed to the patient.

Within a few days that frail little woman was at her post of duty and up to four years afterward she was at work, much improved in health and strength, contented and happy.

Such was the result of the efforts of a woman who was willing to help her weaker sister to help herself.

The **true physician** faces the problems of his patients with impartial and impersonal courage, and with the tenderness of one whose own heart has felt the pressure of these tremendous questions; one so full of love and sympathy for his fellow man, full of cheerfulness, full of strength and optimism and full of helpful hope "That he can move on human life as stars move on the dark seas of bewildered mariners."

CHAPTER VIII.

HYPNOTIC SUGGESTION.

So far I have endeavored to show that hypnotism is nothing more than getting an individual **to act upon an idea or a series of ideas, and to execute them either consciously or subconsciously.** The name matters not except to those who desire to appeal either to the credulity or ignorance of their fellows.

My observation has been that **the physicians** who object most strenuously to the use of suggestive measures, both with and without hypnotism, are the ones who are really doing the most to hypnotize their patients into a serious illness, rather than using suggestion and every other available means to help them get well, and keep well without relying on a physician.

The theologian who raises the greatest objection is the man who is hypnotizing his audience into believing some questionable dogma by an appeal to the emotions, rather than by keeping abreast with the investigation of science and preaching a sane, rational religion that appeals both to the heart and to the intellect.

The educator who most strongly opposes it, is usually the man who is making a great bluff to conceal his own lack of moral stamina or his ignorance.

With the prejudice that exists against the use of suggestive therapeutics by the selfish and uninformed element of our population, from the highest to the lowest rank, I am truly sorry

[11]

that there is so much of meaning in the application of suggestion in its relation to the practice of medicine.

I can but wish that man were **a machine** to be dealt with in
a cold, perfunctory manner, or that he **were a cabbage** instead
of a human being, **or a tree** that needed to be pruned and fertilized and relieved of parasitic infection and then left alone to
see what he would do.

But we cannot get away from the facts that man is an **organism** composed of millions and millions of cells that are susceptible to external stimuli; that these can be stimulated by **any impression that reaches the consciousness** of the individual through
any one of the five special senses; that the higher and lower bodily
functions are so inter-related that **any impression that reaches
the higher centers** is in turn transmitted to the lower bodily
functions; and that through these, every function in the body
and every cell can be influenced.

We cannot forget that man is a sentient being with **intellect**
and **feeling** and **emotion,** which are the highest characteristics
of a human being; that constitute the distinguishing differences
between him and the lower forms of animal and vegetable life.
These cannot be ignored in our consideration of the individual,
composed as he is of mind and body. *Ignorantia legis neminem
excusat.* **Every physician, clergyman, educator, or other human
being,** is playing and toying with these evolutionary factors of
human personality by every idea or impression conveyed to the
human mind, whether he realizes it or not.

Alas! Too often in his refusal to exercise sufficient regard
for the truth, he sets himself in open **opposition to the highest**

and best interests of the health and happiness of all individuals with whom he associates. **Often,** yes, thousands of times and oftener, have I heard physicians refer to suggestion, both with and without hypnotism, and say, "There is nothing in it." These are men who belong to a "learned profession," who are educators and leaders and teachers of the people!

A successful neurologist in one of our larger cities, who considers the greatest element of his success for the last fifteen years due to his employment of suggestive therapeutics very charitably remarked that physicians who opposed these methods really **do not know any better,** and in their ignorance could not be blamed.

In the consideration of any therapeutic measure, the first thought that comes to the mind of the wide awake physician is, what is its advantage over any other method of treatment?

The answer to that question is easy: Its addition to other therapeutic measures enables the physician to **get results** in a very large proportion of cases that come under our observation, **that cannot be secured** through any other agency. The value of any therapeutic adjunct is in direct ratio to the successful results that accrue from its administration. Yet, it must be remembered that **what are possibilities** with any method or kind of treatment, medicinal, surgical, suggestive, or otherwise, are **not always actualities** in the hands of all men alike, and it depends upon the individual and upon him alone, rests the responsibility for what he is not able to accomplish when he is really **put to the test** at the bedside, and this often seriously disturbs our conscience and humbles our pride.

Any physician who expects to use suggestive therapeutics successfully must by practice acquire that confidence in his own ability to succeed with it by familiarizing himself with all the facts and theories and details of his subject.

Yet, I have often noticed an individual who possessed that **inexplicable quality of personality** to get others to do anything he wanted them to do, who had never read a line in psychology or suggestion and was absolutely unfamiliar with the principles of medical science.

Hypnotism is a self-induced psychological condition. You do not hypnotize an individual, you simply get him to do it himself; but to get anyone to act upon an idea or a series of ideas, either consciously or subconsciously, one must **be in dead earnest,** exercise a little enthusiasm about the undertaking and go at it with the will to succeed.

The greatest essential to the application of suggestive therapeutics is a **conviction on the part of the operator** of the value of the treatment as applied to the case at hand and a desire to bring about the recovery of the patient. In fact, this is the important essential which is the *sine qua non* to the success of any kind of treatment.

Yet, if suggestion be of value at all it is of use just in proportion that the individual **accepts and carries out the suggestion** both consciously and subconsciously. **Hypnotism** is but **the art or technique** or method of instructing an individual to act upon a suggestion or a series of suggestions. **There must always be a conscious acquiescence,** consent, or co-operation, on the part of the individual, **not necessarily to be hypnotized,** but to take the suggestion, which is the same thing. Then by suggestion there is induced in the patient a new consciousness whereby he is led to do that which he had previously been unable to do for himself both consciously and subconsciously.

In a preceding chapter I spoke of using suggestion to **inhibit the conscious mind,** as was hypothetically supposed to be accomplished in the hypnotic state. **It would have been more correct** to state that we simply get the patient **to be passive** and allow the operator to induce **a new consciousness** and then to direct the stream of consciousness which produces mental states that react upon every bodily function.

We get our patient to let us **direct and control his psychic activities** and teach and illustrate for him how he can direct and control them for himself. We put our patient **better in control of himself,** all dependent upon the suggestions or sense impressions that are transmitted to his brain cells through the senses while in this passive or suggestible condition. What else does education or theological sermonizing or instruction upon any line accomplish?

Sense impression is the starting point for every psychic action. Every sense impression that is produced by suggestion or otherwise has a determined localization in the brain cortex.

It is assumed by psychologists that every sense impression, according to its degree of strength, produces a molecular change in the nerve cells influenced, which gives rise to the possibility of a reproduction of these ideas or sense impressions by an internal process.

Memory is the result of sense impressions that previous experiences in life have left upon the brain cells. The very ideas or products of thought which are stamped upon the brain cells by suggestion in the hypnotic state, as well as by suggestion without hypnotism, have the **power of being reproduced in mental states,** which gives rise to a new consciousness in the individual.

By suggestion in the hypnotic state we are better enabled to plant sense impressions, ideas, thoughts and feelings which reproduce themselves in the consciousness of the individual and furnish a foundation for his intellectual activities.

In this suggestible condition, we are enabled to drive back certain sense impressions that create unpleasant mental states, obliterate them and wipe them out, and by holding the subject's attention to certain ideas presented to him, **we create a new consciousness** or alter his frame of mind. We render the individual **more self-conscious of potentialities,** dormant and unused within him, which he can call into operation through the combined effort of memory and will, in contrast to previous conceptions of his own personality. **This new conception of himself** and his relation to the outer world contributes to strengthen and develop the self-conscious ego. It is in reality **the development of the ego.**

By suggestion in the hypnotic state we give impulse to reproduce previous sense impressions. Call it strengthening memory or will or character or ego, as you choose, **and the mental process which brings about the logical connection** of sense perceptions or ideas reproduced in this way, **is what is called thinking.**

So, then, by suggestion in the hypnotic state we create new thought habits, mental states or streams of consciousness which react upon every bodily function. We alter the individual's thinking.

The following cases will illustrate the position taken by the author as to the value of suggestion in that condition of induced passivity or receptivity to suggestion commonly referred to as the hypnotic state. **Whether the individual is asleep or not** does not concern us here. It suffices if we have the confidence and co-operation of the patient.

The physician who fails to avail himself of the great therapeutic value of hypnotic suggestion to his patients, in well selected cases, for the relief of conditions and symptoms **that cannot be alleviated by any other method of treatment,** refuses to employ one of the most powerful therapeutic adjuncts available at the present time.

The results obtained by hypnotic suggestion in the following cases **speak for themselves:** I shall only cite enough cases to illustrate the position taken by the author in the preceding pages.

INSOMNIA.

Loss of sleep is a condition that leads to general physical disease. It has innumerable causes, all of which should be considered and treated according to indications, which calls into exercise the complete resources of the physician. It more or less accompanies all diseased conditions, acute or chronic, functional or organic, surgical and otherwise.

It is useless to attempt to break up the habits of nervous, wakeful people by suggestion when the individual lives in open violation to all the known laws of health, or where the system is overloaded with toxic products due to indigestion, caused by overeating, with fermentation, deficient elimination, etc.

Meet every indication in the individual case at hand and, in conjunction with other sane, sensible, rational advice or suggestion, hypnotic suggestion will prove indispensible in many cases.

Make it a rule to **regulate** your patient's **diet, his drinking, and his habits, as well as his thinking.** The question of food and drink habits, etc., will be briefly considered in a separate chapter.

However, there are numerous individuals among all classes **upon whom the cares of life have borne heavily,** who, try as they will, with their imperfect knowledge of self-control and lack of self-reliance, cannot keep back subjective impressions which crowd themselves upon their consciousness when they retire for sleep, and the darkness renders them more conscious of their trials.

Many there are who are still waiting for special divine intervention to satisfy them that their souls are saved. Doubt hovers over them and disturbs their peace of mind. **Others have not learned** the beauty and glory and salutary effects of work and useful employment as a means of strengthening and developing both mind and body.

An unoccupied, idle brain is the reflector of a morbid imagination upon which flit and dance all kinds of annoying mental pictures to the discomfort of the individual who fain would find relief in sleep.

In rare instances an over-expenditure of nerve energy, through work or worry or dissipation, prevents the individual from possessing that inherent quality of nerve force sufficient to exercise self-control. **Uncontrolled emotions,** in the form of sentiments both selfish and altruistic, also contribute their influence to keep awake the restless neurotic.

An irritable nervous system, either hereditary or acquired, is transmitting constantly afferent and efferent impulses to and from the brain, and throughout the entire human frame subjective sense perceptions are interpreted by the individual as nervousness, sickness, pain, disease, etc.

Nutrition is disturbed and toxines of metabolism, or more properly catabolism, are being manufactured to poison all bodily functions and prevent the normal formation of "opsonins."

TREATMENT.

In conjunction with dietetic, medicinal and **hygienic treatment,** suggestion in the hypnotic state should be used, if necessary.

Get your patient to **relax every muscle** and **breathe deeply and rhythmically** for several times in succession, and then with one or two drops of chloroform or any other placebo, or without them, as you choose, tell him that you are "going to put him to sleep, that as you apply this remedy he will get quiet all over, get drowsy and sleepy and go to sleep, and awake feeling better."

Then to hypnotize him, make suggestions as advised in the chapter on the **technique of inducing the hypnotic state.** After he is hypnotized, while you sit beside the unfortunate whose nervous system you have soothed into quietude and passivity, talk to him, using suggestions somewhat like these:

"**You are resting quietly,** sleeping soundly, breathing deeply, perfectly relaxed and passive all over. Now, as you lie in this passive state with all tension relieved, while I am talking to you, you feel your nerves getting steady and quiet and strong. **All nervousness is going away** and by the time I count ten, your nerves will be quiet and steady and strong all over, your nervous equilibrum will be completely re-established from head to foot. One, two, three, four, five, six, seven, eight, nine, ten; your nerves are steady and quiet and strong all over.

"Now, after this treatment, **whenever you think of yourself,** you will find that your nerves are steady and quiet and strong.

"**At bedtime you will relax,** close your eyes and think only of sleep. You will go to sleep and sleep soundly all night long. You will awake in the morning feeling refreshed and rested.

"After this you will **be thirsty and drink more water** than ever before in your life. Every two hours from morning until you retire at night you will drink a glass of water. The increased amount of fluid will cause an increased action of all your bodily functions. Your skin and kidneys, liver and bowels, will eliminate more freely.

"You will be easy and comfortable all over. **You will enjoy eating and work and exercise,** and gain in weight and be happier, feel stronger, and be glad that you are living."

I then awake the patient and give him conscious advice

how to eat, how to drink, how to exercise and **how to relax** so that he can go to sleep. I give him a reason for all the advice that I have given, as well as a reason for the suggestion given him in that induced condition of passivity.

I am often asked, "Do you mean to say that the suggestions will be effective just because they are made to the patient who is hypnotized?" I say **we make sense impressions on the brain cortex** while the patient is in the hypnotic condition that are reproduced in the individual's thought habits. The reproductions of these ideas are **auto-suggestions.** When you substitute **helpful auto-suggestions** for adverse and harmful auto-suggestions, you have been of the greatest help that one human being can be to another. You have put your patient in control of himself. **You have changed his habits of thinking,** and by this means new habits of thought and action in every day life are formed. You have put your patient better in possession of himself, and better enabled him to meet the exigencies of every-day life.

ILLUSTRATION NO. 1.

Syphiliphobia, Insomnia, Neurasthenia, etc.—Mr. Blank, a farmer, who had led an honorable, upright life, had by his indiscretion contracted a gonorrhoea and a chancroid. The chancroid readily healed, but the gonorrhoea persisted for several weeks. **He believed that he had syphilis,** was tortured by a hypersensitive conscience, and for several months had been confined to his room. His physician had re-assured him, **reasoned with him,** and done all in his power to argue the delusion that he had syphilis out of his consciousness.

He had recovered from both these diseases, but there was **a psycho-neurotic element** in his case which was day by day growing more serious. **He did not sleep at night,** was frequently heard crying and praying, when everything was quiet and all were supposed to be asleep. Anorexia, indigestion, malnutrition, a loss in weight of thirty-five pounds in five months, had caused his physician to feel apprehensive of his soon being a fit subject for the insane asylum. In fact, he was so already.

Here were **insomnia, hysteria, syphiliphobia, neurasthenia, delusions, etc.,** all in one case. I explained to him the value of a new and powerful sleep producing remedy (a placebo), that I was "introducing to the profession," and impressed upon him consciously that there was a nervous element in his case that this remedy would relieve.

I let him know that **it was expected to put him to sleep,** and that the result of this sleep would be to relieve the nervous element in his case. **He readily consented** for the treatment to be used, and went into a profound state of suggestibility.

In the hypnotic state I addressed him about as follows: "Now, Mr. Blank, you are sound and dead asleep, perfectly relaxed and passive from head to foot, breathing deeply, your nerves steady and quiet and strong. **As you lie here** while I apply this remedy, your nerves are growing steadier and quieter and stronger, and by the time I count ten, your nerves will be steady and quiet and strong all over. One, two, three, four, five, six, seven, eight, nine, ten, and your nerves are steady, quiet and strong all over. Now, you will not be nervous any more. **After this, whenever you think of yourself,** you will find that your nerves are steady and quiet and strong, and you will realize that you have not had syphilis, that Doctor Blank was right, that he knew his business and that you are now well and all right.

"**You will drink water every two hours,** enjoy your meals, sleep soundly at night, and attend to your duties just as you did months ago when you were well.

"**When you go to bed at night,** you will relax just as you are here now, close your eyes and think only of sleep, then you will go sound asleep, and sleep soundly all night long. If you awake at all in the night, it will be to think of yourself as resting and sleeping quietly, feeling contented, satisfied and happy. **You will enjoy your meals** and take the old-time interest in your farm work, your stock, and business generally. You will go to town as you once did and every day feel thankful for the improved condition of your health."

I allowed him to sleep **for thirty minutes longer** and then awoke him. I told him that this treatment had done him good, that he was going to feel better after this, that he would enjoy his meals, would sleep well at night and would attend to his business as in former times. I assured him that he was in sound health, had been well all the time, and after this would feel differently in regard to his own condition.

He came to see his physician five days after that, and, while lank and lean as a pine fence rail, he was his old self, his rational normal self, as he once was before his misfortunes. Five weeks afterward he had gained twelve pounds in weight and was rapidly on the road to recovery.

By suggestion in the hypnotic state, **new ideas, new sense impressions** had been substituted, **new thoughts planted** in the place of the old ones that were torturing his conscience, preventing his sleep and damning his life. **A new consciousness now possessed him** and he was practically a healthy man.

ILLUSTRATION NO. 2.

Epilepsy, Chlorosis, Anaemia, etc.—This patient, a girl **aged sixteen,** had been treated by five leading physicians of her city for several years without benefit. Her case had been diagnosed as true epilepsy, but I had reason to believe that this was a mistake.

She had epileptic seizures from once to several times a week, was anaemic and chlorotic, her menses were scanty and irregular, she had poor appetite and was badly nourished; slept soundly at night, but her sleep was not refreshing. Awoke in the morning tired, and she took but little interest in anything.

Hypnosis was induced and suggestions were given her while in the hypnotic state, to get her to breathe deeper, and it was also suggested that she would **always breathe deeper,** day and night, asleep or awake, that she would always breathe deeper.

It was also suggested that she would **be thirsty after this and enjoy drinking water,** that she would always drink more water, that she would take a glass of water every two hours from morning to night. It was further suggested that she would **take exercise** freely every day, that her bowels would move regularly every morning, that she would go **to the toilet at least twice a day,** and that her bowels would functionate properly, move freely every morning, etc.

In a case like this, suggestion must be given to influence the individual's **conscious and unconscious psychic or mental activities.** Waking conduct must be guided as well as subjective impressions made to influence the involuntary functions.

My lecture to this girl would probably be about as follows, with my hand upon her forehead or gently stroking her forehead from side to side, made in a monotone, positive, earnest manner, presented **in a way that would transmit words into feeling:** "Now, my dear little girl, you are sound asleep, and while you lie here your nerves are getting quiet and steady and strong, quiet and steady and strong, and by the time I count ten your nerves will be quiet and steady and strong all over. One, two, three, four, five, six, seven, eight, nine, ten, your nerves are quiet and steady and strong from head to foot.

"Now, as I talk to you and place my hand upon your chest you feel your ability to breathe deeper getting stronger and stronger, and by the time I count five I want you to breathe deeply, filling your lungs as deep and full as is possible: One, two, three, four, five, now breathe deeply, deeper yet, [she took the suggestion well]. There, now, rest and breathe naturally.

"Now, after this, you will always breathe deeper, the blood will circulate more freely in your stomach and will better nourish your gastric mucous membrane so that you will have a better appetite and a better digestion. Under my hand here, now, you feel the blood circulating more freely in your stomach, and by the time I count five the blood will be coming freely to your stomach. One, two, three, four, five.

"After this you will be thirsty and drink water every two hours and you will be hungry and enjoy your meals. You will chew your food well and especially enjoy eating fruit and vegetables. You will sleep well at night. When you go to bed you will go sound asleep and sleep soundly all night. You will never again be nervous or have another one of those nervous attacks. You will enjoy breathing, drinking water, and eating, working, exercising and sleeping—you will enjoy life.

"As you eat more and digest your food better, you will be better nourished, get stronger, gain in weight and have perfect health."

About six weeks after this treatment by suggestion, which was followed by three others given by her physician, I learned that she had experienced no more trouble and was a great deal better.

Five years after that, her physician, who assisted in the treatment, informed me that she had never had any further trouble, that she at once began to sleep, eat, drink, exercise, gain in weight, etc. "She went from one hundred and ten to one hundred and forty-five pounds in weight," said he, "and is now married and the happy mother of a fine baby."

The therapeutic application of suggestion in hysteria, neurasthenia, melancholia, indigestion, morbid fears, nervousness, etc., makes use of the same principles as were empolyed in the above mentioned cases. Your suggestions **must be made to meet the individual needs** of the patient at hand. **Burn into his consciousness** or subconsciousness the ideas that you wish to influence both his voluntary waking consciousness and all his or her involuntary physiological processes.

As a rule, **suggest away** whatever subjective impressions, sensations, feelings, thought habits and bodily symptoms that are objectionable, and in their place **suggest what you desire** to influence your patient or become a part of his life.

ILLUSTRATION NO. 3.

Acute Migraine, Neurasthenia, etc.—Telephone girl with acute migraine, but was of neurasthenic and highly nervous temperament at best. Her physician usually began with a hypodermic of morphine sulphate, one-fourth of a grain and atropine sulphate, one-one hundred and fiftieth, and in addition to this, prescribed a brisk purgative of calomel, aloes, podophyllin, cascara, etc.; also hot foot baths and hot fomentations. If constipated, he directed an enema to be given at once.

The girl reached her home at six p. m. in one of her most severe attacks. **At least two days** were usually required for her to get over one of these severe headaches, usually associated with indigestion, and during this time from two to three hypodermics of morphine were required in addition to a dozen doses of coal tar preparations, bromides, etc.

She was a young woman twenty years of age, with an unstable nervous system, and the cares of life were bearing heavily upon her. Her responsibilities were heavy and her work arduous. Her headaches and general collapse were Nature's rebellion against the outrage being daily committed against her weak physical organization. But her suffering was great and she needed help.

[12]

Her physician had already recognized the **harmful effect of the narcotics, sedatives, purgatives, etc.,** which were being demanded more frequently and were used each time with less efficacy.

At 6:30 P. M. I went with her physician to see the girl, suffering with an intense headache, nervous, etc. I told her I could rub her head with a medicine that I had and relieve her headache, and that she would go to sleep.

She readily went under the influence of my suggestions, was easily hypnotized, and I suggested that her head was getting easy and her nerves getting steady and quiet and strong, and repeated this suggestion a half dozen or more times, and ended by saying that by the time I counted ten she would be perfectly easy from head to foot, that her nervous equilibrium would be completely re-established.

We allowed her to sleep until after my lecture and returned at 12:30 to find her asleep. She awoke at my suggestion perfectly easy, thoroughly relaxed, in a copious perspiration. I directed that she be rubbed off gently with a dry towel, drink a glass of malted milk with two eggs in it and drink all the water she wanted. She drank two large glass fulls and then I directed that she shut her eyes and go to sleep and sleep soundly all night. **No, I did not hypnotize her again,** for I had suggested in the hypnotic state that she could go to sleep after I awoke her and every night after that whenever she decided to do so.

Her physician 'phoned me that he went by to inquire about her at seven the next morning, but she had gone to her post at the telephone. I 'phoned him that that was cruelty to animals, for she should have rested that day. What she really needed was shorter working hours, better pay, and more time to devote to outdoor exercise, reading, recreation, etc. But she was in the mill, to have her life ground out of her to enlarge the dividends of an enormous corporation, to be used like corn that is ground to be made into bread to fill our stomachs.

If the medical profession expects to be held in the esteem of the public, which it so eminently deserves, **the physician as an individual should speak out** upon these questions that concern the welfare of our fellow man, not alone in hygiene, dietetics, sanitation, etc., but upon any and all problems that influence the health and happiness of the individual.

ILLUSTRATION NO. 4.

Psycho-neurotic Paralysis.—**Mr. F. E. H., by occupation cotton buyer,** age fifty-eight. His history was that ten years before he was taken with an apoplectic seizure and evidently had a thrombus, as he was unconscious for several weeks and his arm and leg on the affected side were more or less completely paralyzed.

He was sustained by rectal alimentation for several weeks, but could swallow liquid food after six weeks or two months and after six months gradually began to regain the use of his arm on the affected side, and after one year began to hobble with crutches, dragging the affected leg.

He was then taken **with acute sciataca** and confined to his bed for one year longer. At the time I saw him he had been dragging his foot on the affected side for eight and a half years, but was able to get about with the aid of crutches.

During this time he had tried every available method of treatment offered in hospitals, sanitariums, health resorts, etc., as well as some of the modern cults that use suggestion without hypnotism, in disguised forms.

Hypnosis was induced and suggestions made with a view to implanting sense impressions, impulses, or to inducing a self-consciousness of ability to use his leg. When I held the leg up while he was hypnotized and suggested that he would allow it to remain, he held it up without trouble. He then acted upon a suggestion to lift it up, to bend it, and finally I had him walk around in the room while yet in the hypnotic state. It was then suggested that he would wake up and would find that he could walk as well as he ever did in his life.

It was really amusing to see him find himself using the leg which for ten years he had been unable to lift from the ground.

I have treated over a dozen similar cases in patients who have put aside their crutches and walked with perfect ease. The suggestion given is that the limb is getting stronger and stronger, that the normal control and use of it is returning, etc. Repetition and iteration, iteration and repetition, are very necessary in some cases to make a suggestion or suggestions effective.

ILLUSTRATION NO. 5.

Persistent Vomiting.—A gentleman fifty-eight or sixty years old, had **typhoid fever** for three weeks. He had vomited all food taken for **forty-eight hours,** and was nervous and weak, and his physician had used every available means to relieve his uncontrollable emesis. In the hypnotic state I suggested that his nerves were getting quiet and steady and strong and repeated this suggestion several times; that all nervousness or weakness was going away, that his stomach was getting stronger and stronger, easier and easier, and that by the time I counted ten all sickness or nausea or irritability or weakness about his stomach would be gone, and he could retain milk, liquid nourishment and water, and would enjoy them.

I also gave him suggestions to **give him a good night's sleep, etc.** We allowed him to sleep about twenty minutes, and upon waking him, allowed him to drink a glass of fresh buttermilk, which he retained and seemed to enjoy, remarking that that seemed to be the only thing that had tasted right to him since he had been sick. He continued to take milk or some form of liquid nourishment, and was not troubled further with sick stomach. He slept well at night and made a safe recovery. This book is written with a handsome fountain pen presented by that gentleman's son, a prominent jeweler of his city, who said, "When you use it, remember we feel grateful and consider that you saved father's life."

I recall several cases in which well known physicians have relieved persistent, incontrollable vomiting by hypnotic suggestion. There is more or less **neurotic** or **hysterical** or **neurasthenic element in all acute diseases,** which can and should be controlled by suggestion, with or without hypnotism, whichever seems indicated. In **pneumonia, typhoid** and **malarial fevers, the acute infectious diseases,** etc., in fact, **in any case** that comes into the hands of the physician or surgeon, the **psychic factor should never be overlooked.**

ILLUSTRATION NO. 6.

.Psycho-neurotic Indigestion.—Indigestion is **always** accompanied by a neurotic element, with insomnia, nervousness, etc. In numerous instances I have relieved these cases of all distressing symptoms by a single treatment. In general suggestions should be given to **quiet off the nervous element** in the case, to give more plentiful and refreshing sleep, to get them to eat, drink and breathe, and exercise properly, as well as to encourage function. As seeing someone **sucking a juicy lemon** will increase the salivary secretion, so will sense impressions increase the functions of the stomach or any other involuntary function.

A young man, age twenty-four, had a "stricture of the oesophagus" for over two years. He had lived all the while on milk and soup, etc., taking no solid food during this time. **He had an enormously dilated stomach,** due to the large quantities of milk he had ingested. He had been treated as an invalid during the **entire two years or more,** and this itself was a constant suggestive influence to keep up his peculiar psychic condition.

The day I treated this young man, his physician, a most capable and excellent gentleman, had invited two consultants in view of deciding the advisability of making **an exploratory incision to find out the cause of the supposed oesophageal stricture.** I happened to be honored by an invitation to express an opinion in the case, and in a few minutes after I had the liberty of dealing with the young man, I had him eating bananas and drinking water as rapidly as anyone. **A few minutes devoted to hypnotic suggestion** was all that was necessary. After waking him, I advised a diet of eggs, bread and butter and vegetables, with meat once a day, and suggested that the young man be put to work. When heard from two weeks later, he was hard at work and eating anything except milk and soup upon which he had been nourished for the past two years.

ILLUSTRATION NO. 7.

Another Psycho-neurotic Condition.—**A lady about forty-two years old** had been in the John Hopkins Hospital for several months and also had been treated in Southern sanitariums. Several operations, **mostly of a gynecological character,** had been performed. The nervous element in her case, for which she had been operated upon, **was only aggravated** after her return home, and for over two years she had occasional paroxysms of headache, indigestion, hysteria, insomnia, etc. Her physician explained that it usually took **about two days for him to get her relieved,** and then two days longer to get her over the effects of the therapeutic remedies he had used to relieve her terrible seizures.

She was hypnotized and allowed to sleep two hours and suggestions were given to relieve the nervous element in her case, to give her more plentiful and refreshing sleep, to relieve her headaches, to get her to breathe deeper, drink water freely, and aid her digestion. It was also suggested that her nerves would always be quiet and steady and strong and that she would never have another attack. She awoke from the two hours' sleep completely relieved. Five years later she had experienced no more trouble.

ILLUSTRATION NO. 8.

Obstetric Anaesthesia.—N. E., age twenty-two, primapara. Called at 9 a. m. and found patient with light pains and os open the size of a twenty-five cent piece. Hypnotic state induced and suggestion given that when I came to see her again when labor was well established that she would close her eyes and go to sleep and feel no pain. At 10 p. m. I was called and when I told her to close her eyes and go to sleep, and made other suggestions to get her into a deep state of suggestibility, **she easily went into the hypnotic state** and was completley amenable to suggestion.

She would extend her hands to receive help from an assistant and bore down with every contraction, but her expression showed no evidence of pain. **She did not get nervous** and **did not know when the child emerged** until I told her to wake up and look and see her baby.

ILLUSTRATION NO. 9.

Nocturnal Enuresis.—A little factory girl, sixteen years old, arose at 5 a. m. and returned home at 7 p. m. She was about the size of an average child of eleven, had been to school but two or three months in her life and the enuresis had been constant for over two years, but she found no trouble in holding her urine in daytime when awake.

I had a talk face to face with her father and mother, in which I made every effort to burn into their consciousness the enormity of the crime that they were committing in selling their child's brain and blood and muscles for a price. Then I explained kindly to them the importance **of air** and **sunshine and outdoor**

exercise and wholesome food. I should like to have had the owners of that factory take their part of the medicine, and the State authorities also, for permitting such a crime to be inflicted upon children. After this private lecture to the child's parents, I then induced hypnosis in the child and suggested that she would take **exercise night and morning and breathe deeply** and **that she could never urinate lying down again,** that the urine just would not come, her bladder would not let it pass until she got up to use the vessel. I also gave suggestion to relieve the nervous element in her case.

Quite frequently I have had **one single treatment** relieve a case of bedwetting, by suggestion in the hypnotic state. This little girl was heard from several days afterwards and had had no further trouble.

In a number of instances I have instructed the parents to **rock their children from two to six years old to sleep,** and to suggest to them, while going into a natural sleep, that they would wake up and call them when they desired to urinate, that they positively could not wet the bed any more, that without thinking about it they would call their parents or get out of bed on their own accord and use a vessel. In a number of cases the result of this treatment has been highly satisfactory.

ILLUSTRATION NO. 10.

A Retroverted Uterus and its Accompanying Neuroses.— "Good morning, what seems to be the trouble," said I to a negro girl about thirty years old.

"Got de fallin' of the womb, doctor."

"How do you know that is your trouble?"

"Doctor Blank said that was what was the matter with me."

"**I see;** how long has Doctor Blank been treating you?"

"Off and on for five months, doctor."

"**And what has he done** to relieve your womb trouble?"

"Put some medicine in my womb on an instrument with some cotton on it and put some cotton rolls to hold my womb up, and gave me medicine to take every three hours."

"**Do you ever use a hot douche,** use hot water with a syringe?"

"Yes, sir; I use that laying on my back for fifteen minutes twice a week."

On examination I found a decidedly retroflexed and retroverted uterus, bound down by adhesions, with heat, pain and tenderness, and her general temperature was 100.5° F.

"**Have you been able** to work any at all for the past several months?"

"Powerful little, doctor. I tries to do the cooking for a small family and only cooks two meals a day, but I gets awful tremily and weak and I don't sleep at night."

This woman was neurasthenic, suffering with insomina, but little appetite and poor digestion, anaemic and improperly nourished.

She needed her time to make a living; to give her scientific gynecological and surgical treatment was out of the question, for the facilities were not at hand in that locality to care for such patients. I attempted to lift the uterus from out of its impacted position, having put the patient in the knee chest position and applied a Hodge-Smith pessary to hold it. **Yes, I displayed bad judgment** by attempting to use a pessary in that case, but the woman needed help and this was a step toward giving her a little more permanent relief than the continued use of the tampon. My effort to correct the displacement and introduce a pessary gave her much pain, and caused her to be extremely nervous, whereupon I hypnotized her and she went into a profound state of suggestibility.

Here was an ignorant colored woman and my suggestions to her were about as follows:

"**Now, Mary, you are sound asleep.** Sleep on quietly and get the benefit of this treatment. As you lie here (stroking her forehead) your nerves are getting steady and quiet and strong all over. All nervousness and weakness is going away and your nerves are getting steady and quiet and strong all over. By the time I count ten, your nerves will be steady and quiet and strong from your head clear down to your feet. One, two, three, four, five, six, seven, eight, nine, ten, and your nerves are steady and quiet and strong. You are perfectly easy and comfortable all over.

"Now, as you lie here and as I stroke your abdomen, you feel all pain or soreness or tenderness or congestion about your womb and ovaries going away. The blood vessels that carry blood to your womb are drying up and shrinking up, getting smaller and smaller. After this, every minute and every hour and every day you will become stronger and stronger, the blood will circulate freely in your stomach and you will be hungry and enjoy eating and your food will be digested and you will get stronger and stronger every day. You will drink water freely, a glass full at least every two hours. Your kidneys and liver and bowels will act freely.   Your bowels will move every morning after breakfast.   Whether you feel like it or not you will go to the toilet after breakfast and your bowels will move freely.

"You will have no more pain; be easy, sleep well, enjoy eating and improve in health every day.   Whenever you think of yourself, you will find that you are getting better, growing stronger, that you are perfectly easy and you will not be troubled any more."

Do you ask me if I had confidence in those suggestions to believe that they would be effective?   I answer that question by saying that I had desire to benefit that poverty stricken unfortunate outcast sufficient for me to exercise the will to give the suggestions that I wanted to be effective.   The confidence was all on her part.   She had had faith enough in me to save the whole of the previous week's hard earned money and send it to me with a request that I come to see her, "please."

I awoke her from the treatment easily, with the parting suggestion, "you will get better every day now, Mary."

I fully intended calling to see her again after two or three days, but the pressure of my professional engagements for the following week caused me to forget her until about ten days afterward.   Then I thought to myself I had treated her kindly and if she wanted me, I should have been notified.

Eleven and a half months after that visit, I received a call to another house in another portion of my town and found a colored girl suffering with malarial fever.   As I removed the thermometer from her mouth, I remarked, "I have seen you before.   **Where did I see you** and what was your trouble then?"

"You done forgot me, doctor? Nobody ever did do as much good for anyone as you did for me with that one visit you made me most a year ago."

Further questioning recalled to my memory that this was the girl whom I had hypnotized nearly a year before. I had often reproached myself for the unscientific procedure in attempting to use a pessary under such conditions and of my neglect of the case afterwards. I had supposed that she or some physician had removed the hard rubber pessary and that was the end of it so far as I was concerned.

"**Why, girl, have you worn that instrument** all the while and did not consult me about it? Don't you know that is liable to do you great injury?"

"Fo' God, doctor, I ain't had a speck of pain since you walked out of that house and I been doing my work regular up to yesterday."

On examination I found that the pessary was transversely across the vagina, with the uterus sharply retroflexed over it acting only as a foreign body, but that all congestion, soreness, tenderness, hyperplastic condition, etc., were gone. **A very careful examination proved** that there was no erosion or ulceration caused to the parts by the instrument, which had served to keep up a most unsanitary condition. Sexual intercourse, she informed me, had not been painful in the least, but on the other hand, was attended with normal gratification, when the act had been intolerable prior to my first visit.

I removed the pessary and gave her another treatment by hypnotic suggestion, suggesting to her that she would never have the slightest pain or inconvenience from her womb, after that, since the instrument was removed. Her malarial fever rapidly yielded to treatment by calomel and quinine and when this woman was last seen, about two months afterward, she had experienced no more inconvenience.

After that experience, ten or twelve years ago, it fell to my lot to treat a great many gynecological cases, the majority of which, on account of poverty and lack of necessary facilities for radical surgical intervention, were treated conservatively.

I recall a number of cases among both whites and colored where I have relieved by hypnotic suggestions all the painful and nervous symptoms accompanying a **retro-displaced uterus.**

These poor unfortunate women, who did not have money to afford radical scientific surgical and gynecological assistance, were enabled to **meet all the exigencies of life** and be comfortable and happy, carrying a dislocated organ whose reproductive function was not a necessity to their happiness.

As showing the **far-reaching effect of hypnotic suggestion,** in a class of cases usually not considered amenable to benefit by psychological methods of treatment, I report the following three cases:

ILLUSTRATION NO. 11.

Urethritis with Bloody Micturition, Insomnia and Pain.—Lillie H., aged nineteen, married four months, last menstruation six weeks ago. Suffered with painful urethritis causing her to cry out when she voided her urine; passed blood from urethra or bladder when she urinated, which appeared in small clots and shreds in the vessel, suffered constant pain, for which she had

had a daily hypodermic of morphine for a period of one month. During this month she had taken the usual sedative diuretic remedies and the pain had constantly grown worse and the blood in the urine had gradually increased in amount. **The patient wore a distressed countenance,** had but little sleep, and when seen on August 8th, was seated on the bed crying and writhing her body from one side to the other, and was a picture of perfect misery and distress. **Examination of the womb found** it in normal position, a little enlarged, as would have been expected. Diagnosis, congestive urethritis due to reflex disturbance caused by impregnated uterus.

The hypnotic state was induced and proper suggestions were made for relief of pain and cure of all congestion in or about genito-urinary organs. (Note that this was my first visit after this condition had **lasted one month,** and she had constantly had the hypodermic of morphine all the while, thus complicating her case by making her a morphine habituate.)

Second visit eight hours later on the same day, found patient easy, but still discharging blood. **Would not permit treatment by suggestion,** as she begged for morphine. Did not sleep that night, as she had no suggestion to that effect and morphine had suddenly been withdrawn.

Next day she was placed in a deep hypnotic state, appropriate suggestions were given, and she was allowed to sleep four hours; awoke free from pain, and nerves quiet. Treatment by suggestion on same afternoon. Slept well that night, and after that she suffered no more inconvenience from either nervousness or pain. **At the end of one more day** all pain and bloody discharges were gone, the patient was happy, strong, and with good appetite. Two days later the same, four weeks later the same.

ILLUSTRATION NO. 12.

Menorrhagia and Anaemia Accompanying Large Fibroid Tumor of Uterus.—Woman, forty-eight years of age; has large fibroid, profuse menorrhagia for fifteen weeks, greatly emaciated, anaemic, constipated and weak, pulse 140, respiration 60, temperature 102°F. Passing clots as large as a hen's egg and when seen was the picture of distress, with no appetite, very nervous and unable to sleep; suffering also with a remittent malarial fever.

Her case seemed to me to be one in which at best life could not be expected to last longer than a few days. Treatment—Calomel, followed by salines and 15 grains of quinine sulphate daily for the malarial element in her case. Deep hypnosis was induced at my first visit and proper suggestions were made to restore sleep and relieve nervousness, regulate her bowels, to stop hemorrhage, to aid digestion, to give appetite and to build up hope and to change her intuition or belief that she was going to die into belief that she would get well.

From the first treatment by suggestion her nerves were quiet, her sleep was refreshing and plentiful, her appetite was good, and her heart beats slower and stronger and breathing easier. **After four treatments by suggestion** the menorrhagia had entirely stopped. She was then put on a tonic. **Two years later** she was in good health, with her fibroid growing smaller.

ILLUSTRATION NO. 13.

A Unique Case.—A Patient **fifteen years of age** with acute gonorrhea and badly swollen prepuce, had not urinated in thirty-six hours. His bladder in lower part of abdomen felt like a large cocoanut. His pain and suffering were intense. The meatus had in it the large drop of characteristic yellow pus. He had used a hot water hip bath for the relief of his trouble, but without success. To use a catheter would mean to push the disease back into his bladder, giving him gonorrheal cystitis. **Hypnosis was induced** and suggestion made that when he awoke he could urinate freely.

On awakening he expressed the desire to urinate, "oh, so bad," and in one more minute a forcible but small stream began, lasting five minutes. I then gave him a prescription for his gonorrhea, and he went home happy and free from pain. Ten days later he was seen and the case was progressing nicely.

ILLUSTRATION NO. 14.

Another Unique Case.—A physician said to me upon one occasion, "Can you hypnotize this boy so that I can catheterize him." He had acute gonorrhea and was having a catheter used twice a day, in order to relieve his full bladder, which he was not able to relieve in the usual way. Hypnosis was induced and suggestion given to relieve the psycho-neurotic element, and when he awoke **he urinated without catheterization** and continued to do so thereafter.

ILLUSTRATION NO. 15.

Morphine Habit.—This was a patient of one of the **best known physicians in the south.** Her ovaries had been removed,

[13]

cervix and perineum repaired, but the operative procedures had only aggravated the neurotic symptoms that they were intended to relieve. In addition to the aggravated nervous symptoms, she had a pain in one side, which had appeared as a result of adhesions, and to relieve this the administration of morphine had been instituted and continued for several months or more. The pain had subsided, but the demand for the continued use of morphine was imperative, at least from this lady's point of view. Five or six months had elapsed since the beginning of the habit, which was now well fixed.

The patient lived forty miles distant and was ordered to come into the city. Her physician explained to her that I had a treatment which would relieve her of the morphine habit without inconvenience, and both she and her husband consented to co-operate with our plans. She was given at a dose for four doses every two hours, beginning at 2 p. m.

> ℞Calomel, 1 grain.
> Resinous podophyllin, 1-8 grain,
> Extract of nux vomica, 1-6 grain,
> Powdered extract cascara sagrada, 1 grain,
> Aloin, 1-5 grain.
> > M. et. ft. caps. No. 1.

This dose was given in a capsule, every two hours for four doses, beginning at 2 p. m., and the patient was allowed to have her usual hypodermic of one grain of morphine that evening.

The following morning she was given two drachms of Rochelle salts every hour until copious watery evacuations were produced, and this was directed to be given without regard to the action of the purgative dose administered the previous day.

Thorough elimination of the **by-products of morphine** must be secured as well as the getting rid of all retained excreta due to the continued use of morphine. At 11 a. m. the next day a warm bath was ordered, warm enough to secure thorough relaxation, and the drinking of copious draughts of water was also insisted upon for eliminative purposes.

No more morphine was allowed after the dose the day previous. When thorough elimination is secured in this way, morphine can be abruptly withdrawn without any inconvenience to the heart's action; in fact, the patient is less apt to die without the morphine than with it, provided the nervous element in the case is cared for, and this can be controlled by suggestion.

At noon on the second day, after copious actions of the purgative given the day previous and a saline had been given, and a warm bath had been administered, the patient was hypnotized and allowed to sleep for three hours. **It was suggested that her** nerves were steady and quiet and strong, and that her heart would beat strong and regular; that every minute and hour after that her nerves would get steadier and quieter and stronger; that she would enjoy her meals, feel hopeful, optimistic, and cheerful, and after that would have an antipathy for morphine or any form of opium; that she would breathe deeply, drink water freely and take an interest in the affairs of life as she had not done in many months. **It was suggested that at bedtime** she would take three drops of the placebo prescription and go sound asleep and sleep soundly all night and awaken every morning feeling refreshed and well rested.

After three hours' sleep she was awakened and ate a lunch of milk, bread and butter and at once took the train for home, forty miles away. **Five days afterward** I went to this lady's home town, where her husband had gotten the physicians interested in my class work, and instructed a class of physicians at that place, allowing the husband of the patient to be present. She was then sleeping, eating and doing well in every way.

Twenty-seven days after the withdrawal of the morphine, in response to a letter of inquiry I learned that the patient had experienced no more inconvenience, had slept well, enjoyed eating, gained in weight, and was happier and better in every way. "But," said he, "yesterday my wife overexerted herself and I used a hypodermic of one-fourth of a grain of morphine last night, the first that she had taken in twenty-seven days." The only thing left for me to do was to write to him and express my regret that he had acted so unwisely and urged him to use reason, castor oil, Epsom salts, hot poultices, bromides, or do anything else but to deliberately start her on morphine with an already acquired predisposition for the drug.

To educate an individual in the principles of psycho-therapy is one thing, but to get them to exercise the force of character sufficient to apply these principles is something else.

ILLUSTRATION NO. 16.

Chronic Indigestion.—A country editor, age thirty-four, had for several years suffered from indigestion, and in two years he had not eaten meat for supper without spending a restless night and having little sleep, followed by no appetite and a bad head-ache the next day.

He was hypnotized and suggestions were given to encourage a freer flow of blood in his stomach, **to stimulate the cerebral centers that influence this important organ** and also to quiet the nervous element in his case, get him to breathe deeper, and drink more water. Upon awakening him, I advised that he eat some of everything upon the table at his boarding place that evening. "But suppose it makes me sick," asked he. "Then I will pay your doctor's bill," was my reply. "Suppose it kills me?" "I'll buy your coffin and pay your burial expenses," was my answer.

Then addressing him, I said, "Mr. Blank, go and eat as much of everything you have on your table as you desire and especially eat meat, and come tomorrow and tell me how you are feeling." The next day he returned and said he had eaten a hearty supper of pork sausage and broiled beefsteak and never had a better night's sleep or felt better in his life. I laughed and in a friendly way advised him to eat as much of everything as he wished in the future **except printing presses and newspaper editors.** Several days afterwards he was cheerful and happy and had experienced no more difficulty.

It is interesting to me to see the skilled laboratory chemical analysis of the gastric contents, made by some of our physicians, and the diet and medication prescribed according to indications in the light of the teachings of modern physiology. **It is beautiful work, requires great skill,** and proceeds upon exact scientific basis, and I hope some day to be equipped to do such work myself in order more scientifically to report the results of psychological methods of treatment, but my confidence in the brain plasm and its influence over the physiological processes is such that these methods in the large majority of cases seem to me to be quite unnecessary.

In gross pathological changes, however, due to destructive processes, malignant stomach affections, etc., there is presented quite another aspect of the subject, and these methods throw a wonderful light upon the case at hand. However, we must be careful not to **fasten upon our patient by the unconscious use of suggestion a psycho-pathological condition** instead of relieving him of a psycho-neurotic disturbance.

ILLUSTRATION NO. 17.

Subacute Sciatica.—A man aged forty-five was confined to his bed with acute sciatica for several weeks and for five or six months following had used crutches, unable to bear his weight on the affected side. His physician had invited some of his professional friends to witness the treatment of this case.

The history of the case, the time that had elapsed, the rational therapeutic measures, etc., that had been employed, together with the symptoms at hand, convinced me that the severe pain, insomnia, and functional disturbances were unduly **aggravated by the prolonged attention** that had been given to them by the patient, which had **created sense impressions** that **reproduced themselves in the peculiar mental state** exhibited by him.

There is always a tendency for the nervous system to **retain an impression after the cause which gave it birth has passed away.** This proved to be true in this case of sciatica. The patient was hypnotized and suggestions were given to relieve his pain, to quiet nervousness, restore sleep and re-establish the function of the disabled limb. **The man while in the hypnotic state was persuaded** to use the limb, and when awakened stamped his foot on the floor, walked, jumped, hopped on the affected limb, and then turned in all seriousness to the physician and said he was easy for the first time in five months. After seeing him three more times on each of the following days successively, he went to his work. This man was a carpenter and appeared in no sense to belong to the hysterical type, yet this was a psycho-neurotic condition.

ILLUSTRATION NO. 18.

Bronchitis, Asthma, Pneumonia, Etc.—A man, fifty years old, had had chronic bronchitis for fifteen years, with occasional paroxysms of asthma. He now had acute pneumonia, affecting the lower lobe of the right lung only, but had a temperature of 104.5°F., pulse 135, and rapid respiration also. On the fifth day of his acute illness he had slept but little the previous three nights and was extremely nervous and over-solicitous about his condition. There was a large element of fear about his case, which gave rise to very bad auto-suggestions. These were encouraged by an over-anxious family and friends. I had done all within my power to re-assure him by suggestion without hypnotism but to no avail.

Seeing his anxiety so pronounced and the psychic element in his case so adverse to his recovery, I decided that one more day without a change would mean the death of my patient. Taking in my hand a bottle of some placebo, I said to him earnestly,

"Mr. Blank, there is a nervous element in your case that I am going to relieve before I leave you. This medicine, used as I am going to use it presently, will put you to sleep, quiet your nerves, strengthen your heart and help you to get well. Now, it can't hurt you, but will make you stronger. I will stay with you until you awaken, and you will be feeling better and stronger and take quite a different view of your condition when you awake."

A patient in that condition is always easy to hypnotize. **This man readily consented to the treatment,** and while in the hypnotic state I suggested to him that all nervousness was going away and that his nerves were getting steady and quiet and strong. Then I also suggested that his heart was beating stronger and stronger, and that his hands and feet were getting warm, that the blood was circulating freely all over his body, that all congestion and pain about his lungs were going away, and that his fever was cooling, temperature getting more normal, and nerves and muscles and heart getting quiet and steady and strong. I suggested that every dose of the medicine he was taking would quiet his nerves, strengthen his heart, lessen his fever, aid his digestion, and that whenever he thought of himself he would feel that he was getting better, feeling stronger, and going rapidly on to recovery. I allowed him to sleep for twenty miniutes or half an hour. When I awoke him I gave him the answer to my question, which was more an affirmation than a question. **"You are feeling better, Mr. Blank?** This has done you a great deal of good." "Yes, doctor," said, he **"I feel that I am going to get well and have not felt that way before."**

I then took his temperature and found it two degrees lower than it was thirty minutes previously, and his pulse beats twenty a minute fewer than before he went to sleep.

He slept well that night, as I suggested he would, and his pulse and temperature were better the next day. His temperature never went any higher than 102.5°F. after that or his pulse above 120 a minute. His lungs cleared up on the ninth day.

Two years afterwards, that man had not had another attack of asthma, as I had suggested on two or three occasions following the first treatment by hypnotic suggestion that he would never have asthma again, that he would always drink plenty of water, the bowels would move regularly every day, and he would sleep soundly, have a good digestion, and always feel better.

It may be pointed out that in asthma there are always functional disturbances due to deficient elimination causing a general neurotic condition, of which the asthmatic paroxysm is the predominant manifestation, and attracts the greatest attention.

In regard to the use of hypnotism in very sick people suffering with pneumonia and enteric fever, the acute infectious diseases, etc., I have always felt that if I could get the patient to exercise enough self-control to go into the hypnotic state he would be certain to recover. **No possible harm can come from giving a patient suggestions to quiet nervousness,** relieve pain, re-establish function, and encourage the action of all the brain centers, turning this energy represented by the cells that compose the cerebral cortex to the strengthening of every cell and every function in the body.

Hypnotism is only an intensified, and therefore more effica-cious form of applying suggestion and it seems to relieve a very sick patient of a heavy responsibility, when you use his psychic powers for him, direct them, and regulate their control over his body rather than keep him on the alert to do this for himself.

There are yet some physicians who believe that suggestion is of value only in hysterical subjects and that only hysterical people can be benefitted. If that be true, **then all sick people are hysterical,** for there is no acute febrile illness in which the psychic factor does not play an important role in helping or hindering the recovery of the patient.

Remember that there is such a thing as nervous shock, due to sense impressions which give rise to fear thoughts that hold the attention of a very sick patient. The physician who can **change these psychic states,** changes the mental attitude of his patient, encourages all involuntary physiological processes, **and helps his patient to recovery.**

It is **hard to hypnotize an hysterical patient,** while, on the other hand, **a normal nervous organization always best responds to suggestion** and makes the best hypnotic subject. This I have demonstrated and proved to the satisfaction of **several thousand American physicians,** notwithstanding the opinion of a few pre-judiced neurologists, who are self-hypnotized by their precon-ceived convictions, to the contrary.

ILLUSTRATION NO. 19.

Dressing a Painful Wound.—A gentleman, thirty-two years old, had his foot infected with a gas-producing germ which caused the leg to swell enormously. To give him the only chance to recover the surgeon amputated the limb at a point about seven inches below the hip joint and dressed the amputation wide open, not allowing the flaps to close, in order to secure thorough drainage. **Large quantities** of gauze came away at each dressing literally soaked in purulent discharge, as the infection had extended above the amputation.

The patient's reserve forces were being drawn upon heavily and his toxic condition left him unable to withstand pain. He did not appear hysterical, but at each dressing of the wound he could be heard crying all over the hospital, on account of the severe pain. He was placed in a suggestible condition, using a placebo medicine as an aid, suggestions were given to produce anaesthesia, and the wound was dressed without the slightest complaint on the part of patient.

ILLUSTRATION NO. 20.

Hysteria, Neurasthenia with Delusions, Hallucinations, Etc. —**A delicate, high-strung, nervous young woman,** with ambition while in college three times in excess of her physical strength. A decidedly neurotic tendency, always over-sensitive and morbidly conscientious. This condition had been encouraged by overstrain in education and by one incident after another which proved to be a shock too great for a nervous system so unstable; yet not more than a normal individual could easily withstand. **Finally came an attack of typhoid fever,** and when the patient was seen several months later she had for five months been confined to her room with hands and arms fastened, **with delusions of persecution,** and impersonating one character after another sent down to earth by Prometheus, etc.

She drank but little water, taking only a small quantity of milk for nourishment; her bowels moved **only under influence of purgatives;** there was **constant enuresis,** sleep was secured only by hypnotics, bromides, etc. **She had a furred tongue, fetid breath, rapid pulse,** was extremely nervous, with an excitable, over-active brain, and finally would become exhausted and lie with head hot and bathed all over in perspiration. At my first visit I released her arms and **acted as if I had perfect confidence in her,** had her exercise every muscle, breathe deeply, drink one glass of water, and after an hour another glass. I then put her into **a light state of hypnosis** and gave suggestions to **quiet nervousness,** to relieve an **over-excitable brain, secure sleep, cure enuresis, correct delusions, create appetite and thirst, and to regulate bowels, etc.**

Besides releasing her from the fastenings on her arms, **all medicine was withdrawn at once** save a one-eighth grain dose of protoiodide of mercury, which was ordered to be given at bed time for its general tonic effect. **From the first treatment by hypnotic suggestion** she became quiet, slept well at night, ate three wholesome meals a day, had but few delusions, enuresis was stopped, pulse quiet and normal, talk rational, and the whole picture of the case was changed.

After one week she was eating, sleeping, drinking water freely, exercising and resting alternately, practicing deep breathing, and presented every indication of great improvement, while previously she had been gradually growing worse for several months and probably several years. **After two weeks' treatment,** she made up her own bed, swept her own room, took walks in the park, and assisted in the housework, busying herself with fancy work, etc.

The outcome of this case is for time only to decide. **The permanency of the results obtained by suggestive therapeutics depends altogether upon the stability of the nervous system.** A favorable out come in a case like this will depend upon our ability to bring about those conditions **necessary to physical development,** sleep, food, drink, exercise, mental quietude, as well as directing her habits of thought and action into healthful, normal channels. Yet, **the results so far** show the possiblities for help even in this unfortunate class of cases.

Sanity or insanity is not to be ascertained by any definite standard. They are terms that cannot be defined, for one merely denotes the absence of the other. They are both only relative terms. It is absolutely impossible to find a person of so healthy a mind and body that some form of degeneracy cannot be observed. As a well-known psychologist remarked, **"No one can be accused of being hopelessly sane."** Yet, if an individual is **unable to look after his affairs and is dangerous to himself and others,** and interferes with society, he may undoubtedly be said to be of unsound mind. At any rate, insanity is not revealed by any one symptom. The change is displayed by everything both physical and mental. The degeneration **affects the body as a whole.**

Not every person that is sick, then, should be counted as insane, for all disease affects both mind and body in a degree. **There are many people that are insane,** however, who, had timely treatment been instituted, could have been completely restored to a normal condition of health in both mind and body. **"Treatment," in the sense used in the above remark** involves education environment, dietetics, exercise or employment, and all that contributes to the evolution of the individual.

Suggestions, both with and without hypnotism, in the hands of a thoughtful physician can do much toward bringing about those conditions under which recovery may be rendered possible.

HYPNOTIC SUGGESTION IN SURGERY.

One physician who had taken my personal instruction in suggestive therapeutics informed me six months afterwards that he had used hypnotic suggestion for anaesthesia **in not less than five or six hundred cases** of minor surgery with complete success. Another stated that he used suggestion both with and without hypnotism, in obstetrics and minor surgery so frequently that **it had become an unconscious habit with him.** All physicians use suggestion, consciously or unconsciously. Only those who have studied and understand the use of hypnotism use it systematically and scientifically, so as to get the **most efficacious results** from its employment.

An anaesthetist who understands the systematic and artful use of suggestion will, in some cases, use not over one-fourth of the amount of chloroform or ether that would be required by another, who does not properly use suggestion, and will thus greatly lessen the danger of anaesthetics. **In giving chloroform, or ether,** engage the attention of your patient. This should be done tactfully, so as to gain his **spontaneous attention** without letting him know that you are making an effort to impress him. Examine his heart and pulse and affirm: "You are in fine condition to take an anaesthetic; now, I want you to do as I request and this will put you in a sound sleep without the slightest danger. Given by the method that I use, it only makes your circulation and breathing strong and regular, while all other functions are inhibited. Now, close your eyes lightly, breathe through your mouth, and think of going to sleep. As you inhale this remedy, you will get quiet all over and get drowsy and sleepy and go to sleep and awake after the operation feeling fine. **You will not be sick at your stomach** or nauseated in the least degree. We are going to take good care of you and you will get along all right. Now, breathe this down and go to sleep, sleep, sleep, sleep," etc.

I employ the same suggestions as are used to induce hypnosis, and at the same time use chloroform or ether, only to the minimum extent required.

If you expect to push the chloroform or ether to the extent that sense impressions could not be made on the brain or suggestions be presented to your patient, suggest to him before he is fully under the anaesthetic that he will be perfectly relaxed and limber, that he will breathe deeply and regularly, that his heart will beat strongly and regularly, and that he will have no feeling, that all sensation will disappear. Then proceed with the anaesthetic.

Frequently, however, **I start off with ten or twenty drops of chloroform** and hypnotize the patient while he thinks the anaesthetic is producing the result. In that case I suggest to the patient, after hypnosis is induced, that all feeling, all sensation in the field of operation, is going away, that the part is becoming perfectly dead, and that by the time I count ten the part will have no feeling in it.

ILLUSTRATION NO. 21.

Suprapubic Cystotomy.—The operation was decided on, the patient being a man about forty years of age, who had an infection produced by a catheter being thrust through the urethra, behind the bladder into the peritoneal cavity, an abscess being formed, extending above and in front of the bladder. **It was the "other fellow's patient,"** and I had been invited to go with the consulting surgeon to see what could be done for the unfortunate. The surgeon said to the sick man, **already in a subconscious condition,** due to his anxiety over his serious case, "This is a physician friend of mine and he will give you chloroform and put you to sleep and we will do the right thing for you. Do just as he tells you and he will take good care of you."

With a piece of gauze on the bottom of my hand and with ten drops of chloroform on it, I said to the patient, **"Close your eyes, breathe through your mouth, and think of going to sleep.** As you inhale this chloroform, you will get drowsy and sleepy and go on to sleep without any trouble." I then exercised suggestion on him, using the formula described in a previous chapter to induce hypnosis. (Hypnotism demonstrated.)

With a piece of cotton saturated with water, after the patient was hypnotized, I gently touched the area to be operated on, saying to him, "All feeling is going away; this part is becoming perfectly dead, no feeling in it at all, and by the time I count ten it will be perfectly dead and without feeling."

In the midst of the operation the surgeon asked, "How much of this is suggestion and how much is chloroform?" I answered him by holding the man's arm up and suggesting that he allow it to remain until the operation was completed. We afterwards awoke the patient with nerves steady and quiet and strong, as suggested to him, and he stated that he had experienced no pain and felt much better. In this case we used not over twenty drops of chloroform by actual measurement.

Always tell your patient how he will feel before waking him. That will determine his feeling after he is hypnotized. It is **not only what you do** and what you say that brings success, but the **way you do and how you say it.** This is true of the use of suggestion both with and without hypnotism.

In reducing dislocations, setting fractures, opening abscesses, sewing up incised wounds, and numerous other conditions, hypnotic suggestion is applicable. Yet, so much depends upon the environment, for an adverse environment produces a counter influence by unconscious suggestion, that it is often impossible to overcome. **In private practice,** however, we have an ideal condition for the application of suggestive therapeutics. It is here that the best results are always obtained, for there is a closer personal relation between the physician and his patient.

ILLUSTRATION NO. 22.

Operation for Adenoids.—This patient was **a little girl ten years old,** with adenoids to be removed. She was hypnotized, and the suggestion given that when the doctor examined in her mouth and back of her throat and nose, it would only tickle her a little, that the parts back there were dead, had no feeling in them, and that when I said "Wake," she would awake laughing ·

[14]

and see some blood come out of her nose and mouth. The operation was done by a well-known specialist, and with perfect success. The little girl did not shed a tear.

ILLUSTRATION NO. 23.

Suggestion in Dental Surgery.—**A young man twenty-four years of age,** by occupation a drug clerk, had serious valvular lesions, and cocaine or chloroform or ether was positively forbidden by his physician. **At his request** I hypnotized him in the presence of three well-known physicians and surgeons, and two large molar teeth were extracted without pain, and he was less nervous after the operation than before he took his seat in the chair. Two of the physicians examined the heart before and after the operation and remarked upon the improved nervous condition. After inducing hypnosis, I suggested that he open his mouth, and then applying a small quantity of an antiseptic solution upon some cotton around his tooth, suggested that all feeling was going away, that his gum and tooth and jaw were becoming perfectly dead, and that by the time I counted five, that entire side of his face **would have no feeling in it,** that the dentist could extract the tooth, without the patient's feeling any pain.

To use hypnotism or suggestion with success in surgery or dentistry, you must have the confidence of your patient. In fact, the best results from suggestive therapeutics **in all classes of practice can be obtained only** where a perfect confidential relation exists between the patient and the attending physician. **For that reason,** suggestive therapeutics will never be particularly applicable to general hospital work, but in private sanitarium work, where the physician is brought into close relation to his patient, an ideal condition is presented.

ILLUSTRATION NO. 24.

Psychical Impotency.—**A young man had been accused** by a jealous wife of worshiping a foreign goddess. This he strenuously denied. However, upon one occassion he walked by his home with the lady in question and was observed by his suspecting wife. Though he assured her that his being with her upon the occasion was only a coincidence, his assurances did not allay his wife's suspicions, and she then and there demanded that he prove his fidelity by his ability to perform the sexual act. Though the young man was innocent, the psychic effect of being put to so crucial a test, so suddenly, was sufficient to completely inhibit his ability to meet the demands. **Then the exacting wife turned** with double vehemence upon the unfortunate husband, and the sense impressions or suggestions produced by her declarations that she had proof positive of the correctness of her suspicions, rendered the poor fellow impotent, in her presence, for a month.

The stability of his home was in jeopardy, and threats of abandonment were made by the wife, who felt that she had been wronged. His physician sent for me and my treatment for the young man was by **instruction and education** as to how he should steer himself out of his dilemma. **He was also hypnotized** and special suggestions were given to combat the psychic effect of the suggestions that had so completely subdued him. This was on Saturday, and on Monday he reported that the psychic atmosphere of his home had been completely changed and that the treatment was a decided success.

The psychology of the sexual relation is a most interesting and important subject, and involves the consideration of the physical, emotional, intellectual, ethical, aesthetic and moral qualities of human beings. It is related to every phase of life— educational, religious, social and moral — and plays an all-important part in the production of health and happiness. **The highest function of the physician** is to be prepared to give sane, wholesome, sensible advice where needed in such cases, and to save such as are seeking help from the vampires who live and thrive upon the distorted imaginations, credulity and suggestibility of those who are honestly and earnestly seeking relief.

ILLUSTRATION NO. 25.

Insomnia Treated in a Unique Manner.—" Doctor, I wish you would give me something to make me sleep better at night," said the wife of a hard-working man upon whom the cares of life were pressing heavily.

" Why can't you sleep, Mrs. Blank ? " said I.

" Oh, I just toss and roll about for hours and hours, and last night I didn't close my eyes until after one o'clock."

This lady was a great religious character, and I knew this was her most vulnerable point from a psychological stand-point; so I asked her if she believed that if two people agreed as touching any one thing it could be done for them. " You know I do, doctor," she answered.

. " All right," said I. " Let's agree that you are going to go to sleep right now." I was standing at the foot of her bed, and, looking into her face for a moment, I said in a calm monotone voice: **" Just look at me and think of sleep.** As you do, your eyes will become heavy and you will get drowsy and sleepy and go to sleep. Now, close your eyes lightly and go to sleep, sleep, sleep, sleep. By the time I count ten you will be fast asleep, one, two, three, four, five, six, seven, eight, nine, ten and now you are asleep, fast asleep."

Then coming up to her I gently soothed her forehead with a few strokes on either side with my fingers. " You are sleeping nicely, having a calm, refreshing sleep. Sleep soundly for two hours and then awake. Your sleep will be restful and refreshing. After this you will be able to go to sleep at any time you desire to do so. Just close your eyes and relax every muscle and think of sleep, and you will go to sleep and sleep soundly all night, and awake feeling refreshed and rested every morning. **You will drink water freely** every two hours from morning until you retire at night. You will enjoy your meals, have a good appetite, find pleasure in your work, rest when you get tired enjoy the companionship of your husband and children and friends, and always feel happier on account of the improved condition of your health."

Two years afterwards this woman's husband reminded me of this experience. He said his wife had slept well and enjoyed her meals, had no more headaches and was greatly improved in every way. **" Nothing ever did her so much good,** doctor, as that one visit of yours, but we lost our baby with cholera infantum two months ago and my wife is 'just all in,' and I want you to see her again." This was on a passing visit to my home and I could not see his wife as requested, but I have always felt that I missed a great pleasure in not having the opportunity to infuse into her sad life some of my own strength and optimism by another suggestive treatment.

ILLUSTRATION NO. 26.

A Psycho-neurotic Condition.—A young lady twenty-two **years old,** the beautiful daughter of a prominent physician, had not been able to eat any meat without it causing gastric disturbance, since the death of her mother two years before, and since that time she had been nervous, suffered with insomnia, and lost considerably in weight. I gave her two suggestive treatments, having first secured a suggestible condition. **Two weeks later she reported her case,** and had gained in weight, slept well at night, ate all the meat she desired without the slightest inconvenience, and felt better and happier in every way.

ILLUSTRATION NO. 27.

Nausea and Vomiting of Pregnancy.—A Physician once **stated** to me frankly that he had no confidence in anything pertaining to these methods and could not possibly become interested in a subject that he had so disregarded. **He was an excellent gentleman,** but like so many physicians in our profession, had not troubled himself to look into the subject of psychotherapy.

A day or two later he said to a patient of his, the wife of a leading banker in his city, who had suffered with gravid nausea persistently for several days, "If you don't get better, I will bring a physician here who will treat you by hypnotic suggestion."

Her mother, who was present, urged that he do so, and referred to a physician who had relieved her brother, the Reverend Blank, D. D., a prominent educator, of a most distressing supra-orbital neuralgia, after no benefit had been obtained from other methods of treatment for over two weeks. His patient also urged that I be called in to see her. In his conveyance, while on our way to see this patient, I asked why he desired to use a a method in which he "had absolutely no confidence," and had so expressed himself only two days before, wherein he related to me the circumstance just referred to.

"For this visit she is my patient as well as she is yours, doctor," said I, "and I expect to get a fine result."

The preconceived mental attitude of your patient is of great psychic significance in determining the results of any kind of therapeutic measures. I had this lady's confidence before I ever saw her, and this was an ideal relation.

After talking with her for a few minutes, I turned to her and said I was glad to have the opportunity of demonstrating to Doctor Blank the efficacy of the method of treatment which I was introducing to physicians, and in this particular case it would be a genuine pleasure for her sake, as well as for my own and Doctor Blank's.

I had that lady hypnotized or in a suggestible condition before I suggested that she go to sleep, yet I placed her in a deep subconscious or hypnotic condition and made appropriate suggestions.

She was allowed to sleep twenty minutes, and awoke comfortable, ate some bread and buttermilk, as I suggested, and as she drank it down, stopped to ask her mother if she remembered that she went to the refrigerator upon her return from her graduating exercises four years before, and remarked that no milk had ever tasted so nice before or since until she got this glass, and she proceeded to drain its contents. **Her comments upon that glass of buttermilk** reminded me of how I relished nice buttermilk when a boy on the farm, and I asked for a glass and drank to her health, and it was fine, too. I hypnotized my patient, but got hypnotized myself into drinking a glass of milk before I left the room.

That lady ate her evening meal, slept well that night, enjoyed her breakfast and was out driving the next day. A year later her mother reported to me that **she went for several weeks without inconvenience,** but after that, the destruction of some choice flowers by a stupid gardener brought on the return of her trouble, but "it was never so bad."

ILLUSTRATION NO. 28.

Supraorbital Neuralgia.—The case of the prominent educator mentioned in illustration No. 27, who had supraorbital neuralgia, was an interesting one, and is worth relating here, as it brings out some important features in connection with the application of suggestive therapeutics, and at the same time **clears up some misapprehensions** in regard to hypnotism and its application to the higher grades of intelligence. **The gentleman in question** was the president of a well-known college in his State. When I met him he apologized for his "stupidity" and explained that his case had resisted all treatment for two weeks and was getting the best of him. He said that twenty-five grains of quinine daily and two one-quarter grain doses of morphine sulphate had been his dose for the past several days, besides using static electricity, hot applications, different standard neuralgic remedies and all the modern "antis."

"Let me relieve you by suggestion, doctor," said I.

"What, do you mean to hypnotize me?" he replied, somewhat astonished.

"Yes, get you to take a suggestion."

"But I never thought I could be hypnotized," said he.

"Only weak minded persons cannot be hypnotized, cannot be induced to execute an idea or series of ideas, for the lack of ability to exercise self-control, and certainly one cannot hypnotize a strong minded person who does not care to be hypnotized. Of course, you belong to the latter class, but if you will consent, I will show you what can be done for you."

"My dear sir," replied he, "I will consent to anything that even holds out a hope of relief." We very promptly arranged to give him the treatment and I left him in a condition supposed to be sleep, having made appropriate suggestions.

Ten days later I saw him again, and he was quick to thank me for the very prompt and efficacious relief given him by the treatment, and said he had not suffered one iota from that condition since I left him, "But, doctor," said he, "I don't think I was asleep. I wanted to tell you that I was easy before you left, but promised to lie still in the condition as you requested!"

That was just where he consented to act intelligently upon and execute an idea or take my suggestion. All that is necessary is the intelligent co-operation of the patient; so I repeat again for I desire to drive this point home, that hypnotism is nothing more or less than getting an individual **to act upon an idea or series of ideas, either consciously or subconsciously.**

Get out of your mind anything you ever saw on the stage in exhibition of the amusement features of hypnotism. Even there, however, you see an illustration of the subject under discussion. **Boys like fun.** It is in their line—in accordance with their thought and conduct—and they go on the stage having perhaps unconsciously decided **to act upon or execute any idea or series of ideas given by the hypnotist.** Your patient does the same thing when he co-operates with you in any ordinary method of treatment.

ILLUSTRATION NO. 29.

Alcoholism and its Accompanying Neuroses.—Once, in one of our great American cities, a well-known physician telephoned me to know what I could do with a case of acute alcoholism. I replied that I had good results in my private practice in such cases, but that it all depended upon the character of the individual.

He wanted me to come at once to treat a patient of his who had been drinking too freely for a week or more, had taken not less than fifteen drinks that day, but was anxious to quit. **His patient was a fine man,** who proved afterwards to be one of the most delightful men I ever met, but he had his vulnerable point and his friends had led him too far.

If I can talk to an individual for a few minutes I feel the personality of the man sufficiently to approach him with a degree of certainty or with uncertainty as regards results. I suppose this is acquired by experience. Anyway, I was not in this gentleman's presence five minutes before I said to his physician, " Doctor, we are going to get along all right. I am ready to proceed with the treatment." **The patient, a business man and capitalist,** about forty-eight years old, was nervous, emotional, irritable, miserable, and had suffered with insomnia, anorexia, etc., and just felt that something had to be done for him. **Even in the condition described,** the man was a gentleman, showed that he had a great soul in him, and I could feel that I had in him the elements of a man to use on his own behalf, which he, from inability to express the supreme function of consciousness, the will, had failed to use for himself.

I induced the suggestive state and allowed him to sleep for three hours, giving him a glass of water at intervals of an hour apart without arousing him from the existing state of suggestibility.

He was then awakened and advised to take a walk for half-an-hour or more with his wife, a bowl of chicken broth being ordered in the meantime. In the suggestive state I had made such suggestions as would quiet nervousness, relieve soreness in the epigastric region, restore self-confidence, produce an antipathy or hatred for whisky, and arouse the highest element of selfhood into action.

It was also suggested that after his walk he would eat a bowl of chicken broth and then go to bed and at once go sound asleep, that he would sleep soundly all night, and that if he became restless during the night, his wife would give him a glass of water and he would go sound asleep again. I impressed on him that he **would not wake until nine o'clock the next day,** at which time his wife would awaken him. Then, as has been my custom, I told him he would feel rested, refreshed, self-sufficient, and not want whisky any more.

At eleven o'clock the next day his wife phoned me, in response to an inquiry about his condition, using these words: "Oh, doctor, he is doing beautifully. He slept all night long, taking water twice, and looks so calm and self poised this morning. **He says he does not want any more whisky,** and I never saw him look and talk like this after a spree before."

I saw him only twice more and talked to him face to face as friend with friend. Several weeks later, when I was ready to leave that city, he came to my room at the hotel, again expressing his thanks, and like the real man that he was, he said, "Doctor, you have helped me more than anyone ever did in my whole life. You have given me a new conception of myself and made me feel in regard to myself as I never felt before."

I had awakened in him a higher self-consciousness or an appreciation of a higher self hood, and the memory that I have of hundreds and hundreds of such experiences is to me one of life's greatest rewards.

> "Conversion is suggestion just disguised,
> The new man, is the old man hypnotized."

It is a great thing to have confidence in human beings; faith in humanity is faith in God. It is to recognize the divine in human life.

The individual or individuals who have helped me the most

in life have been those who were able to discover the germination of a higher selfhood as an actuating impulse in my own life and conduct.

ILLUSTRATION NO. 31.

Pulmonary Tuberculosis.—**In a southern town a few years ago** the thermometer suddenly dropped and the weather was uncomfortably cold. At the hotel a lady from a different state, in a well-advanced stage of pulmonary tuberculosis, was visiting. Cough, cough, cough was all that she could do. **Her weakness aroused my sympathy,** and I said to her: " Mrs. Blank, I can help you a great deal by suggestion, and should be glad to do so while I am here for the pleasure I should get out of seeing you benefitted."

" Why, Doctor Munro, I have consumption. Pray, how could hypnotism help me? This is no imaginary disease."

" Mrs. Blank, you are evidently very nervous. I heard you say you did not sleep two hours in all last night, and I noticed that you ate practically no breakfast this morning."

" Yes," she replied, " I am so weak and nervous I can scarcely walk. **This bandage on my hand** is the result of an injury received from a fall yesterday. No, I cannot eat or sleep, and this miserable weather is terrible on me."

She had a forlorn, downcast look, but I honestly believed that I could benefit her.

" Mrs. Blank," said I, " by suggestion in the hypnotic state I can quiet that irritability of your nervous system, give you a good, refreshing night's sleep, and yet you can relieve yourself by expectorating when necessary in your sleep. **Getting** a good night's rest, you will conserve your energies and will awake with a good appetite and strong, quiet nerves. Then, as you eat more, sleep better, and get stronger, I will get you to breathe deeper and take in more oxygen. **The increased amount of air** will mean much to your general health, for oxygen is a food that many people do not take in sufficient quantities. Along with the influence of more oxygen upon all bodily functions will be an increase in elimination, both of carbon dioxide from your lungs, and from a freer activity of all bodily functions. "**In your particular case** I have confidence in the benefit to be derived from deep breathing in other ways. Increased function means increased blood supply, and by breathing deeper your lung substance will be better nourished and its resistive powers increased, and your chances to recover strengthened ten to one as compared to the present. There are other ways that suggestion would prove of benefit, but though you could not understand if I attempted to explain them to you, I feel warranted in saying that I know you will be benefited to a remarkable degree."

" Doctor Munro, **I am ready whenever you are,** and as often as you see fit to give this treatment," she replied.

Calling her friend, Miss Blank, into a room to be present at the time of the administration of this treatment, I proceeded to put her into a condition of suggestibility and gave suggestions to quiet her nervousness, restore more plentiful and refreshing sleep, inflate the lungs, and, above all, to stir all latent psychic activities into action, to increase her resistive powers, etc.

This young lady present told me that when she was a school girl Mrs. Blank was a fine singer and had a lovely voice, so at another time while she was hypnotized I gave her a suggestion that **she was again a school-girl,** and was going to sing while her friend furnished the music. The song was the " Angel's Serenade," and she sang, too. She reached the highest note in " Hosannah in the highest, Hosannah to his name."

I then appreciated as I had never done before with any patient, what I had done for her. All that I did was out of kindness and sympathy, but with optimism and faith. There was no money in this case. There was no selfish motive in it.

After four days she had been sleeping, eating, drinking, exercising, and singing as she had not before in years. **Six weeks later** I learned indirectly from her husband in another town in that State that she had gained six pounds, and was rapidly improving every day.

When I left the town where I treated this lady, she thanked me sincerely, and gave me a note which she had prepared to send to me at the train by the porter. In this she expressed her gratitude that she had received through me the ability to **eat and sleep,** for **the relief from pain, nervousness,** etc., and ended by saying, " **You have put into my life a bit of blue, where all before was smoke and cloud.**"

Four years later this lady was enjoying life and much improved in health.

I shall hope that every reader of these pages may do as much for many individuals who do not need medicine, but do need to have aroused in them **a self-consciousness of dormant potentialities awaiting utilization.**

CHAPTER IX.

THE OPINION OF A "NEUROPATH" AND OTHERS.

The inconsistency of some men and their attitude toward certain phases of psycho-therapy but reflects their own limited conception of the subject.

Prof. F. X. Dercum has thought fit, in his work upon Suggestion, Hypnotism, Etc., to classify the phenomena of hypnotism as belonging **"unequivocally to the domain of hysteria,"** and asserts that **"the state of hypnosis is beyond doubt pathologic,"** but remarks that **"suggestion without hypnotism is susceptible of scientific application and is often profound and far-reaching in its effects.** So easily do men acquire a one-sided way of seeing things! **Their outlook** is colored by the hue of **their own subjective limitations.**

Dubois, on the other hand, says: **"The suggestible condition is normal.** One can boldly say that everybody is hypnotizable and suggestible. The subjects who prove refractory are those who are temporarily in an unfavorable psychological situation; under the sway of skepticism, fear, or distraction."

On the other hand, *the pathologist of one of our greatest Eastern universities, a medical school **second to none upon this continent,** whose graduates all over the United States reflect the high character of their alma mater, in an unsolicited letter

---

*Personal letter to the author from Dr. Allen J. Smith, pathologist to the University of Pennsylvania and formerly dean of the University of Texas.

in reference to my work among the physicians, commits himself as follows: **"If it be of any value to you,** that I should express an opinion of your efforts to disseminate a more intelligent idea of the value of suggestion in the treatment of disease, you are more than welcome to this note.   I do not think your claims are in any way excessive, as I can from experience substantiate all I have heard you say as to the efficacy of the measure as an adjunct in ordinary therapeutics.   Your explanation of its mode of action, while necessarily not of completeness, I believe to be based on sound principles, and your methods of inducing hypnosis in order to effectively apply suggestions, have added, to my mind, several valuable details to the methods commonly taught.   I am particularly glad to see an effort to have suggestion applied in a logical mode to **appreciated pathological conditions** as underlying the manifestation of symptoms, rather than made in an indiscriminating way for the mere relief of symptoms without concern for their cause."

The professor of principles and practice of medicine in one of our great Western universities remarked to me: "Munro, I have been to Europe five times within the last thirty years and have kept up with the progress of psychotherapy **from the early Charcot days** to the present time.   I have at least thirty volumes written by as many different authors in my library upon this subject, and I do not hesitate to say that **you have a simplified conception** and easy method of teaching psycho-therapy that should be in the hands of every American physician.   Now, take my advice go and give it to them in a book."

[15]

It is hard for me to conceive of a man occupying an important position in the medical profession clinging to such a distorted, antiquated conception of this subject as that enunciated by the prominent neurologist before mentioned, **unless he is himself** in a psycho-neurotic condition, which the reading of his comments upon hypnotism and suggestion would indicate.

Out of between four and five thousand men put into a degree of suggestibility by the method I have explained in a previous chapter, with the assistance of **as many American physicians,** to **a degree that anesthesia could be induced** by suggestion, during the past seven years with a success of **at least ninety-eight per cent,** the only failures were upon **hysterical** or **extremely neurotic** individuals. In all cases **the more normal nervous organizations** made the best subjects for demonstrative purposes.

The phenomena of hypnotism, and all forms of suggestion, are **in accordance with the normal physiological processes. It is a physiological** condition, and to conceive of it as being anything else, shows the hysterical, **perverted mental condition** of the man who is attempting to hypnotize the profession into believing otherwise.

Between these two great American medical schools situated as they are, on the Atlantic and the Pacific, hundreds and thousands of American physicians, many of them occupying professorships in other reputable medical schools and **standing high in the profession,** have said to me, "I know from experience that what you say in reference to the utility of suggestion in the practice of medicine is true."

So, **in the face of the facts** that I have presented in the preceding pages, upheld as they have been by **physicians of the highest professional attainments,** I am constrained to believe that the man who opposes the judicious, conscientious use of suggestion in any form applied in the hands of the well-qualified physician as an **adjunct to his therapeutic resources,** does not know any better.

If suggestion be of value at all, the most efficacious form of suggestion is the most valuable. It is all hypnotism or it is all suggestion, **each is a phase of one and the same thing, pertaining to psycho-therapy,** a mode of influence, and the **personality of the man** who is using it determines **its use or abuse,** just as is the case with all other therapeutic measures.

It will be twenty-two years before my day of Oslerization comes, and I hope to be able at some future time to give the profession a more scientific presentation of the subject at hand, backed by additional facts, supported by new evidence tests and clinical experiences.

The majority of cases that I have reported have been those treated for my colleagues and the facts set forth in all such cases **can be substantiated by their testimony.** My explanation of the *modus operandi* is in accordance with modern scientific knowledge and stands upon its own merits. **The permanency of the results** of suggestive therapeutics depends entirely upon the **quality of the individual subject's nerve and brain plasm.**

The least satisfactory results are obtained in hysterical, neurasthenic, weak-minded, and degenerative nervous and mental organizations. yet **in this very class** of unfortunates it has within it the promise of **more benefit** than can be obtained by any other method of treatment.

For seven years I have made good my claims for the efficacy of suggestive therapeutics in the presence of **critical physicians** and I am ready to **stand by the facts** as I have found them, notwithstanding the opinion of a **few psycho-neurotic neurologists** who seem afraid of encroachment upon their specialty if this branch of professional equipment became a part of the general practitioner's therapeutic armamentarium.

The cases here reported are given simply as an index to the **broad scope of the usefulness** of suggestive therapeutics in its application to the general practice of medicine and surgery, as yet only partially appreciated by a small portion of the medical profession. The subject, when studied in its broadest aspect, is some day certain to occupy the prominence in therapeutics, that it so eminently deserves.

The more intelligent and better educated laymen are becoming wide awake to its importance and there are those in the profession who are ever ready to adopt **what is true and useful** notwithstanding the prejudice of the ignorant and superstitious element of our age.

Physicians who have studied and employed these methods have frequently said to me frankly: "Suggestive therapeutics is all right, but there is no money in using those methods; the people prefer to pay a man who will **exaggerate their symptoms,** as is usually done by one who does not appreciate the psychic factor in his consideration of the symptomatology."

What we see in our patient's symptoms depends altogether upon the way we see it. **As our mental perspective broadens,** we interpret symptoms in a new light and what we see has a new meaning.

By all means let us "tell our patients the truth" in medicine and in religion and education and on all lines, but let it be "the truth" as **the more enlightened people see it.**

Absolute knowledge on any line does not exist.

Because we can study anatomy and pathology with the miscroscope and the test tube, we are liable to overlook the factors of human personality of which anatomy, physiology, and pathology are but expressions or manifestations.

We may not know what the mind is, but we are learning what it will do, and if mental methods of treatment will get results, **then as broad-minded men** we want them, for we want anything that will alleviate sickness, weakness and unhappiness and help to cure disease.

A well-known physician who did over one hundred major surgical operations a year, for fifteen or twenty years, very earnestly remarked that as soon as he began to **study the results** of these cases for one year, five years, and ten years afterwards, his conscience hurt him so that he now treated his patients more conservatively; that while such work was far less remunerative, the results, so **far as his patients were concerned,** were much more satisfactory, and that he himself slept sounder and was less disturbed in his dreams.

All over the country physicians have called my attention to cases where surgical intervention has been resorted to for the relief of some **psycho-neurotic condition, associated with a minor structural abnormality,** where the symptoms were only aggravated instead of benefited by surgical procedures. **Yet in these very cases** the operation was a " brilliant success," because the temporary psychic effect gave the patient a boost, which enables the surgeon to collect a good fee and hypnotize himself into believing that he was all-important.

Other physicians say that while they recognize the value of these methods of treatment, they find that they feel as if they were carrying a heavy load of responsibility on their shoulders which is too burdensome for them to endure. They feel as if they were assuming the responsibility that the patient should take upon himself. **The fault in such cases** is not with suggestive therapeutics, but with the physician's methods of using it. **The physician himself** was probably in need of psychopathic treatment, for the real aim in the application of suggestive therapeutics is **to help your patient to help himself.**

No kind of work is more conducive to the mental and physical vigor of a physician than the effort to make suggestions that will produce such sense impressions **as will give rise to healthful mental states** in your patients, for the very attention on your part to such ideas causes the effort to be **of therapeutic value to you** as well as to your patient.

CHAPTER X.

SOME OTHER PRACTICAL POINTS.

Unquestionably the fine art in applying suggestive therapeutics lies in the employment of suggestion without an effort to induce a sleep-like condition. Yet, if the individual can be induced **to act upon and execute your suggestion,** either consciously or sub-consciously, it is by the use of the same method; call it reasoning, persuasion, advice, preaching, education, suggestion or hypnotism.

Upon one occasion when I was **standing by a cigar stand** with two physicians, and holding in my hand **a small phial of water,** a third physician, a stranger to me, walked up and asked, " What is that in your hand?"

" **Liquid electricity,**" was my reply.

" **Liquid electricity;** why, what is that and what is it for?"

" **It is used locally** as an anaesthetic, to relieve pain, cure headache, or to extract teeth and do minor surgery," said I. " Hold out your arm and I will demonstrate its efficacy."

The physician extended his arm and rubbing some of the water on the back of it for half a minute, I withdrew from my pocket a small steel pin, and holding it between my eyes and his, said to him, **" You see this pin.** I am going to stick it through a fold of skin on your arm, but **you will not feel it.** Your arm is perfectly dead and if that hurts you in the least, let the physicians present know it. Look at it; here it goes," thrusting the pin through a large fold of his skin.

" **Did that hurt you?** " asked one of the physicians.

" Not the least bit," was his reply.

Taking me by the arm the first physician said, " Come back this way, Dr. Munro; come back with us Blank." In his office he turned to me and said, Dr. Munro, shake hands with Dr. Blank."

" **I want some of that preparation of yours,**" said he.

When I explained that the medicine was only water and that I had been talking to the other physicians present about the efficacy of suggestion, he laughed heartily and seemed to appreciate the experience.

Such experiences have been mine in hundreds and hundreds of instances, not only experimental and demonstrative, but also with a direct therapeutic aim. I state this experience in detail to bring out this point—**the unconscious use of suggestive methods is the most effective.**

In three-fourths of the cases where an individual requests that he be placed in the hypnotic state, we fail to get him into a state of suggestibility sufficiently effective **to induce anaesthesia** by suggestion, but by **suggestion in disguise,** we frequently succeed in a hundred cases, consecutively without a failure. A physician in a Western city **questioned the above statement,** as have many other physicians who had to be shown.

Upon the occasion of my lecture and demonstrations, one physician, after inducing hypnosis, proceeded as usual and induced anaesthesia and made other tests. **Then another did the same** upon an entirely new subject, to the extent that a large pin was thrust through the fold of the man's face without his evincing the slightest evidence of pain, and he also was made to sustain a weight of 200 pounds on his body with his head on one chair and his heels in another, to demonstrate the efficacy of suggestion.

At this juncture the physician who had questioned our ability to successfully hypnotize such a large percentage of individuals, asked if I called that hypnotism. "Why," exclaimed he, "you are getting those men to do that **through auto-suggestion.**"

"**Certainly, doctor,**" was my reply.

"Well, why don't you call your work by the right name and say you are demonstrating and teaching **suggestion and autosuggestion?**"

Other physicians present who were men of the highest professional attainments, assured the physician in question that they had never witnessed more successful demonstrations of the efficacy of suggestion, having seen work both in America and Europe, by competent men.

The extreme ignorance manifested by some men in regard to the practical and theoretical phases of psycho-therapy is pitiful. **They expect to find** in hypnotism some **uncanny influence by** which they can dominate and control people without regard to their wishes or knowledge, as has been claimed by every kind of outlandish faker advertising to teach all sorts of absurdities.

The only class of people that we can **dominate,** as distinguished from simply aiding them to execute an idea or series of ideas, is those of an unstable nervous organization, in whom a consciousness of self-control has never been evolved. **Such**

people are so suggestible that they readily take suggestions put in the form of positive affirmations in the waking state, but for therapeutic purposes they are the least satisfactory patients, although the very ones that most need our help, and the class of cases for whom suggestion is more useful than any other measure.

I have experimented with hypnotism and suggestion in every possible manner, both for amusement, demonstration and therapeutic application. **The more normal,** reliable and strongest nervous organizations have always produced the most satisfactory results, because they could best exercise self-control and were better able **to act upon and execute** a suggestion both consciously and sub-consciously. We can treat by suggestion **any individual who seeks our services as a physician.**

Never, under any consideration, let a patient suggest to you the kind of treatment you must adopt.

In the case of unstable and degenerative nervous organizations, the problem is to bring about those conditions that increase **their protoplasmic energies,** as well as to direct those energies into normal, useful, healthful channels. **I have often prescribed** a placebo to satisfy the patient, while I only too well realized, that his benefit and recovery depended altogether upon my influence upon his **habits of thought and conduct.**

A neurotic lady for whom I prescribed a teaspoonful of compound rhubarb and soda mixture at bedtime for sleep, and **advised to relax and breathe deeply** and **rhythmically** for ten minutes when she retired, so the medicine could have full effect, complained that she slept so soundly that she felt "dead all over" the next morning. **I accepted that** as evidence of a splendid result of the treatment, but advised her to **reduce the dose one-half,** drink more water, and take more exercise in open air and sunshine, assuring her that the "dead feeling" was only her "nervousness dying out."

Never use hypnotism or suggestion for amusement upon any occasion.

The physicians over the United States who have felt that their practices were injured by their use of suggestion and hypnotism have been mostly those who have given parlor entertainments, etc. **I have yet to find a single man** who employs suggestive measures in a dignified, conscientious manner, but whose success has been augmented both therapeutically and financially.

I can cite some men who have stated to me **five years after** taking my instruction in suggestive therapeutics that the knowledge derived from the one lesson had benefited them more than a three-months' course of post graduate instruction. **They were men** who had not before **realized their own worth,** and by the lesson in suggestive therapeutics they awoke to a **higher appreciation** of themselves.

Contact and close proximity breeds sympathy between two people of **opposite sex,** and when an easily impressible neurotic woman seems to be possessed of the hallucination or self suggestion that you are unduly fond of her, a single suggestion or a look of indignation is quite sufficient to plant a sense impression of an opposite character that will dispel her delusion.

It has been asserted that a patient who has been frequently hypnotized has been robbed of self-reliance and become so helpless that he must lean upon his hypnotizer for support. **On the**

contrary, I have frequently planted suggestions into the mind of a patient that have rendered them so independent and capable and **self-reliant** that they have refused to have further suggestions from me, taking their lives into their own hands, being guided by their own reason, while we remained the best of friends.

A man had been so crazed by a long drunken spree that he became delirious and rushed out of his house in the dark, ran into a fence, and landed in a neighbor's house, begging him to protect him, his face bleeding from the obstacles he had encountered. **Beside his bed** was found an iron poker and on either side of him were respectively **a pistol and a large knife.** His stomach had at last become his best friend and given him a chance to end his siege of alcoholic poisoning by rejecting all whisky he attempted to put into it, **as well as all medicine** given for the relief of his miserable nervous and mental condition. **He felt, however,** crazed as he was, that I was his friend and I did my best to prove worthy of his confidence.

I placed a cold towel upon his forehead and began my suggestions to hypnotize him by telling him that the cold application would quiet him all over and make him drowsy and sleepy, and that he would go to sleep and sleep soundly all night and awake in the morning feeling all right. **Though I had secured thorough relaxation,** with his eyes closed and with him breathing through his mouth, when I suggested that "this cold towel will put you to sleep and you will sleep sound all night," he took a deep inspiration and said, "Lord grant it," showing how he acquiesced in the treatment. **He was hypnotized,** and suggestions were given to quiet all nervousness, to relieve his irritable stomach, to get him to sleep soundly all night, to excite a disgust or antipathy and hatred for whisky; and above all, to awaken within him a consciousness of manhood and duty to his family.

He slept soundly all night from 5:30 p. m. until 7:30 a. m. the next day, and as I approached the front door on my return visit, his wife, whose nervous system had been shattered by such experiences for several years, met me with the exclamation, "Oh, Dr. Munro, do you reckon Mr. Blank will ever wake up?"

"Why, certainly, Mrs. Blank; he is breathing, is he not?"

"Yes, he has been resting nicely, and I was able to retire last night and get some sleep for the first time in three weeks."

Upon awakening the patient in question, who was a large, strong, well educated, successful business man, I congratulated him upon having a good night's sleep and assured him that he would not care for more whisky and was going to be a man after that.

That evening I said to him, "Mr. Blank, I desire to put you to sleep again," and extending his hand, he said, Dr. Munro, you c-a-n-t do it. I thank you very much for the treatment last night and **shall always appreciate it,** but I do not expect to touch any more whisky and I shall get along all right."

I assured him that I was very glad indeed to hear him talk that way, and that for his wife's and daughter's sake, as well as his own, I knew he would feel happier. However, I turned to an attendant and directed that a **placebo capsule** (of powdered licorice root) be given at eight o'clock and in case he did not sleep soundly by nine, to give a second capsule, suggesting to the patient that he would sleep soundly all night. **He refused hypnotic suggestion** but took the placebo capsules and slept soundly.

It is very easy to get an individual to accept a suggestion that is in accordance **with his natural desires. Some people do not want to get well.** They enjoy the sympathy and attention of an over anxious family *ad nauseum*. **In such cases** a suggestion given to set up a reaction may become necessary.

A physician had a pneumonia patient who had insisted that he was going to die on a certain night. The family had asked that another doctor be called in and that each of them stay on watch during the night.

The attending physician had kindly assured the family that there were no alarming symptoms and also did all he could to reason with and reassure the patient. **Nevertheless** at the appointed time the young man sent for his family and began bidding them good-by, when at that juncture the attending physician walked into the room, where the new recruit had for two hours been on watch.

He was a man who did things in his own way, so he insisted that all the family go out of the room and demanded of the patient, as if he was mad enough to fight, what all this commotion meant? When the young man assured him that he was going to die and could not get well, etc., the wise old physician answered, **"Well, die ⸺ you, die and be in a hurry about it;** make haste and let me see you." **Then placing his hand** on his forehead he called the boy by name and said to him kindly, "I am tired of all this foolishness. **You are going to get well.** You can't die, it matters not how hard you try. Now, close your eyes and go to sleep and let me hear no more from you." **The patient was relieved** of his morbid psycho-neurotic condition and made a nice recovery.

A hypodermic of one-tenth of a grain of apomorphine has served the author as a most valuable means of suggestion.

In some psycho-neurotic cases a **Paquelin cautery** heated to a cherry red heat before the patient's eyes and brushed with quick light strokes down the spine proves a most valuable expedient as a means of suggestion. **Hundreds and hundreds** of physicians are using the static machine at so much per treatment. **Says one,** who is honest enough to admit that it is only a suggestive means of treatment: "It matters not what be the trouble, **I give them all the same dose."**

A man who will exercise the courage to do so can use suggestion and get results when all such subterfuges are worthless. **He can take his equipment with him** wherever he goes and the general practice of medicine is unquestionably the field for its most valuable and effective employment.

In my work among the physicians it has been a matter of observation that psychotherapy is being appreciated just in proportion **as culture and education** are most in evidence. **Its successful employment,** as with all other branches of medicine, depends largely upon the personality of the physician. **There is no disease or condition** where its use is contraindicated, provided the **right suggestions are given** to help the patient.

If used to benefit the patient, its employment will make friends for the physician. **No selfish, cold blooded physician** who is in the practice of medicine solely for the money and who has not **his patients' interest** more at heart than the desire to secure a fee, can ever be a successful psychotherapist. **It is best employed** by the man who is most willing to stand up for his weaker brother, who is most anxious to help his patients to help themselves. Character, which is educated thinking, desiring, willing and acting is a valuable asset in the make-up of a physician's therapeutic armamentarium. With such an asset his conduct towards his patients will be governed accordingly.

CHAPTER XI.

THE PSYCHOLOGIC FACTOR IN OBSTETRICS.

It was once my pleasure to be present at a medical society meeting at which, from a psychological point of view, the discussions of a most highly interesting and instructive paper upon the use of " **Forceps in Obstetrics** " interested me very much.

One physician related his experience in a recent case where he, and another physician present, had found it necessary to make several prolonged and strenuous efforts at traction upon the fore-coming head before they succeeded in a delivery which resulted in a badly lacerated cervix and a most completely lacerated perineum, stating in the conclusion of his remarks that he found it frequently necessary to resort to the use of forceps, and for this reason he highly appreciated the paper.

Another physician referred to a recent high forceps operation, and the difficulty in applying forceps before the head began to descend and while the os was as yet but partially dilated. **A third referred** to the frequency with which he had found it necessary to resort to the use of forceps in obstetrics, and how he dreaded such ordeals. **Still another** speaker emphasized, among other valuable ideas, the small amount of traction with which she had been able to deliver her forceps cases, even while the patient had been thoroughly chloroformed.

Among those who discussed the paper was yet another, a large, self-possessed and magnificent looking physician, a little past fifty-five I should guess, who rarely ever had to resort to the

[16]

use of forceps, and he urged the advisibility of not being in a hurry, and giving the natural physiological processes time to accomplish their work, rather than of hastily resorting to instrumental assistance or interference.

I do not claim to be perfectly accurate in my passing references to the discussion to which I have referred. **But the features brought out in those discussions** illustrate conclusively the importance of more attention being paid to the psychologic factor in obstetric practice.

It was quite evident that the large self-possessed physician to whom I referred did appreciate the psychologic factor, and hence, " rarely, if ever " had to resort to the use of forceps; and it was also equally evident that of those present, some physicians were rather inclined to be nervous, and unconsciously had been a potent factor in producing the condition in their patients which necessitated the use of instruments.

More than in any other part of the practice of medicine, in obstetrics the physician should be well poised and self-possessed, and should maintain a quiet demeanor and keep well conserved his mental and nervous equilibrium in the presence of an excitable, frightened and nervous patient.

In the early years of my professional work I assisted three times in the instrumental delivery of a lady who at the time of her fourth delivery fell into my hands. **Knowing the difficulty** that she had experienced with her previous deliveries, and seeing the depression that her condition and the approaching ordeal produced upon her, I had her come to see me quite frequently and positively assured her that I had her on a treatment that would insure a safe and easy delivery, and before her confinement I had eliminated all element of fear. When I was called to see her at the time of delivery, after making a careful diagnosis, I again **positively assured her** that it was absolutely impossible for her to do otherwise than get along nicely, and I have never attended an easier delivery than hers.

Where it has been possible, it has been my habit to see the prospective mothers often enough before parturition to keep well *en rapport* with them. I have frequently placed them in the suggestive state two or three times during the last weeks of pregnancy, in order to insure a perfect psychological attitude at the time of delivery.

The influence of the mind upon metabolism is well established. To keep our prospective mothers in a buoyant, hopeful, cheerful state of mind helps to prevent albumenuria, eclampsia, and other complications. All other essentials requisite to the well-being of our patient of course should not be overlooked. A wholesome vegetable diet, with milk and eggs, as well as regular out-door exercise, should be insisted upon.

When called to see your patient when in labor, manifest a kindly interest in her well-being and make her feel that you are kind, firm, and self-sufficient, by your conduct in her presence. After carefully making your diagnosis, do all you can to calm her spirit, assuage her fears, and inspire her with confidence in your ability and intentions to do what is best for her. **Assume absolute command** of the situation and allow no environmental influence, such as over-anxious expressions of friends, to influence her. Let her feel the masterful, helpful, encouraging influence of your personality, as well as get the benefit of your kindly assistance.

When the members of the medical profession become awake to the importance of the psychological factor in obstetrics, forceps deliveries, lacerated cervices and perinei will be far less frequent.

While in a Southern city four years ago, a well-known physician requested me to see with him a woman in labor, and I quote the following from his report of the case: " About 2 a. m. I was called to Mrs. W., a young primapara, who was frightened, exceedingly nervous, and hard to control. At 4 a. m. Doctor Munro came at my request and demonstrated the efficacy of suggestion in a most satisfactory manner, by substituting for the extreme nervousness a condition of placid repose. The rapid heartbeats became normal, the patient slept peacefully between contractions and ' bore down ' to her pains without complaint. It proved especially efficacious during that nagging stage of dilatation. Later on, with the aid of only a few drops of chloroform, the case was conducted to a finish with perfect satisfaction both to myself, my patient, and her friends. I am fully convinced that when physicians learn to practice intelligently what for ages we have all been practising ignorantly, i. e., suggestive therapeutics, then the obstetric couch will be robbed of its horrors."

TECHNIQUE OF APPLICATION.

Labor is well established, the os is dilated to the size of a fifty cent piece, more or less, the contractions and all indications are that there is to be no cessation of symptoms until your patient is delivered.

She is begging you to do something for her. You have made out your diagnosis and reassured your patient, but now the severity of her symptoms is such that she feels that she must have help. **You have the reputation of using chloroform,** and she would not be satisfied unless you did use chloroform. You are waiting for the right psychological moment, she has patiently endured her sufferings and feels that she can hold out no longer without help that she has not received. **You have assured her** that she is doing well, that every indication is for a safe delivery, and that you are going to use chloroform so that she will not suffer. **The urgency of the occasion** grows more imperative and you decide to make another digital examination.

As this is completed, say, " All right, madam, be patient and bear strong and hard to the next pain and **just as that leaves you** I will give you chloroform so that you will get well under its influence by the time another contraction comes and you will not suffer any more."

Just as the contraction has expended its energy, synchronously with the first inspiration after a long bearing down, shake about **thirty drops of chloroform** upon a handkerchief in a paper cone or that you have placed in a tumbler, and placing that close over her nose and mouth, suggest to her strongly, " Breathe this down now, and go to sleep." She takes a deep inspiration, and you quickly and strongly suggest, **" Breathe it in again,** and now again, away down deep."

The three deep inspirations from the thirty drops of chloro-form administered in this way at this particular moment have sufficient physiological effect to annihilate completely the receding contraction; and also the three deep inspirations in succession, together with the physiological effect of the chloro-form, secure the thorough relaxation of your patient. **She is now in a receptive condition,** and you must quickly, but em-phatically and distinctly, follow this up with your suggestions to get her into a deeper suggestible condition or into a hypnotic state.

So, removing the cone or glass about two inches from her nose, you proceed to suggest, "Now, go to sleep, sleep, sleep, sleep. Now you feel quiet all over. Your muscles are relaxed. Everything is dark to you. You do not hear anything but my voice. You are drowsy and sleepy, s-o-o-o-o sleepy. You feel the sleep coming over you. You are going to sleep. Sleep, sleep, sleep. By the time I count ten you will be fast asleep. One, two, three, four, five, six, seven, eight, nine, ten, and you are asleep, fast asleep. By the time I count five you will be sound and dead asleep. One, two, three, four, five, and you are asleep, fast asleep, sound asleep, dead asleep, and you will not awaken now until I tell you. Every second your sleep becomes sounder and sounder and deeper and deeper. You will not hear anything or feel anything or know anything except what I tell you. Sleep on quietly now until I awake you."

Your patient is now in a deeper condition of suggestibility, but you want to take an additional precaution to secure more thor-ough relaxation, so, without the addition of more chloroform you bring the cone or glass closer to her nose and suggest, **"Breathe deeply,** deeper yet, once again away down deep. There, now, you are thoroughly relaxed."

Then stroking her forehead gently, make suggestions about as follows: "Sleep on quietly. Now, your nerves are getting steady and quiet and strong, steady and quiet and strong all over. By the time I count ten the last bit of nervousness will be gone and your nerves will be steady and quiet and strong all over. One, two, three, four, five, six, seven, eight, nine, ten, and your nerves are steady and quiet and strong all over."

"Now, on account of the sedative effect of the chloroform upon you, you feel all pain or aching or soreness or hurting about your abdomen or back or womb going away, you are getting easier and easier, and by the time I count five you will be perfectly easy and not suffer any more. One, two, three, four, five, and you are perfectly easy.

"Now your labor will be regular and normal, you will labor hard, but will feel no pain. Your contractions will be strong, the mouth of your womb will dilate and open easier, but you will feel no pain.

"Sleep on and when the next contraction comes, reach up your hands and bear down strong and long, but you will only feel a pressure; you will not experience any pain."

As the contraction again becomes evident, say to your patient, "Bear down hard now, it will not hurt you. That is fine; stronger yet, more yet! There now, take more chloroform and go into a deeper sleep."

Here you put about **twenty drops of chloroform** on the handkerchief in the cone or glass and make a few additional suggestions about as follows: "Sleep, sleep, sleep, sleep, breathe deeply, sleep sound. Now, sleep on quietly until the next contraction and then don't wake up, just reach up your hands and bear down, but sleep on."

As this contraction recedes you give about ten drops more of chloroform and make a few additional suggestions.

By that time your patient is sufficiently amenable to suggestion to the extent that I have frequently had patients **go two hours in labor without more than the slightest complaint,** getting them to relax thoroughly after each contraction and making a few additional suggestions.

Toward the latter part of the second stage of labor, with the last two or three expulsive pains, it is best that you give chloroform at the beginning of the contraction for its physiological effect, using it freely and effectively as it enables you to manipulate the head and perineum and render such assistance as best to prevent laceration.

I have yet to see the first case of post partum hemorrhage in a case where suggestion was used; though I have always followed the expulsion of the child with my left hand and grasped the fundus of the uterus after Crede's method. **Post partum hemorrhage** is largely a nervous phenomenon and properly directing and controlling the psychic factor is a safeguard against it, though I never neglect any other precaution, consequently I have never had any trouble on this score.

A rigid os indicates an irritable involuntary nervous system and it rapidly disappears when the psychic factor is properly directed as above outlined. **Your success will be in the direct ratio** to that in which you secure thorough relaxation of the patient and properly make suggestions.

The patient need not necessarily be asleep; a merely partial subconscious condition is attended with excellent results, provided you have the **confidence and co-operation of your patient,** and this it is your privilege to gain very quickly after you enter the room.

A nervous physician is undoubtedly a menace to the welfare of an obstetric patient, for nervousness begets nervousness and fear begets fear. Self-control and self-confidence on the part of the accoucheur carry, all unconsciously, a wonderfully helpful influence.

Don't neglect any other therapeutic resource. An obstetric patient of mine had two sisters, each of whom died of eclampsia in her first labor. The effect of such a family record was most depressing upon her. During the last weeks of pregnancy I saw her every few days and assured her positively that the treatment I had her on would prevent any such occurrence. She was a plethoric, full-blooded woman and the secundines were removed with practically no hemorrhage at all. A severe headache, extreme nervousness, and rapid, full pulse which followed, required not only large doses of veratrum hypodermically, but free bleeding also, as well as suggestion in the form of reassurance, persuasion and encouragement, with **large doses of calomel and jalap.**

To a patient who had aborted after four months and had considerable hemorrhage and was almost pulseless, I suggested strongly and loudly, upon making an examination, **"You will be all right!** Be brave, madam, you will have no trouble, etc.," though I proceeded to clear and pack her uterus.

In a case of twins, I "chloroformed" my patient with alcohol administered by inhalation and suggestion, used forceps on the first child and internal version on the second, with perfect success.

Ten drops of chloroform given to a patient after each contraction while she is thoroughly relaxed, passive, eyes closed and breathing rhythmically through her mouth, **and suggestions made in a monotone, conversational way,** to quiet nervousness and render the patient conscious that something was being done for her, is attended with excellent results, without any farther effort to induce hypnosis.

The confidence of the patient in her physician can be considerably augmented by properly directing the psychic factor in obstetrics, and the welfare and safety of the patient are rendered far more certain.

In a case of an abortion at five months, before the expulsion of the uterine contents, which was attended with much hemorrhage, I packed the vagina and put on T bandage, **hypnotized the patient, made appropriate suggestions,** and went away, returning in three hours to find that the patient had been easy, but upon removal of the packing both foetus and secundines came away together.

A patient who once has the assistance of a physician who properly directs the psychic factor will instinctively feel that she has never before had the right attention in her previous confinements.

A number of physicians of my acquaintance have been able to execute successfully the above described methods greatly to the satisfaction of themselves and patient.

Your success in obstetrics, as in all other classes of work, will be in direct ratio to the integrity and stability of your patient's nerve and brain plasm, on the one hand, and your ability to present suggestion properly, on the other.

CHAPTER XII.

TRAINING THE SUBCONSCIOUS SELF.

A RATIONAL BASIS FOR AUTO-SUGGESTION.

Every sense impression or perception or idea that has come within our individual experience through education or environment has left its impress upon the brain cells, and these brain cells stimulated by ideas of a similar character reproduce the memory pictures gathered by experience and this process is what is called thinking. Thinking in logical sequence constitutes reasoning. Thinking gives rise to mental processes or states of mind or conditions of consciousness that are constantly changing, so that the conscious mind or ego of one moment is not that of the next.

So inter-related are our psychical and physical processes that much has been learned of our subconscious psychic activities by observing the influence of the mind over the body.

The subconscious self corresponds to all mental and physical processes which lie beneath the stream of consciousness. We often flatter ourselves by believing that we control our thoughts, when, as a matter of fact, thinking is but a reflex of the sense impressions that have been made upon our cerebral cells by all that has gone to make up our experience in life.

Yet, education, travel, association with people, and all other like experiences, benefit us only as we react to them.

Every impression or idea that is made upon the conscious mind of the individual throughout his entire life is one of the factors that collectively constitute the training of the subconscious self. The result of this training constitutes our assets, as represented by body, mind and character.

Our ability to react upon and be benefited by the experiences of life is dependent upon an inherited quality of brain plasm, on the one hand, and education, on the other. **We can be benefited** by the experiences that come into our lives only as we are prepared by knowledge gained from previous experiences.

That which influences us most is what most persistently holds our interested attention. The kind of thought or line of endeavor that most receives our purposeful attention sustained by reason, will and determination, so reacts upon our bodies and minds that we unconsciously become moulded by that particular kind of work.

The mind, like the body, becomes strengthened or weakened by mental and physical action. The blacksmith who uses a sledge hammer day by day develops a muscle of steel, while the bookkeeper who lifts no more ponderous weight than the leaves of his ledger from week to week, has muscles that have become atrophied and shriveled. **The man of genius** is only distinguished from other men by his exceptional power of attention to one given subject. On any line of work in all professions the individual who becomes most proficient is he who most persistently gives attention to his specialty.

It has been well said that the mind set habitually and strongly in any one given direction loses the power to think upon any other line.   **The Christian Scientist,** who ignores the material aspect of disease, **and the physician** who does not appreciate the psychical, are good illustrations of the above statement.   **The particular line of thought** to which we constantly give our attention, and by which we habitually act, makes us what we are.

To be strong, capable and free is the ideal that every individual should strive to attain, but strength in mind and character cannot be attained by neglect of the body, for the interdependence of mind and body is such that the highest development of the one quality depends upon the other for its support.

Use your faculties and live, grow and develop, is a decree of Nature from which there can be no escaping.   Some day, sooner or later, each individual awakens to the realization that his life is a fight between himself and the entire world.   **We are so related to each other,** however, that the duty of the individual and his dependence upon other individuals and their dependence and relation to the great whole must never be left out of consideration.   Yet, **the individual** must stand upon his own feet, see the world with his own eyes, do things with his own hands, and interpret the problems of life with his own intellect.

To be prepared for this conflict, this contest, this body, mind and character tryst, is the problem of training the subconscious self.   **Life itself** is the greatest incentive for living, and to attain the highest development and expression of the subconscious self renders the individual capable of enjoying life, not only for his or her own sake, but because to him or her comes a double pleasure of being better equipped to help make life more worth while to others.

Since we are endowed with a little infinitesimally small portion of the universal life, wisdom, intelligence and force that exists in the universe, the highest privilege of every human being is that of being a chooser; the privilege of exercising a choice between what shall and what shall not receive his attention. **The ideas which we encourage** become stronger, last longer, and exercise the greatest influence on our habits of thought and conduct.

Even in the case of what are commonly held to be involuntary mental processes which crowd themselves upon us unwelcome and unbidden, when we are consciously all unaware of their existence, coming as the result of previous experiences—**we can encourage** those that are desirable and inhibit others that are undesirable to a very large degree. **But while we can only partly** inhibit those memory pictures that are undesirable, we can as choosers decide what shall in the present and in the future claim our conscious, intelligent attention.

Everything that claims our conscious attention strongly and persistently constitutes "food stuff" for the subconscious self, which contributes to the remoulding and rebuilding of our physical and mental constitutions. **Character itself** is evolved in accordance with this same law.

As choosers, then, the privilege is ours to be open and receptive to whatsoever is good, true, and useful in the realms of thought—as expressed in the literature of poetry or fiction, philosophy, religion, or science, or from association with individuals —that may be of use to ourselves or other human beings. We should study it honestly, appropriate its truths, and live by them in all departments of life.

In the same realm of human experience, with respect to whatever is not good and not true and not useful for our best growth and development, let us exercise the courage of our convictions and reject it, even though it has the time-honored sanction of conventionalism and authority. **We should let truth herself** sum up the case and guide our lives and conduct in accordance with the light and knowledge of the present age. **This is the clue to the correct training** of the subconscious self.

Then, too, since we realize the power of mind upon mind and the influence of the mind upon the body, both for our own good and for the benefit of others, we should encourage mental states that make us hopeful, optimistic, and cheerful. We should look upon the bright side of everything and strive to say and do something to cheer the lives of others. As we sow, that shall we also reap, is the law of Nature in the realm of both thought and action. **Whosoever uses suggestion to help others** is using the highest form of autosuggestion to help himself. Our effort to create healthful mental states in others reacts upon our own subconscious selves, so that what we are is to a great extent the result of what we have given to others.

Individuality and strength should be our highest and most constant aim in life.

The great subconscious self, with its millions and millions of living cells of brain and blood and bone and muscle, all reservoirs of expressive energy, is for us to educate, train, and develop in accordance with the laws of evolution. **Each individual is the maker of himself** in a far greater sense than is realized by the pessimistic philosophers of our age, who would surrender all to heredity and environment. **The limitations set by heredity and environment** of course, are beyond question, but when once we become strong enough to think for ourselves and to rely upon the powers and capabilities inherent within the cells of our organism, then those influences that would fetter and mould a weaker individual and hinder bodily and mental growth and development become for us strengthening and wholesome exercise.

Each individual contains within himself an ideal man, and to bring forth this individual harmoniously and symmetrically developed in all the qualities of selfhood should be our constant endeavor. What the man or woman of the future is to be depends upon our habits of thought and conduct today. No proposition is more true than that by constant endeavor we can day by day gain in strength of body, mind and character.

The great trouble with the majority of people is that they have not an adequate appreciation of the potentialities and possibilities inherent within the cells of their own organism, which are ever ready to be trained into active, useful service. **Others are satisfied as they are** and they constitute a large percentage of our population. They are drifting along day after day without making any special effort at self-development and almost wholly dependent upon others to think and do for them. **Depend upon others** to think and act and do for you and you become incapable of thinking and acting and doing for yourself. That which makes a man strong in all the qualities of self, social, intellectual, physical, moral, business or ethical, is action, effort, concentration, persistency, determination.

[17]

Recognition of our defects and desire for self-improvement are the incentives which urge us to higher growth and development. Those who feel that they are self-sufficient and are all that they care to be, have not been stirred by the influences which induce a self-consciousness that gives rise to the impulse to make effort. Perhaps they are unfortunate and have not been awakened to a consciousness of what they are as compared with what they may become.

The hope of humanity lies in the law of the "survival of the fittest!" The great mass of the people do not think for themselves above the most elementary questions of life. In problems of health and education, ethical and moral ideals, their views are more a matter of inheritance than based upon intelligent conviction as the result of careful investigation. **The physician who can arouse them to observation,** reflection, and self-activity, is doing them the highest service that an enlightened mind can render.

The problems of health are the problems of life and pertain to all questions of human interest. Body, mind, and character are but reflections of the great subconscious realm with its inherited or acquired impulses, habits, instincts or ideals, and these, like the flower garden, need to be continually uprooted and reset. The false and barren and useless should be rejected, and new varieties planted in keeping with knowledge and experience.

Surely this line of thought has a practical application in the practice of medicine. Stand any day you choose on a street corner and see the masses as they pass, and with pencil and paper in hand make a mark for everyone who is weak and living, minus the qualities of a normal, healthy individual, and you will find that at least fifty per cent of our population have weak bodies and imperfect nervous organizations.

The great majority of those who are sick need to be taught how to keep well, how to eat, how to drink, how to exercise, how to work, and how to sleep—in short, how to live. More than at any time in any age does the individual need self-reliance and the feeling of independence and freedom. This belongs only to those who have achieved sufficient self-hood to dare to exercise the courage to stand by their convictions.

Self-reliance is nothing more than one's own recognition of his or her ability to act and think and live according to the dictates of reason and judgment. Each individual has a different problem to solve. All people are not "born free and equal," so far as heredity and environment are concerned, but all are born with the privilege to think, act and do for themselves, that the greatest health and happiness may be maintained.

People as a rule are not sufficiently educated to take their lives into their own hands. In their efforts to do for themselves and to struggle with the problems of life, they make many blunders which react with ill results to both mind and body, and **as experts in the healing art,** our aid is sought to help them. **They do not always need medicine,** but they do always need education, knowledge and guidance.

The physician must have more than professional knowledge and skill. He should be an expression of the highest thought and culture of his age, to be prepared to take his place as a leader and teacher of his fellow man.

The practice of medicine offers great privileges for real, genuine, unselfish service. The opportunities for being of real help to our fellow man are the greatest of any calling in the list of human achievement. In no other profession are such conditions offered for brain development, self-reliance, and altruism.

The people have a right to make every effort to keep healthy and strong without relying upon us to administer to their physical necessities. It should be a part of our work to help them to so help themselves and then the followers of the different non-medical therapeutic systems would no longer continue their hold upon the people.

So long as new-born babies come to gladden the hearts of the men and women of the world, physicians will be in demand. **While human endeavor continues,** accidents will happen and the surgeon will be needed. We have not yet subdued the mosquito so as to prevent his carrying malaria and yellow fever germs, or eradicated vice to prevent the diseases of physical degradation due to infectious germs.

The Klebs-Loeffler bacillus, the bacilli of anthrax, and typhoid fever, and the thousand other germs of infection do not respect even a healthy human organism, and for all these conditions the services of the physician will be invoked. **The astigmatic eye** and other refractive errors are here to stay to cause reflex disturbances and functional diseases of both mind and body. **Infantile diseases** will claim our little ones as long as it is human to err in dietetics and the world remains the abode of

Weischesbaum's bacillus of meningitis and other infectious diseases. **The great white plague alone** claims one out of ten of all human beings. In spite of our knowledge of mental therapeutics **women will grow tumors** and a million years of special effort will not annihilate the physical results of **inebriety** and **syphilis** or prevent insanity in its various forms.

The one sure event in the pathway of every human being is death, sooner or later, and the one hope of every individual is that his life will be prolonged. **Let us, then, do all we can** with all therapeutic measures when the people are sick, but by all means let us help them to keep well by teaching them how to live so far as possible to maintain healthy bodies.

The benefit to be derived from work and exercise and water and laughter and rest, food and companionship, education and environment and self-development in a thousand ways should be ever kept before them. All these things should be studied by the people and all this constitutes the correct training of the subconscious self.

CHAPTER XIII.

CORRECT DIAGNOSIS A SAFEGUARD AGAINST BLUNDERS.

It goes without saying that a good clinician has a wonderful advantage over the individual who has not had sufficient training and the necessary experience to interpret the symptoms of a disease, and quickly couple those symptoms with its etiology, pathology, prognosis and treatment.

As has been stated in previous pages, suggestive therapeutics should be applied with an understanding and comprehension of the anatomical and physiological relations of the organism as well as of the pathological conditions to be alleviated.

Good men in our profession who do not sufficiently appreciate the psychic factor in therapeutics are frequently so engrossed with pathology that they forget to tell the patient what he can expect in the way of recovery and to keep this idea constantly impressed upon him. **They do, however,** often impress him with the seriousness of his condition in a detailed explanation of its pathology, but they fail to inspire him with a conviction of recovery. **Such physicians** leave the patient depressed, and if, forsooth, he happens to fall into the hands of a quack who has sufficient personality to lift him out of the depression thrust upon him, and recovery is not incompatible with the pathology of his disease, the patient " is cured " and the physician's reputation is injured.

As bearing upon this subject, in a discussion of a paper read by me in one of our larger cities, one of the best known men in the medical profession thus expressed himself: "Now, gentlemen, you know as well as I that there are a great many people in this city that have been treated by some of our very best physicians for months and years, and yet, satisfactory results have failed to be attained by them. **Yet, those same patients,** after going the rounds from one physician to another; finally land in the office of some of the most notorious quacks in the city, and do obtain the relief so vainly sought at our hands. When we know that such things as this exist all about us, it seems the time has come when we can afford to study some of the secrets of the quack, for what they can do for morbid processes, we can do also."

At that same discussion another physician in the course of her remarks said: "Doctor Munro dares to speak out aloud what all thinking physicians have recognised, but do not express, except at low breath, when among themselves."

This line of therapeutics is undergoing a rapid evolution, and the true and useful and good that is in it is being sifted from the false and useless. Those of our profession who take a stand against it are doing much to encourage the followers of the modern "creeds" and "cults," "ists" and "paths," who go to extremes in their views of the influence of the mind over the body.

People easily believe that which it is to their interest to believe. Physicians are educated to their view that medicine is the natural recourse of the sick man, and it is hard for them to recognize the psychologic factor, because it happens to be the basis of all forms of quackery. **Yet, the thinking portion** of the American people are on the alert, and they are ever ready to accept and support anything true and useful, it matters not how strong their prejudice may have been. **Christian Science, weltermerism,** etc., have served a useful purpose. They have stimulated the people to reflect and exercise more self-control, but they have made, and are destined yet to make, many gross and painful blunders before their fanatical zeal is quelled.

In several instances within my knowledge disastrous results have followed the vigorous methods of those who use massage as a means of suggestion. In a case of acute articular rheumatism in a little boy of twelve, the inflammation which followed this treatment by vigorous massage was such that an amputation of the limb was necessary to save the little fellow's life.

In a case of diphtheria the methods employed served only to increase the inflammatory exudate, and a speedy death followed; whereas the timely employment of anti-toxin in diphtheria has reduced the mortality of that disease to a very small death rate.

A case of acute mastoiditis, resulting from a neglected middle-ear disease, was treated by the methods of the Christian Scientist whereby surgical intervention was withheld until too late to be effective.

In several instances it has come to my knowledge where appendicular abscesses were ruptured by massage with fatal consequences, to say nothing of children with gastro-entero-colitis who died under Christian Science psycho-therapeutics while legitimate, prophylactic, antiseptic, medicinal and dietetic methods were withheld.

I once witnessed the removal of sixty-five stones from the gallbladder of a woman who had been taught to ignore such " errors of mortal mind " ; but after becoming weak, jaundiced, and anaemic, with all bodily functions disturbed, she at last yielded to the rational advice of her friends in time to resort to surgical procedures for relief, and recovered.

At a Christian Science service not long since, just in front of me sat a young man who was rapidly losing his hair as a result of an infection of the hair follicles with the germ which causes seborrhoeic eczema. The psychic effect of his religion upon him was great, but the germs went on with their work just the same.

Christian Science was held before the attention of the audience by readings, songs and prayer, as a sovereign remedy for sin, sickness and death; but over on my left sat a lady in mourning. With her head drooped and lips closed tightly, she sat there, not at all receptive, and took her medicine, though her expression showed a consciousness that realized the mockery of all that was receiving her attention. Her face was sad because her husband was dead, and this experience was setting up a mental reaction to all the negations that fell upon her ears.

Over on my right sat a gentleman with eyes open like full moons and his lower jaw dropped as if it had no muscles to support it, with a well fixed gaze upon the reader of the suggestions that had been prepared to hypnotize the audience. He was suffering with locomotor ataxia, and though credulous, receptive and suggestible in the most complete sense, he walked away upon two " errors of mortal mind," usually called crutches.

Yet, physicians are far from infallible. All their patients do not get well, **neither does absolute knowledge upon any subject exist,** while every conception or theory or viewpoint represent some relative phase of truth to be determined by individual experience.

While we know what mercury will do in syphilis, and quinine in malaria, and sulphur in itch, and antitoxin timely administered in diphtheria, and what the result of corrected errors of refraction will bring in the relief of headaches and numerous functional disturbances, and what relief surgery will bring in gross pathological changes, etc., yet there are many conditions confronted in all lines of professional work in which **we do not know** absolutely what the outcome will be, and no physician has done his full duty until he has given his patient the full benefit of every therapeutic aid. The rule should be " While there is life there is hope."

Two cases here cited that have been brought to my attention will illustrate the blunders that may be made by too quickly jumping at conclusions without due appreciation of the psychologic factor in therapeutics.

A well-known physician and surgeon was consulted in reference to a patient of another physician with an incipient malignant affection of the cervix, and he strongly advised operative procedures as the only safe course to pursue. The operation was deferred, and several months later this patient was taken on a litter to a prominent surgeon in one of our larger cities. After carefully considering the case, together with the assistance of a well-known pathologist who made a microscopical examination to determine the exact character of the disease, he declined to operate, as he believed this would only serve to transplant the disease to more vital structures and hasten her death. Discouraged and hopeless the lady finally yielded after much protest to the solicitation of a Christian Science friend, and consented to do so because this was the only promise held out to her for a possible hold on life. **After three or four months'** treatment by Christian Science psychological methods, that lady had gained twenty pounds and returned home, walking erect and strong, **and after three years** would occasionally call upon the consulting surgeon in her home town, who advised the operation in the incipiency of her disease, and laugh heartily over the incidents connected with her case. **The facts in this case** can be well authenticated.

Again in a Western city a gentleman about thirty-five years of age had been treated for pulmonary tuberculosis for a period extending over many months, and was finally advised to go to a higher and drier altitude, his physician assuring him that this was the only hope offered for him. He went to a town situated just west of the Rocky Mountains, and carried with him a letter of introduction from his home physician, together with a **report from a competent pathologist** showing sputa teeming with tubercule bacilli. **After examination and observation** for several days this physician advised the sufferer to go home at once and die among his friends and relatives. **He then sought the assistance** of a Christian Scientist, and after two days did return home inspired with hope, and having been able to sleep and eat under the psychic effects of their method, **he was much improved,** and put himself under the care of a Christian Science " practitioner " at his home town. **When I saw him,** he was holding the position of city attorney, and in his hands **he held the report of the pathologist,** as unquestionable proof of the correctness of his history, which he flaunted while he enthusiastically related his experiences at one of their mid-week meetings, stating that he had gained thirty pounds and was **enjoying life, eating, working and happy.**

As illustrating another phase of the subject at hand, however, in another Western city a well-known physician advised an immediate operation for an incipient malignant disease of the cervix. **Seeing his patient a few weeks later** he very naturally greeted her and expressed his pleasure at seeing her looking so well. " Oh, I have never been sick, doctor. That was all an 'error of mortal mind.' I am perfectly well." **Her phraseology** at once " put him next," so with the salutation, " I wish you well, madam," he modestly left her.

Several months later she returned to his office. The temporary psychic stimulation that had for awhile held her up in spite of the existing pathological conditions, had reacted, and now that characteristic, sallow, cachectic hue which attends this disease was plainly in evidence. She was weak and anaemic, nervous and over-anxious about her condition. She had at last decided to have him operate, but she had waited too long, and there was nothing left but to leave her to face the inevitable.

In the first case of " malignant disease " it is probable that the pathologist was mistaken; and tuberculosis, under favorable climatic conditions, and when not too far advanced, **is by no**

means an incurable disease. **Good food, dry open air, sunshine and optimism** often do wonders in the way of giving the recuperative powers of such patients an opportunity to overcome pathogenic bacteria and re-establish a condition of health. **In less serious affections,** especially, should the influence that the psychic factor exerts, be well kept in mind before an unfavorable prognosis is rendered. For there are numerous instances in which the prognosis may determine the outcome of the disease, on account of the part played by suggestion in aiding or retarding recovery.

In many diseases, an exact diagnosis is not always possible, though few expert diagnosticians will admit this, and even in psychiatry and nervous diseases those that are amenable to treatment, either curative or palliative, are benefitted just in proportion as the bodily functions, both voluntary and involuntary, are encouraged into activity.

No possible harm can come to the individual by suggestive measures, used either with or without hypnotism, which are only a means of getting the individual to rely upon the properties, faculties and functions inherent within the biological elements of the cells of his organism. By suggestion we can stimulate all bodily functions, both voluntary and involuntary.

All other sane, sensible measures are, of course, not to be neglected, such as rest or exercise, dietetics, hydrotherapy both internal and external, relaxation, deep breathing and materia medica agencies, as the individual case indicates. **Yet, there are many cases,** not incompatible with complete recovery in which the patient would get well, due attention being given to the psychologic factor, but which would not recover without its aid.

In all cases let us give the patient the benefit of the doubt.

CHAPTER XIV.

PHILOSOPHY AND RELIGION AND THEIR RELATION TO HEALTH.

From a psychological standpoint all religious services of all denominations are especially interesting. If we attend them to learn, we usually find our lesson between the lines.

The psychic effect of the comingling of several hundred male and female voices, with sentiments of love expressed in song; with the martial spirit of soldiers battling in unison and marching as conquerors from victory to victory; amid music and beautiful flowers, fine clothes and suggestive mottoes, and mystical carvings; all these combine to have a significance but little appreciated by one in a thousand of the people of our times. **They** subtly and gently stimulate all the involuntary cells of the body and temporarily lift the individual out of his self-conscious physical and psychical weaknesses, and, in general, **when free from emotional excitement,** prove to be an experience which, like other deviations, reacts with benefit upon both mind and body.

Suggestion is to be seen in all such experiences from start to finish. The methods adopted by the clergyman of getting *en rapport* with the audience; the unconsciously induced condition of receptivity by quartettes composed of male and female voices; the reading responded to by the audience, followed by a female solo; **all create a psychic condition** which renders the individual forgetful of self and his surroundings.

For the time being he is completely amenable to the suggestion given from the pulpit orator, who from thirty to sixty minutes has the opportunity to create sense impressions and present ideas or suggestions that **are beneficial or harmful,** as the case may be. **They are wholesome, beneficial and helpful** suggestions just in proportion as they are the reflection of a broad, well educated, truth-loving mind or personality.

It has been my privilege to hear such men in all denominations, both Protestant and Catholic, Jew and Gentile, Mormon and Free Thinkers, as well as promulgators of Oriental philosophies and religions, containing **much that is true and useful and good.**

Just in proportion as the people are becoming sufficiently well educated to comprehend in some degree the cosmic order of the universe and the laws of its evolution and to appreciate the part played by **heredity, environment and education** in determining the ideas and ideals which go to construct the religious beliefs of individuals, are they becoming more open to accept **the contribution made by science** to our moral and religious philosophy.

The more enlightened element of all denominations now admits that science has in numerous instances unquestionably demonstrated that religious teachings have at times been wrong as to matters of fact. **Be that as it may,** man is a religious being, for he is by nature a truth seeker, and everyone must either have a philosophy of his own in reference to the questions of life or be creed-fettered by some fixed religious dogma, which seeks to mould him according to prescribed ideals.

At no time in the world's history were the rights of the individual so much appreciated as now. All religions are useful just in proportion **as they contribute to the development of the individual** in body and mind.

As long as religion appeals to the intellect and renders the individual conscious of his privilege of being a thinking, reasoning, responsible entity, with the power to exercise choice as to **what shall and what shall not** enter his life; as long as its promulgators inspire men and women **with high ideals** and point to sane, rational, sensible rules of conduct both for self-betterment and for the health of his fellow man; as long as it teaches him self-appreciation and altruism and its influence is for what is good and true and useful for human happiness and health and growth, **the beneficial influence of religion for the evolution of the individual** cannot be questioned.

The sublime faith that carries with it a conviction that is unshaken, that brings peace, eliminates fear, and makes life serene, **or a reasonable philosophy** that is entirely satisfactory to the individual in regard to his past evolution, present conduct, and future development, is as essential to the life, health and happiness of a rational human being as is food or water, exercise or sleep or air, congenial associates or other life essentials. **It is here that the mind takes refuge** in those problems that are forced upon the attention of all civilized races.

Yet, when the emotions have been wrought upon and the individual is led into that extreme state of mono-ideaism which exists in religious ecstacy with crying, shouting, or other manifestations of joy or grief, pleasure or hope, and he **or** she is no

[18]

longer under the guidance and control of reason, it can but be regarded **as psychical prostitution pure and simple.**

The psychical correlation between religious emotion and the animal passions is now recognized by all our ablest psychologists, neurologists and psychiatrists. **The erotic and religious feelings** are so closely associated that the step from the emotional religious enthusiast to the sexual prostitute is but a very short one.

As bearing upon this subject, Howard says: "Religious emotion springs from the animating power of the sexual nature, and through the emotion thus aroused we deify and worship the inspirational source of our spiritual longings."

Kraft-Ebing remarks: "How powerfully sensuality expresses itself in the histories of religious fanatics and in what revolting scenes, true orgies, the religious festivals of antiquity, no less than the meetings of certain sects in modern times, express themselves. . . . . . **Owing to the correspondence in many points** between these two emotional states, it is clear that when they are very intense the one may take the place of the other, since every manifestation of one element of mental life also intensifies its associations."

The reader is aware that the more enlightened leaders of all religions now openly oppose any form of emotional excitement in religious services and regard it as a **deplorable relic of ancient barbarism.** **But, be that as it may,** it has been my experience to attend such meetings all over our country and the consciousness of the degrading influence of such meetings on innocent, impressible, and highly suggestible boys and girls, men and women, who are the victims of these induced endemics of temporary emotional insanity, has been particularly painful and revolting to me.

Children, as well as men and women, who are not sufficiently educated to think for themselves upon these questions, are, when the emotions are stirred, suggestible in the highest degree, and any method of coercion which incites fear, plays upon the imagination and dethrones reason, is prostitution of body and mind. **One neurotic boy** of my knowledge remained in a subconscious state all night long and his nervous system never reacted from the shock or sense impressions of that experience. He was weak minded and hysterical ever afterward and finally became insane and died in the asylum. **A neurotic woman,** after having been subject to religious excitement for several days, began having cataleptic seizures and had kept this up constantly every day for two years, being all the while in a state of religious fervor, and was frequently visited by her minister, who would talk and pray with her, thus keeping up this morbid, psychoneurotic condition.

It has been my experience to be called in consultation to see two persons, ill with an acute disease, who died as a result of the effect of having been for several days subjected to the injurious sense impressions **produced by a fanatical, emotional revivalist.** The timely use of suggestion to drive back these perverted mental states and plant new sense impressions in their stead would, no doubt, have altered the results, but neither of these patients was amenable to treatment at the time I visited them.

The conviction of sin and fear of hell and the awfulness of the "Judgment Day" were impressed upon them until every organic function had been disturbed, they had been unable to sleep, food and medicine had not been assimilated, and they died of diseases from which under different conditions they should have made a speedy and sure recovery. **Such has been the experience of hundreds** of physicians of my acquaintance as a result of emotional religious excitement.

But aside from the danger that such pernicious influences exert upon life itself, the positive harm to the development and growth of body and mind is the worst. **To speak plainly,** the effect upon the entire individual is identical to that of excessive sexual intercourse and it is questionable if the results upon mind and body of sexual prostitution are not even less injurious.

Every intellectual state is accompanied by definite physical manifestations. The physical concomitants of such psychical states as where the individual is under the sway of emotional religious excitement are vasomotor phenomena, respiratory phenomena, and motor phenomena or phenomena of expression.

The vascular modifications that take place are felt in the form of arterial pulsations, heaviness and a sense of choking, all of which are usually ascribed to being "the power of the Holy Spirit" acting upon the individual. They all denote a state of tension of the organism and of concentration of effort. **Such emotion is contagious.** Mental states beget similar mental states in others who are so situated as to receive sense impressions from those thus affected. **The tension produced** upon the nervous system and the physical reaction to such experiences for several days in succession leaves such individuals nervous and weak with all bodily functions disturbed. Sleep is hindered and they are often pale and indifferent to interest in all other things except religious matters.

We all realize that this is nothing more than a condition of hysteria, but such hysteria is contagious and when often repeated forms a habit, and such habits are positively injurious. **To be exposed to such influences** interferes with the growth of both mind and body of children, and the habit of having one's psychic life controlled and played upon by an emotional enthusiast, in the personality of an individual of the opposite sex, is positively destructive to the essential conditions of a happy marriage relation.

To educate an individual to be guided and controlled by **emotion** or **passion** in religious matters and expect him **to exercise reason and judgment** in reference to other phases of his life's conduct, would mean to teach him to act directly contrary to his religious teaching.

The over-expenditure of nervous energy from such emotional religious experiences and the habit of being psychically aroused by such experiences reduces the individual to a condition of mental and physical inertness. **It is horrible to contemplate,** but there are thousands of ardent female religious devotees whose psychic life is so dominated and controlled by their church executive or "spiritual adviser," that their husbands find no more place in their higher nature than a dog finds comfort upon the grave of his buried master.

This state of affairs reduces such marriage relations into nothing less than legalized prostitution. Whoever holds the attention of an individual, stirs his emotions, and directs his thoughts, governs his actions and controls his life both consciously and subconsciously; **and when married women are so dominated and controlled,** the higher social affiliations and more complete amalgamation of personalities between man and his wife are rendered impossible. **Such marriages, then,** are a fraud and a farce, and the result is unhappiness and nervousness, functional disorders and disease. **Such practices might be** excused in old maids and widows who are safely beyond the danger of ever getting married and who have **no ambition to attain in life;** but no growing young man or woman or wife or prospective mother should be exposed to their pernicious influences.

Adolescence, especially, should be kept free from an environment of religious fervor, which holds their constant attention and causes a useless expenditure of nervous energy to the neglect of the development of all other physical and mental attributes that should be cultivated by directing their lives into the normal, healthful, useful lines of thought and action.

The religious training of a great many individuals has but served to educate them into a psycho-neurotic disease, which practically unqualifies them for the duties and responsibilities of life.

To maintain a robust, vigorous state of health and physical well being while adhering to such religious practices is an absolute impossibility.

It is from this class of religious neurotics that Christian Science largely draws its membership and its dogma of negation and affirmation is only a suggestive means **to drive back morbid states of consciousness** produced by sense impressions made in times gone by and forgotten, and to replace these by conceptions, ideas, **sense impressions, or suggestions** that give rise to a new consciousness, to mental states that are **more pleasant, more hopeful, less emotional, more optimistic and cheerful,** and these react favorably upon the body. **With all its absurdity** Christian Science is a stepping stone, perhaps not an indispensable one, to the evolution and revision that is today taking place in the religious philosophies of the world. **To the man who is broad enough** and generous enough and wise enough to detect the kernel of psychological truth buried beneath its capsule of religious dogma, this cult serves as an illustration for an important lesson namely, that **the mind and the influence exerted upon it through religious worship plays an important role in the cause of disease and the maintenance of health.**

People are not to be blamed for their religious beliefs or habits of conduct in life. As a rule they are creatures of circumstance, fettered by **environment,** unfortunate **heredity,** and deficient **educational** advantages.

The clue to the situation was unconsciously admitted by a country clergyman in the South, who, in discussing the evolution that is taking place in religious ideals among the more enlightened centers of our country and the part that education exercises in shaping our religious beliefs, answered "Yes, but we care nothing about such ideals and education down here." **And so**

it is with everyone in reference to his philosophic and religious convictions. He instinctively feels that he is right from his viewpoint, and he is. His religion fills an essential need to his life and he has as much right to it as he has to life itself. And so has the individual who has acquired a broader perspective the same right to reject the false, worn out, and useless, and to interpret the problems of life for himself.

We are still only half civilized.

Ten million years of growth, evolution and development will not have remedied all the consequences of the ignorance that exists today.

Institutions, organizations and religions are a necessity. When they do not interfere with individual liberty and expression, they are useful. The majority of people are incapable of thinking and reasoning for themselves. They have not as yet acquired strength of intellect and knowledge of the universe sufficient to give them the confidence to take their lives into their own hands.

To them the power, strength, authority and privileges of the self-conscious ego are as much a stranger and as intangible and useless in the choice as to what shall govern and control their life, as if they never existed. Indeed, such a self-consciousness to them does not exist, for this quality of human personality is also developed according to the general laws of existence through heredity, environment and education.

However, individual responsibility cannot be evaded.

Men and women who know better and have evolved moral courage sufficient to give them the impulse to act up to their convictions, **are impelled by immutable law under which they cannot decide** to do otherwise than press forward and onward and upward, and they are increasing their strength day by day according to the law of development by use.

We live in a new age and are confronted by new conditions. New opportunities are thrust upon us. We must live up to our privileges or take the consequences. We must turn opportunities to good account. We must each go our route. We can't live and do as any other individual in this world today or in any age has done.

The great need of the world is men and women to interpret life and its meaning in the light of modern education and enlightenment; such as will speak out aloud and tell the truth as the more enlightened people of this day see it, and who will not be intimidated by the bulwarks set in our way of progress by the **ignorance** and **superstition of ages past and gone.**

At least to us as physicians there is no other time but now, and no other place but here, and a billion of years will not make it otherwise.

CHAPTER XV.

CONSERVATION OF ENERGY.

EDUCATION AND CONTROL OF THE EMOTIONS.

BREATHING, RELAXATION, DIETETICS, ETC.

More power, strength and ability is a radical craving of the human being. Such cravings are as instinctive as the desire to live.

Each individual is endowed with latent potentialities or energy expressed in the millions of cells of his organism, according to their quality, and these he may use or abuse as he decides for himself.

How to create and conserve the highest expression of personality as represented by body and mind, in order that the greatest happiness may be maintained, is worthy of the serious consideration of every intelligent human being.

When we take stock of ourselves, we find that we have all the qualities of the lower animals, and others, besides, which are the distinguishing characteristics between human beings and the lower forms of intelligence. **Appetites, passions, emotions,** feelings, desires, and a consideration for others of its species, belong to the animals beneath us. **Man alone** of all the animal creation is capable of thinking and reasoning and of communicating his ideas to others **in spoken and written language.**

No rule of conduct can be pointed out as a guide as to the best methods for the individual to pursue in order that the highest degree of physical strength, intellectual development, and moral character may be maintained. **That is the problem** that confronts every individual. **It is the problem of life** which each one must solve for himself; yet, how many there are who fail to live up to their privileges!

When we as physicians are brought face to face with the problem of treating disease we have but to reflect for a moment to see that the **real problem for the individual is** how to live.

The most fruitful cause of disease and weakness of body and mind lies in uncontrolled and misguided appetites, emotions, and passions, and a failure properly to conserve and direct our mental and physical energies into healthy channels of thought and conduct.

With the properly developed individual the intellectual functions and physiological processes are so under his control that he can by practice **direct any selected one as he chooses.** The true purpose of education is to teach the individual self-control and a just consideration for the welfare of others.

The sexual function, of the natural instincts, is second only to the instinct of self-preservation. In some individuals it is perhaps the strongest of all the bodily appetites and passions. **The healthy, vigorous glow of sexuality,** when not debased by sensuality, is the crowning glory of a man or woman. **We have but one Energy** and this is expressed by the individual in every manifestation of his life's conduct, whether physical, intellectual, or emotional in character.

Scott* has well said that **"purity is the crown of all real manliness,** and the vigorous and robust, who by repression of evil have preserved their sexual potency, make the best husbands

*Scott, The Sexual Instinct, E. B. Treat & Co.

and fathers, and they are the direct benefactors of the race by begetting progeny who are not predisposed to sexual violation and bodily and mental degeneracy."

The tendency of rational Medicine is getting more and more toward the prevention as well as the cure of disease, insanity and degeneracy in its numerous manifestations. **Educators and teachers** are at last awakening to the importance of defending ignorance and innocence **against morbid moral processes** as well as to protect them from smallpox and yellow fever; so the day is not remote when children will be taught in our common schools to regard the care and preservation of their bodies as paramount to their lessons in English grammar and arithmetic.

Monogamy will modify all excesses in the sexual line and **right thinking** will eliminate all habits which may be destructive to an individual or against the best interest of the community.

Aside from a condition of lowered vitality that is frequently maintained in both men and women by such indiscretions, emotional religious feelings, too much social excitement among enthusiastic, exuberant young people, over-eating, excessive chewing and smoking of tobacco, whisky and beer drinking, worry and over-anxiety about business, anger, envy, jealousy and fear, irregular habits of sleep, work and recreation, all contribute their quota to hold the individual in check and prevent the highest and best expression of individuality in body and mind.

A lady who had emerged from an excitable emotional religious revival, weak and nervous, after being sick for a day, was anxious to return, and when I admonished her of the danger of such dissipation, and remarked that death itself was not infrequent as a result of such indiscretions, she answered suavely that " it would be a lovely way to die."

In the same spirit another patient whom I advised to abandon the use of tobacco and whisky if he expected to get well, replied that he would rather not live if he had to give them up; that he had reached the age when his sexual powers had failed, and he now felt that these offered all that went to make life worth while.

It is hard to realize, until one stops to consider this subject, in what complete slavery many human beings are held by their appetites and uncontrolled emotions and passions.

A country parson once sent for me, and very seriously and confidentially explained that the physicians of his town did not understand his case. That he had for years suffered so much with indigestion until he was unable to do mental work, and, though he " loved his work and was completely in the hands of the Lord," that it troubled him to be unable to prepare sermons that would hold the people. He was six feet high and weighed two hundred and eighty pounds. After he had related his tale of woe, I informed him that the external evidence in his case did not coincide with his interpretation; that instead of suffering with indigestion he gave every evidence of digesting and assimilating too much food. **Then turning to his wife** I asked how much he ate for breakfast as compared with the other members of the family, and she answered, as much as herself and their four children combined. **I reasoned with him** and explained how it was impossible for his stomach and his brain each to perform the highest function at the same time, and outlined a reasonable diet, advised that he walk ten miles a day and cut his own wood, work in his garden, and take such other physical exercise as would reduce his weight. **He took my advice kindly,** and two weeks afterwards informed me that he felt like a new man. He had been so completely occupied in getting individuals to " save their souls," that he had forgotten the present salvation of his own character sufficient to control his bodily appetites.

I was once introduced to an aged physician, then ninty-one years old, who had just returned from a six-mile ride on horseback on a visit to a patient in the country. I inquired why he did not leave such trips to "the boys " in the profession, pointing to two physicians who were themselves between sixty and seventy years old. I shall never forget his answer. He died of pneumonia several months afterwards, but that answer of his contained a fine lecture on psycho-therapeutics. **His reply was: " I don't want to die.** Do you not know that as long as a man is at work, he is thinking, and that when he is working and thinking, he is using his brain cells, and that the brain cells kept in constant use give strength to every part of his body ? "

For sixty-five years, this physician, old Dr. Smith, of Oxford, Mississippi, had kept in harness, frequently making trips on horseback for sixty miles in the early part of his professional career, and he furnished a good illustration of the salutary effect of continuous exercise and useful employment.

The only safe way to control our emotions, appetites, and passions, is to direct our energies into channels of wholesome and useful effort, whether it be physical or mental effort. The result is strengthening to both mind and body, provided it is done cheerfully and with a purpose.

The emotional part of our nature, when guided by reason, is expressed in enthusiasm, a quality which is essential to success in any line of effort. **Be it man or woman,** the continuous and persistent pursuit of some steady work or useful employment will react as health and strength-producing factors to both mind and body. **This very effort** conserves our energy, guides and controls the emotions, and cultivates all the positive qualities of human character. **The proficiency** which comes from continuous persistent effort achieves a self-reliance that eradicates fear.

Worry is only our own recognition of our inadequacy or or inability to be equal to the exigencies of life. It shows a lack of self-reliance, without which man is but the plaything of chance, a puppet of circumstances.

Envy and anger and jealousy are all characteristics of weakness and incompetency. Such negative qualities can find no place in the life and character of a real man or woman.

There is a retroactive degeneracy of wealth which, as history has shown, proves the destroyer of the idle, the proud, and the self-conceited.

The sooner every human being can learn that the real elements that create health and strength and happiness and success in life are inherent within him, and that reason should be the guiding star by which he should direct and control and develop and use the potentialities within his own organism, the sooner will he realize that upon him alone depends the responsibility of so living that he can maintain sufficient resistive power in the cells of his organism for health to become a habit and happiness and success the rule of his life.

We have only a few medicines that can be relied upon in their application to the treatment of disease, and in some instances it is really remarkable how well people get along without any medicine at all.

In one little city of 25,000 inhabitants, the physicians informed me that a non-medical practitioner in that town was doing more work than any two physicians in the place. He had taught school for a good many years, and had gained quite a fund of general information in regard to psycho-therapeutics, dietetics, hydro-therapy, massage, exercise, etc., which, coupled with a good personality, enabled him to practise with remarkable success.

Now, I am not a therapeutic nihilist. We should use medicine when indicated, and there are conditions in which is it absolutely indispensable, but in the great majority of cases that come to us for aid, we should display **more confidence in our patient's brain plasm** and in the recuperative powers inherent in the cells of his organism under proper conditions, to reestablish a condition of health.

Without the co-operation of the patient, it matters not what be our therapeutic measures, we are handicapped very seriously. It is not what we do for the patient with materia medica agencies that is the greatest factor in therapeutics, but the environment which we create for him and what we get him perhaps unconsciously to do for himself. **If his brain cells do not respond** to the sense impressions made upon them so as to get him to act upon and execute our ideas both consciously and sub-consciously, then may we expect very little benefit to be derived from the administration of medicine. **It is what he eats and what he drinks, how he acts and the way he thinks,** together with breathing and relaxation, fresh air, pure water, work and sunshine, that are the real helps to get a sick man well.

Thousands of the ablest physicians place little or no confidence in more than a few medicines, aside from the confidence that the patient has in their efficacy. **Is it not time** that we should deal with our patients squarely and honestly, and, while giving medicine when indicated, either for its physiological or psychological effects, let them know that the real source of health and happiness depends upon their own control and direction of their conscious and unconscious psychic activities into normal, healthful lines of thought and conduct. **Where an individual needs such advice,** and the majority of them do, I should deem myself untrue as his physician and false to my Hippocratic oath, did I not express my honest convictions relative to the real elements that contribute to his health and well being.

Thousands of American people to-day are magnificent examples of what intelligent, systematic, physical exercise can do in the way of developing a vigorous, robust, healthy body.

[19]

A large percentage of our most successful physicians are physical athletes as the result of intelligent physical training.

As yet not one person out of five knows how to breathe, or realizes that sufficient oxygen taken into his lungs from the inspired air is as important as the food that he eats.

Water, pure, wholesome water, as a functional stimulant, a toxine eliminant and health-producing agent has not occupied the place it deserves in our therapeutic armamentarium or in the appreciation of the people, whose privilege it is to use it without our advice.

Most of our people still overtax their nervous systems with an excess of meats, as an article of diet, and thus maintain a lowered power of both mind and body on account of such indiscretions and excesses. **The tests at Yale University,** made by Professor Irving Fisher, have proved beyond all question that " a low proteid, non-flesh or nearly non-flesh dietary " is conducive to a greater mental and physical endurance than the ordinary American diet.

The use of the corset as a fruitful source of disease yet needs to be impressed upon the minds of our women.

Intemperance or lack of self-control and the use of reason in eating, in dress and business activities, and religious worship, and sexual matters, and emotions of all kinds, and passions of every description, should all be kept in mind by the physician who intends to make such suggestions as will redound to the greatest benefit of his patients. **Self-control is** humanity's greatest, highest, noblest achievement.

CHAPTER XVI.

ROUGHING-IT AS A MEANS OF HEALTH.

Disease is a condition where the cells of a part or of the entire organism do not properly perform their function. At any rate, it denotes an absence of health. These are only relative terms, for what might be a condition of reasonably good health for one individual would be so far below the normal standard of another as to be considered disease for him.

A problem that confronts every human being is how to maintain the highest possible degree of resistive power in the cells of his organism so as to render them invulnerable to pathogenic germs and other etiological factors of disease. **This can not always** be accomplished by tonics, reconstructive agents, etc. In many instances it is simply a question of getting the individual to conform to those conditions and habits of life which bring an increased degree of resistive power to the cells of his organism as a consequence. **Such habits can often** be brought about as the result of an idea put strongly into the brain plasm of your patient. **Before you can succeed** in putting such an idea sufficiently strong to get your patient to act upon it so as to change his habits of thought and conduct, you must believe in the efficacy of the means to secure the desired end. **Confidence begets confidence** and conviction creates conviction; courage begets courage and health begets health.

So, if a physician is weak, discouraged and tender-footed, before he can get others to act upon an idea, either consciously or subconsciously, he must get right himself.

To bring about this end, try "roughing-it" as a means of health, and get your patients to do likewise.

The finest reconstructive agent at our command is an idea conveyed to your patient that will create hope, expectancy, confidence and optimism. **All these encourage anabolism** or constructive metamorphosis, and this is doubly true when it moves one out **into the sunshine and fresh air** and **enforces exercise** and deep breathing, resulting in sound sleep, good appetite, and increased digestion and assimilation. **It means new blood** for the patient and all this contributes to health.

Along with this comes a rest from the routine path of life, the dropping of business cares and perplexities, and a chance to catch something of the inspiration that comes from associating with birds and wild flowers, trees and rocks and running streams. **The psychic and physical effect** for the good of the individual of all such measures cannot be overestimated.

We are told that one death out of ten in the world today is the result of tuberculosis. It is not so. **The people who die** infected with tubercle bacilli do so because they do not live so as to maintain that high degree of resistive power to enable the cells of their organism to withstand the onslaught of this pathogenic enemy.

In offices and street cars, in places of business and on the street, we in cities are exposed to the tubercle infection every day of our lives. **We do not contract the disease** because we are alive enough to resist its invasion. **The factors of disease** are here and ever will be. It is up to us to learn how to live.

No better illustration of the value of roughing it can be cited than where thousands and thousands of individuals with this disease are yearly going to the high altitudes along the range of the Rockies and dropping all home comforts, having the will and courage to face hardships in the West, living out of doors in open tents, and in this way making the fight for their lives. **The very decision to do** that which they believe will result in their recovery is the important essential which, favored by a dry high altitude and the conditions for living in the open air and sunshine, and encouraged by the optimism and cheerfulness of those who have been in that section long enough to have dropped the title of "tenderfoot," brings about a restoration of health.

Life is a struggle with us all. **In order to live** we must dare to be. We need sufficient resistive power in the cells of our organism to combat the etiological factors of disease, and this **can only be secured** by conforming to the requirements for creating and maintaining that high standard of healthfulness that will secure this quality.

In all classes of practice, medicine is only an aid. With its assistance the individual's chances of recovery, when sick, depend upon the **natural recuperative powers** of the cells of his organism.

In thousands of instances during warfare individuals have left their homes of comfort and luxurious ease and for years have endured the hardships of camp life and the stress of battle, on scanty food and insufficient bedding without shelter, only to return after the campaign strong and robust and in a perfect state of health.

During the cowboy days many young men, reared in wealth and affluence, went as physical weaklings to the Western plains and astride a broncho followed a herd of cattle and endured the hardships of camp life and simple diet, until they were rewarded with health and vigor of mind and body.

The very process of learning to be content with little to make one comfortable and satisfied with extemporized substitutes, cultivates a mental and physical stoicism which, as a means of health, is hard to overestimate.

We watch with interest a game of baseball or football on the hottest day of summer and wonder how the participants can so ignore the heat and enjoy such sport; such "roughing-it" brings its reward and produces physical athletes.

At a temperature of 110 degrees in the shade I watched a gang of men working for hours and hours in the hot sun engaged in laborious manual labor with pick and shovel. This acquired physical resistance came "by roughing-it," and the men were healthy and happy.

A month after the earthquake of San Francisco, when a hundred thousand people were in improvised tents and on plain, coarse food, the health of that city was officially reported as being better than at any time in its history. Neurasthenics who must have a cup of coffee with snowflake crackers in bed before rising in the morning were, after one month of "roughing-it," enjoying a breakfast of onions and beans.

The health and vigor that rewarded the early settlers in the pioneer days of our country when they were compelled to labor hard, live simply and have but little, also has its lesson.

To the thoughtful observer it is plain that our artificial methods of living at the present time are not conducive to the highest development of manhood and womanhood.

When education interferes with physical development it strikes a weakening blow at the quality of brain plasm of the individual, an element that must be kept at a high standard to attain the best results in mind and body building.

It has often been observed that the most successful men in all professions, and in all lines of business, in our large cities, have been, and are, those who were reared in the less populous towns and rural districts, where those natural conditions of simple living, fresh air, pure water and sunshine, quiet surroundings and wholesome food, exercise and employment, furnished the enviornment under which the highest standard of physical development could be produced. **Such conditions favored the growth** and development of a quality of brain plasm that manifested itself in the facility with which the individual was enabled to withstand the arduous duties and responsibilities amid the more complex environment of city life.

The boy reared in the fields, well acquainted with the woods and familiar with the chop-ax and the wood pile, thought he was having a hard time; but we know better now.

The country girl that rides horseback to school, carries a cold lunch in a bucket, and grows up among the birds and flowers, with cheeks painted by fresh air and sunshine, has a mental and physical equipment for life that far surpasses the accomplishments of her more delicately formed city sister. **Let this be supplemented** with a liberal education and she is prepared to withstand the exigencies of life under any and all conditions.

"Yes," said one physician, "granting that all you say about the value of physiological and mental therapeutics be true, if we put the laity in possession of such knowledge, we physicians are likely to be out of a job."

To entertain for one moment such a selfish idea or to give expression to such sentiments is not in accord with the spirit that actuates the leaders of our high and noble profession.

No better illustration of the absolute absurdity of the idea that any one therapeutic resource in the form of psycho-therapeutics disguised as Christian Science or osteopathy, or any physical culture or dietetic fad could ever supplant the rational work of the physician can be made than by quoting here from that excellent article appearing in the **American Monthly Review of Reviews** entilted, **"The Doctor in the Public Schools,"** by **Dr. John Cronin,** of the health department of the City of New York.

No better illustration, also, of the influence exerted **by the body upon the mind** and of the criminal neglect that fanatics are likely to bring upon the children of our country, by failure to have proper medical attention given for the correction of physical defects, could be presented than are made plain by the facts brought out in this report.

After relating the history of the movement for the inspection of children in the public schools as instituted by the board of health and relating the facts showing the necessity for a more thorough physical examination of children in the schools, Dr. Cronin says:

"Of 99,240 children examined in the schools of the Borough of Manhattan from March 27, 1905, to September 29, 1906, 65,741—or about 65 per cent.—needed some form of medical treatment. Of those 99,240 children, 30 per cent. (30,958) required correction of defects of sight, in most cases by eye-glasses. A still larger percentage (39,778) needed attention to their teeth. There were 38,273 children with swollen gland, in the neck, indicating some present or past trouble in the throat, noses ear, or some abnormal constitutional condition. Enlarged tonsils, with their baneful effects, including liability to tonsilitis and diptheria, were found in 18,131 children. About 10 per cent. of all the children examined (9850) were found to have adenoid growths in their throats—a condition which predisposes to affections of the ears, the nose and the lungs, and which interferes most seriously with the child's general health and mental development. Heart disease was found in 1659 children; disease of the lungs in 1039, and deformities of the bodies or limbs in 2347. Of the children thus far examined 2476 have been found mentally deficient; but probably the percentage of such children in our schools is slightly greater, as the figures thus far quoted include largely the primary grades, in which the mental development of the children is not so easily judged as in the upper classes.   .   .   .   .

"But perhaps the most striking results in the way of physical and mental improvements have been noted in the children who have adenoid growths or large tonsils removed. The amazing change which these children have undergone can scarcely be believed unless actually witnessed. From dullards, many of them have become the brightest among their fellows, after the operation.   .   .   .   .

"It has been shown that 95 per cent. of 'backward children' and of mentally deficient children have physical defects which can be remedied, thus improving their mentality as well as their physical health.   According to the City Superintendent of Schools, 40 per cent. of the children of the schools of New York are below the grades in which they should be according to their ages.   The Department of Health has found that 2 per cent. of all the children thus far examined were mentally deficient, and in nearly all these cases adenoid growths, defects of vision, or other remedial disabilities existed.   In the special classes for defectives in Public School 110, 95 per cent. had adenoid growths in the throats.   .   .   .

"Moral obliquity, of which truancy is the first manifestation in school life, goes hand in hand with physical defects.   Thus, among eighty-three truants examined by the Department of Health in the Special Truant School in this city, 87 per cent. were found to have physical defects, in most cases of a remedial character.   Truancy, and its kindred ills—the 'street habit,' and the 'gang habit'—lead to crime unless speedily checked. The records of the Children's Court in New York and of the similar court in Chicago showed that nearly all the youthful criminals that were brought to these courts were truants, and, what is more, that 85 per cent. of these children were found physically defective.   .   .   .   .   .   .

"To sum up, we may say that we have shown beyond peradventure that physical defects exist in about 60 per cent. of all school children in New York; that in most cases these defects are remediable by proper treatment, and that the early discovery of these defects is the prime factor in the maintenance of the health of the school children and in enabling them to pursue their studies.

"We have shown, furthermore, that backward, mentally deficient, and truant children can be vastly improved by the early recognition of physical infirmities which underlie their mental or moral defects, and that by appropriate treatment, if applied early enough, we can save these children from illiteracy, from drudgery in factories at small wages, or from an almost inevitable criminal career.

"In view of these facts, what can be more important than a systematic individual examination of every school child at stated periods, and what can be of more lasting benefit that the early application of the proper treatment in all cases in which physical defects are found? .   .   .

The facts, however, brought out in this report show also the ill results of an environment that does not furnish fresh air and sunshine, pure food and good water, and a mental quietude that is conducive to sound sleep and a healthy body.

That such ill conditions exist is no fault of the medical profession, whose work it is to meet conditions as it finds them.

Disease usually attacks the most vulnerable point, and where a low state of physical resistance is maintained, it is manifested in numerous ways.

Correction and treatment of physical defects in children and adults by all means should not be overlooked when we are brought face to face with such conditions, **but what is of far greater importance** is that people be so environed that health and vigor of mind and body would be the natural consequence of such an existence.

We all have noticed the benefit resulting in health and strength to a city-bred boy or girl who had spent a short time "roughing-it" in a country home.

CHAPTER XVII.

ARE ALL SPECIALISTS EGOTISTS?

Egotism and altruism are the distinguishing characteristics of an enlightened mind. An individual with the first quality only, however, without the second to balance it, is converted into a character that would be more aptly described by some other adjective. **Such men are everywhere,** in all professions and avocations of life. They are those who have acquired a one-pointed view of seeing things. **They follow the path illumined** by the light of a narrow intellect so long until their faculties for any other conception or interpretation become dwarfed and useless.

The tendency of the human mind is to run in channels carved out, as it were, in the brain plasm by sense impressions most constantly and frequently playing upon it. **The reflex of these impressions** is what gives rise to every individual's peculiar way of thinking and reasoning. So that a man who continually looks at any problem, be it that of a physician, facing the complexities of disease with all its numerous manifestations, or any other individual facing any problem **from a restricted viewpoint,** is liable to be mistaken.

Specialism in medicine, from the very nature of things, is a necessity. It has come to be regarded as synonymous with proficiency, and is, as it ought to be, here to stay. Furthermore the men that compose the rank and file of our specialists are for the most part, broad-minded and well educated physicians.

The specialist's association with the general practitioner and the men who follow other special lines of work than his own is usually a safeguard against his acquiring a narrow way of interpreting the symptoms of disease. Much of his work is referred to him by his colleagues, who, in some degree, feel the responsibility as sponsor for his treatment. **He is usually a man** who has followed the law of adaptation and his particular branch of medicine is chosen in view of special qualifications and fitness, and he continues his specialty according to the law of the " survival of the fittest."

Granting all this, and much more that could be said in his favor, there is a strong tendency for the physician to exaggerate the importance of his special line of work as a contributing factor to the welfare and happiness of the human race. **His very proficiency** and success and belief in himself and his methods, all combined, have a tendency to produce an unconscious temporary psychic beneficial result to his patient, as an accompaniment of other special treatment; and frequently a relapse of the patient into ill health follows, indicating that an important element in the case had been overlooked. **Finally,** the patient, usually a woman, seeks another specialist, on an entirely different line, who discovers what he regards to be the real source of her illness, and she is again temporarily benefited. **The results prove** that this physician also was correct, but the patient has added to her consciousness an increased awareness of her complications.

After a third, or perhaps a fourth, physician, each of a different specialty, has conscientiously and correctly treated the patient, she has been unconsciously suggested into a state of invalidism.

She then falls into the hands of some non-medical system of treatment, a Christian Scientist for example, where she becomes educated to disregard the medical profession and for the privilege of outpouring her abuse upon all physicians, she unconsciously adopts a stoicism that enables her to exist in a reasonably fair state of health, while she daily declares that it is all an " error of mortal mind." **The very egotism of her leaders** and the self-assertiveness of her new environment gives her the psychic stimulation and encouragement to tolerate her existing physical disabilities, which, in reality, are improved because she ceases to give them attention. **Her morbid self-analysis,** with its despondency and fear, has been replaced by a positive antagonistic attitude to the medical profession, and she becomes so preoccupied in deriding physicians that she forgets her physical disabilities much to her betterment.

It has been my experience to find many such cases as outlined in the above description. Just such a lady once sought my advice, luckily having visited only two physicians. **Her neurotic symptoms,** insomnia, headaches, indigestion, etc., were the natural accompaniments of a pronounced error of refraction and a catarrhal endocervicitis.

After proper glasses had been prescribed by a competent oculist and her endocervicitis appropriately treated, it was an easy matter to secure habits of plentiful and refreshing sleep by suggestion, following which was a good appetite and digestion, improved nutrition, a relief of all neurotic symptoms, and a rapid return to health.

Neither the " neurasthenia " of the neurologist, the " subacute gastritis " of the stomach specialist, the " catarrhal endocervicitis " of the gynecologist, nor the " astigmatic error of refraction " of the oculist, treated alone, as applying to this case, could have resulted in the relief of that patient. **Furthermore,** she could have had the benefit of all the specialists in the medical profession, and if she were under a **religious environment** that maintained a psychoneurotic condition, with its disastrous consequences to the normal physiological processes of the body, her reduced physical resistance thus maintained would have precluded the possibility of perfect health under any circumstances.

The egotism of the specialist, then, becomes a dangerous and abused quality of human personality the very moment he unduly exaggerates the importance of his specialty, to the neglect of other lines of sane, sensible, rational therapeutic measures, be they surgical, gynecological, medicinal, environmental, hygienic, dietetic, psychologic, mechanical and physical or physiological.

No one is more prone to commit this unpardonable sin against his profession than the psychotherapeutic fanatic, who is also in evidence, and such specimens of narrowness and bigotry have done much to retard the progress of this branch of therapeutics within the past twenty years.

Let us remember that we are human beings, as are, also, our patients; that we are physicians as well as specialists, and as physicians let us acquire a broad and generous perspective of our patient and his welfare, and of his and our relations to others, and not unduly exaggerate our importance. **No man has a right** to expect the support of his colleagues in a specialty who is not first a well qualified, all-round physician.

We should be prepared to give our patients the benefit of all that modern professional skill and knowledge offers, and should have **the courage to manifest the egotism and altruism** to insist upon his or her conformity to all conditions and means that contribute to health, and then the people would not so often find it necessary to resort to measures outside of the medical profession, for relief that we fail to give.

Man as a whole, a being both physical and mental, composed of qualities designated as mind and body, must be taken into consideration.

CHAPTER XVIII.

PERSONALITY AS A FACTOR IN THERAPEUTICS.

The personality of a physician is an important asset in the makeup of his professional equipment.

The achievement of personality is the goal sought by everyone beginning the study of medicine; and everything pertaining to medical thought, colleges, books, hospitals, clinics, operations, laboratories, dissecting rooms, class associates, quiz masters, instructors and professors, all combined, furnish the environmental and educational factors which collectively go to convert the aspirant into the type of *genus hominis* known as a physician.

Aside from his scientific medical training, the personality of a physician is the greatest factor in the make-up of his professional armamentarium. So much so is this true that we often hear the expression that " the physician is born, not made." **Such an expression** usually implies that there is an inner quality of personality that manifests itself in the dealing of a physician with his patients, that does not exist equally in all men equally trained in professional knowledge. **There seems to be an inner spring** or quality of character that counts when such men are put to the test in the office, or at the bedside, in daily intercourse with others, on any and all occasions, which is a *sine qua non* to the successful practice of medicine.

There is in every one a quality of personality that either attracts or repels others. It is not necessarily an accompaniment of any special type or physique or nervous organization.

[20]

It is found in men of small build and of neurotic type as well as in those that are robust, phlegmatic and heavy. **Such men frequently make serious blunders** in their professional work, but still they hold the people.

Individuals sometimes wait one, two, or even three days for a physician to sober up from a debauch and go for him with their own conveyance and assist him to the bedside of a sick wife or child, and declare that they would prefer him drunk to any other physician sober. This has been an occurrence in a city whose medical profession compares favorably to that of a town of equal size anywhere.

It has been a matter of personal experience, in my own work among the medical profession, that I have frequently grasped the hand of a stranger and instantly felt that I had found a warm personal friend before we had exchanged any more than a mere formal greeting. **On the other hand,** I have frequently felt so repulsed, at the first glance of a physician, that I refused to acknowledge him as a man whom I wished to meet.

Upon one occasion I called upon a physician of high professional attainment, whose conduct, when I approached him, was discourteous in the extreme. I looked him squarely in the face for a moment, and extended my hand, saying, in a quiet monotone, " good-bye, doctor." The effect of this upon him needs no comment. He shook hands with me, but learned a lesson. **In his reception room** he had but one patient and that one appeared to be an old stand-by. This was no surprise to me, for that physician had given me a taste of his quality, and I never cared to see him again, and so it was with his patients.

From this office I went to see another physician, in the same specialty, who was courteous and human, really showing me more deference than I felt that I deserved. He had won a high place in the esteem of his colleagues by hard work in his home city, and his office was full of patients. **The treatment accorded a stranger** by that physician was a sample of the quality of the personality of the man, and such a quality as the people liked, and he is doing a great work.

Invariably those of the medical profession who are competent men and who possess this happy streak of personality above illustrated, are making a success of their work.

There is a lesson for us as physicians in the following verse:

"There are loyal hearts, there are spirits brave,
There are souls that are pure and true;
Then give to the world the best you have,
And the best will come to you.
Give love, and love to your heart will flow,
A strength in your utmost need;
Have faith, and a score of hearts will show
Their faith in your word and deed."

A little display of those qualities typified by the great religious reformer about two thousand years ago, kindness, sincerity, sympathy, earnestness, fearlessness, bravery, magnanimity and altruism, is an inestimable element in the personality of the physician. **It helps to get control of people,** not by force, and better enables him to put them in possession of themselves.

Here is the clue to the explanation of that indefinable psychic quality that the most successful physicians carry with them which proves a power in therapeutics; and this is manifested all unconsciously by him in every move of his life. It **begets the confidence and trust** of his patient and the respect and co-operation that is a most essential factor in the successful treatment of any disease.

Especially is this quality in the physician necessary in the treatment of enlightened and self-respecting people. It begets a reciprocation of that respect which such people feel is due them. **They positively refuse** to be driven, but it is only an evidence of their high intelligence when they are willing to be led for their own good by the skillful direction of a cultured, competent, conscientious physician.

A sensible display of tact and diplomacy will often enable a physician to win the confidence of a patient, and thus secure the co-operation so essentially necessary for the best results, when the being too blunt and abrupt would render him utterly helpless.

To see one physician so manage a little fellow as to get him to submit to the skillful dilatation and treatment of a suppurative dacryocystitis with hardly a whimper, by his firmness and kindness and tactful persuasion where another would become nervous and excited and spend a much longer time in accomplishing this result, his patient crying vehemently and suffering a needless amount of pain on account of his resistance, is an illustration of what personality means in a certain class of work.

It is a great help to a physician to be able to get hold of people and use them to help themselves to get well. We all help or hinder the recovery of our patients, far more than many realize, by the way we deal with them. We unconsciously use suggestive therapeutics at every step in our routine work.

People buy goods of the merchant they like, the groceryman they like, the dairyman they like. In all trades this personal factor is taken into account. A dry goods clerk brings a better price because people like him, he knows how to deal with people and to help them to suit themselves in their purchases; but more than in any other department of life does the personality of the physician count in helping people to get well. **A patient cannot get into your office** and walk out without your personality having made some mark upon him. **There are people** in whose presence you are always at your very best, and for whom you can render the best professional service.

It is a recognized psychological law that we become like those whom we habitually admire. Thus we become a part of all with whom we have associated during our existence. **In all of our experience with literature** and personal association, this law continually operates, so that all men are reproductions of other men.

In all sections of the country are neurologists, who, from constant association with a certain class of patients, seem to have become the living embodiment of all the objectionable, mental and physical characteristics of their patients. **A patient who had twice** been to see a physician of that type, remarked that he felt worse after each visit, and did not care to return again.

Another neurologist who was himself the personification of physical strength and mental vigor and optimism, remarked to me that he never felt as though he had done his duty unless he sent his patient out of his office feeling better for having come to see him. It is needless to remark that he is one of the most successful men in his specialty in the profession to-day.

The reader will pardon me if I seem critical or personal in my remarks in this chapter, but the importance of the subject at hand is such that I should deem my effort futile did I not drive home the point under consideration.

We all have our short-comings. **Day by day do I have added** to my consciousness an increased awareness of my own deficiences as compared to the knowledge and competency of some of my colleagues with whom I have been privileged to associate. **Only my experience** and the results obtained by careful observation of the personal factor in therapeutics and the encouragement of physicians **who have also personally tested these methods,** would give me the courage to express my honest convictions at all hazards.

I fully realize that the hard knocks and criticism that may be fired at me will only serve to educate the profession in the sane, rational use of the measures advocated, and if such be the case, my efforts will not have been in vain.

It is a great thing to be able to make a hair-splitting diagnosis, the correctness of which is infallible, and I shall unceasingly strive to attain such proficiency.

It may also be a great satisfaction, and it is of unquestionable benefit to the physician who can do it, to give a minute and detailed delineation and description of the pathology of a disease to the satisfaction of his professional associates, but such an elucidation is never of value to the patient.

Physicians themselves become the easy victims of any disease as soon as they become conscious of the seriousness and gravity of the diagnosis rendered by their colleagues in attendance. **Their very knowledge of its etiology** and pathology renders them unduly self-conscious of their condition, and such a self-consciousness gives rise to morbid mental states that inhibit the normal physiological processes, prevent sleep, and seriously retard recovery.

When I see a physician sick and half dozen of his learned colleagues lined up around him, all rendering him more self-conscious of the seriousness of his condition, I can but wish that only one of them had been called and that he possessed those qualities of personality that, **in spite of the physician's knowledge of pathology,** could drive back those existing morbid sense impressions and substitute in their stead mental states that would enable him to put up a more creditable fight. **If the life** of a physician is worth anything the end would justify the means. **So while giving due appreciation** to scientific professional knowledge and training in pathology and diagnosis, **what is of far greater importance** is, that we so use our knowledge as to help our patients to get well.

Every visit of the physician is an opportunity to help accomplish such a result, and here is where the personality of the physician is often detrimental or helpful to the recovery of the patient. **The very self-consciousness** induced by a physician at his visits, and the mental states which follow in consequence of such an induced self-consciousness, are the deciding factors for the good or harm of the patient. **The influence of personality** is contagious. We set up mental states in others around our patients that prove helpful or harmful in the sick room.

Out in New Mexico a young man walked out of a physician's office looking downcast and dejected, with lips tightly closed and with jerky inspirations. " A lunger up against it good and hard," is the way they refer to such patients out there.

That night I lectured to a class of physicians and the next day that patient went out of the same office with a smile on his face, and a bright animated expression, having taken the first step towards recovery, as the result of sense impressions or suggestions strongly made upon his brain cortex by his physician. **He ate more that day,** slept well that night, and reported that he had coughed but little, was not so nervous, had enjoyed his breakfast, and felt stronger. **All because his physician** had the personality to exercise the **egotism and altruism** to look him squarely in the face after his examination and say to him, " I have some good news to tell you. You are much better to-day. Already a marked improvement has taken place in your condition, but you will be very much better by to-morrow. You will enjoy your food to-day, have a good digestion, sleep well to-night, and improve every day from now on."

Physicians themselves frequently have invalid wives, whose invalidism is maintained in consequence of the constant association of a husband whose personality depresses them. **The**

affection displayed by such men for their wives may be beautiful to contemplate, but the accompanying emotional, sentimental sympathy, is weakening in the extreme.

Reader, if you happen to be of that type of individual, get cured of your miserable psychoneurotic disease, and don't live as a parasite infecting the lives of those with whom you associate. My prescription for you is, to associate and amalgamate with the wide-awake element of the medical profession who constitute the upper ten per cent. of our ranks. Sages, poets and philosophers of all ages have repeated this message to the world, that men and women make men and women.

If there be anything of value in these expressions, that I so feebly echo here, they are but the reflex of impressions that association with other personalities has left upon my cerebral cortex.

If the quality of my brain plasm were of higher standard, and my previous environmental and educational advantages had been more propitious, my opportunities would have borne better fruit.

We all have our capacity, and, under equal opportunities, we can only react upon sense impressions or suggestions in proportion to our qualifications.

Whatever be our deficiencies as a result of heredity, environment, and education, each of us can give our patients of our highest, truest, and best self, as an aid to their recovery.

Some men bring a reproach upon the profession on account of a failure to exhibit those character qualities which alone constitute the highest type of professional personality and manhood. **By the correct use** of your personality as a factor in therapeutics, you help people to help themselves. But there are instances when you advise a nervous patient who is suffering with insomnia and a train of functional disorders, to relax and practice deep rhythmical breathing, and to concentrate his mind on sleep as a means of self-help, and **the neurotic patient says, " I can't."** The stability of his nerve and brain plasm is below par, and he lacks the will power and determination to execute your advice or simple suggestions.

" Then I will relieve that uncontrollable nervousness for you, so that you can lie here and let this medicine have its effect." **The patient believes in the medicine,** but not in himself. Only a placebo is used, but by kindness, firmness and persuasion, I got my patient to relax and exercise that self-control which he believed that he was incapable of doing. **By the aid of my suggestions** he easily goes into the hypnotic or suggestive state. **Then I plant new ideas, impressions,** and feelings upon his brain plasm, and he awakes from the treatment with a new element added to his consciousness. He now feels that he can relax, breathe deeply and rhythmically, and go to sleep. **In the waking state** I reinforce these suggestions.

" That treatment has greatly benefited you. You can relax and will sleep well to-night. You will always feel better after this."

A new quality of self-hood has been added to that patient's personality. Brain cells have been encouraged and persuaded into action. What I did for him was in a spirit of kindness and for his best interest, and he appreciates it as such. **He leaves my presence in gratitude** and feels that I am his friend.

The fear that some physicians have that people will object to the employment of these methods is a self-confessed weakness. They are too proud to express a favorable opinion. Fear never accomplished anything for the good of the physician or his patient. Some of the best friends I have in the world to-day were those made in my efforts to get them to control themselves, who took my suggestions given either consciously or sub-consciously, and through such aid learned to rely upon themselves.

In the employment of suggestion, both with and without hypnotism, you are only helping your patient to help himself. Yet many physicians will denounce and ridicule it and go on filling neurotic patients with such medicines as lessen in every way the patient's self-reliance; making the patient absolutely dependent upon them.

A man who practices medicine in that way may make money, but he also encourages the business of the undertaker. He can only be excused upon the ground of ignorance.

CHAPTER XIX.

THE ABUSE OF PERSONALITY.

In order to make myself understood, I will give you an illustration of how personality is abused in the practice of medicine, and the picture here presented is an apt illustration of the conduct of many of the general practitioners, who do not take into consideration the psychological factor in therapeutics.

All observing individuals have noticed that in every locality there are physicians who have more "very sick" patients, in proportion to their patronage than others. **That the personality of a physician** is frequently the prime factor in producing these "very sick patients" is beyond question.

Here is an illustration of the usual conduct pursued by such men in the treatment of an ordinary case of pneumonia, a disease in which the correct use, or abuse, of the personality of the attending physician, **more than in any other acute disease,** determines the recovery or non-recovery of a patient.

"Give this medicine very carefully, and watch her closely until I see her again. I will call this evening."

True to his promise he is punctual in fulfilling his appointment, much to the satisfaction of the family, who anxiously await his coming. **During the day** the sick mother has grown more nervous, her temperature is higher, her pulse rate faster. She is by this time over-anxious about her condition, and this in turn has made her family extremely anxious about her.

The physician has, by his conduct, demeanor, words, and action, made a strong impression upon both patient and family, and the fear that he has thus implanted into the minds of all in the household has kept up a depressing environmental influence which has got in its effective work upon the patient.

The lady in question is suffering with acute pneumonia. She feels a decided pain upon breathing, experiences a sense of suffocation, and the paroxysms of coughing have rendered her decidedly conscious of her illness; and now the physician in whom she has placed her trust has looked serious and given directions in a way that speaks louder than words in unduly exciting her. **Not one word has he said** to allay her anxiety, soothe her mind, assuage her fears, or inspire hope.

Upon his second examination he finds his patient decidedly worse, as might have been expected, and now he is serious, sure enough. His fatalities in the treatment of pneumonia have been particularly large, and he much dreads this disease; and seeing his patient with a higher fever, a more rapid pulse, flushed face, more anxious expression, and remembering his past record with such cases, he makes no effort to conceal his gloomy forebodings.

Again giving directions for the night, he starts for his conveyance, and when out in the hall the members of the anxious family, who have followed him, turn with pleading faces and inquire, "Doctor, how is mother?"

"Very sick, very sick," is his reply. "Watch her carefully tonight. Keep the house as quiet as possible, and if she should get worse before morning, be sure to call me."

Before the next day he has been called, for his patient has been unable to sleep, and from his point of view a hypodermic of morphine is decidedly indicated.

On and on this management goes, and if finally his patient recovers after two weeks of severe illness, which she might possibly have done in spite of her physician, that family are grateful to God and the doctor for having "pulled her through."

I remember once going to see a lady about fifty-five years old, **with acute pneumonia,** a decided congestion of the lower lobe of the right lung, and after carefully making out my diagnosis and prescribing for her medicinally, I turned to the patient and gave her a talk about as follows: "You have pneumonia, Mrs. Blank, but only a mild case, temperature only 103.5°F., but a good pulse and everything is favorable to a nice recovery. **You are in pain,** but a hot poultice I have ordered will relieve that very promptly. You will soon get comfortable and will rest well tonight and be feeling much better tomorrow when I see you again. Now, be patient, and in from seven to ten days you will be well. **The medicine prescribed for you** will keep you comfortable, strengthen your heart, keep your nerves quiet, steady and strong, and all will be well with you."

With tears of gratitude in her eyes, she answered, "Oh, doctor, you make me feel like I am well already. I feared that I had pneumonia and felt that I never would get well."

"You are going to get well all right," said I, "going along nicely to recovery. Your daughter will have entire charge of your medicines, and knows just what I want you to have in the way of nourishment. **After the hot poultice** is applied, you close your eyes and go to sleep, you will rest nicely and feel much better when I see you tomorrow."

Upon my return the next day she smiled pleasantly as I entered and bade her good-morning, and when I felt her pulse and remarked, "You are better," she answered, "I feel much better, doctor."

"Going right along to recovery, madam. Now, I shall see you day after tomorrow."

"See her every day if you think best, doctor," exclaimed her son. "We want mother to be well real soon."

"I can't trust everybody as I can you, so I will not come tomorrow unless you call me. She is going to do well. Keep out all visitors, continue all directions, and I will see her again day after tomorrow."

I saw that patient only twice more, and at the last visit assured her that it was a pleasure to come into her pleasant family, but that I was going to turn her over to the entire charge of Mrs. Blank, her daughter.

"If you feel it necessary to consult me again, just whistle and I will come."

In about seven more days the son came to know if his mother had better have a tonic; he said she had had no fever for three or four days and was entirely well. Her lung cleared up upon the ninth day of her disease.

I do not mean to say that all pneumonia cases should be seen only four times. In fact, a daily visit or two is indicated in most cases, but the case in question serves to illustrate the part that the psychological factor plays in an ordinary case of illness.

Many people die who would get well if given a chance to allow their protoplasmic energies to assert themselves.

Out in California I was invited by a physician to go with him on his rounds through the County Hospital. **Six pneumonia patients** were in one of the wards, four of them old men. The majority of these were chronic alcoholics and only one was delirious or appeared seriously ill.

"But one death from pneumonia in five years, in this hospital," was the physician's record up to that time.

"How do you treat them?" I inquired.

"Keep them comfortable, give them hospital tea (sweet milk) and let them have old Frank to keep them feeling good." **"Old Frank,"** as the hospital physician styled the genial German superintendent, carried sunshine and good cheer into those wards at least twice a day. **He had then been in his place** for seventeen years, and the therapeutic value of his personality to that institution would be hard to estimate. He knows how to get the confidence of men and women and how to keep them feeling good when they are sick. **Many a poor tramp,** who has only seen the rough side of life, has felt soothed by his kindness, and buoyed up to recovery by his optimism, while being controlled by his firmness.

There is no disease in which the influence brought to bear upon the mind of the patient so determines the recovery or non-recovery as pneumonia. **It is a self–limited disease** and those influences which soothe the mind and quiet the nervous system bring about a complete re-establishment of the nervous equilibrium, allowing the blood to circulate normally through the peripheral blood vessels of the body, and thus relieve the tension or high pressure upon the heart and inflamed lung, with its fatal termination to pneumonia patients.

One of Old Frank's characteristics is kindness, which is encouraging in contradistinction to sympathy, which is depressing and weakening.

There is more or less mental depression in all pneumonia patients, as the individual is rendered painfully conscious of his helplessness. This results in fear, and such sufferers enjoy sympathy as they enjoy morphine, which inhibits the normal physiological processes and stealthily lessens their resistive powers to the disease. **No worse influence** can be exerted over the patient than the presence of a highly emotional person, who lavishly pours out sympathy to the destruction of all the optimistic and strengthening qualities of mind and body. **So great are the influences** brought to bear by the mind over the physiological processes of the body that a physician who unconsciously uses the power of suggestion to the detriment of his patient, actually makes a very serious condition out of a trivial disorder.

On the other hand, by the intelligent and judicious use of suggestion, we can make a very trivial disorder out of a seemingly serious pathological condition, so far as the results are concerned.

The injury done to the unsuspecting public by physicians who are ignorant of the use and power of suggestion, is far greater than is commonly supposed. **Whole communities** have

[21]

become fear-stricken by the exaggerated serious reports of this class of physicians, who frequently ride day and night to see the victims of their perverted influence. **Their very influence** in the community in which they live spreads like a contagious disease, emanating from a focus, which stealthily moves among, them, reaping financial reward for their indiscretions.

"Very sick, very sick," is their watchword, as they implant fear in their trail.

While the laity are properly being educated in the necessity of self-protection from the contagiousness of tuberculous disease, malarial and yellow fever carriers, and other infections, for the safety of their own lives, they should also be protected from that **pest to any community,** the physician who unduly exaggerates the condition of his patients by reporting all cases as being seriously ill.

CHAPTER XX.

ENVIRONMENT--ITS INFLUENCE IN THERAPEUTICS.

Only the practical aspects of this subject remain to be considered.

A physician in general practice must not only treat his patient, but be in absolute control of the environmental influence brought to bear upon him as well, in order to secure the best results.

The sick room, especially in the small towns, and rural districts, is often the meeting place for gossipers, who unconsciously exercise a great influence upon the patient, frequently preventing recovery in an otherwise curable disease.

To say nothing of the value of quiet, rest and sleep, which is hindered by this procedure, the discussion of other cases of a similar kind that have terminated unfavorably and which had come within the experience of the visitor, or remarks relating to the procedures of another physician whose methods are different from your own, all exercise an unconscious influence that makes the patient nervous, excites fear, and proves destructive to that confidential relation which should exist between patient and physician.

The physician who is timid and allows this state of affairs to exist, to the detriment of his patient, is jeopardizing his professional reputation.

A loud-mouthed, self-assertive woman, who is the unconscious drummer for a competitor, is to be found in every locality.

Seeing the harmful influence of such an individual upon a patient with a continued illness, the simple instruction to "admit no visitors" is usually sufficient; but the madame in question is not always repulsed so easily, as she unduly exaggerates the importance of her presence to the welfare of the sufferer, and enforces her entrance in spite of your injunction, which she considers does not apply to her.

My own custom has been, under such conditions, to give my patient or his family the choice between my services and those of this unfriendly visitor.

Useless antagonism, however, never pays upon any occasion, but where the welfare of your patient is at stake, people will appreciate any stand that you take in his behalf. **"Do what's right,** come what may," is a safe rule under any and all circumstances, and the self-respecting physician should exercise the courage and self-assertiveness to face these problems and leave no stone unturned that might retard the recovery of his patients. **The successful men** in the medical profession are those who have the stamina to stand by their convictions and allow no intervening meddler to poison the environment of the sick room.

In a large class of cases it is absolutely impossible to obtain successful results in private practice, on account of our inability to secure the right environment, and here is where sanatorium and hospital facilities give the physician a wonderful advantage. In such places the environment is absolutely under his control and direction.

We should overrule any factor in private practice, however as far as possible that will in any way set up an undesirable mental attitude on the part of the patient as regards his own condition, or that will create mental states that are injurious; for mental states influence metabolism, and encourage or retard all the normal physiological processes, and wonderfully help or woefully hinder the recovery of your patient.

In all classes of professional work, there is a fine art in adapting one's self to whatever environment one may be thrown into, and in maintaining that prestige which the successful physician must never surrender. **When to be dictatorial,** when to to coerce, when to be lenient and kind, and when even to soothe and palliate by your presence, and at the same time be in absolute control of the situation, are all important considerations in the successful practice of medicine.

People sometimes need to be aroused and lifted out of mental states which prove to be adverse to their recovery, and new ones substituted in their place; and this applies not only to the patient, but to everyone coming into his or her presence. **It is our duty as physicians,** to create an environment wherever our patients are to be found that will help to make them get well.

To illustrate, here is a patient sick with pneumonia, a disease that frightens the majority of people. On my second visit I find the family and others in attendance depressed and downhearted, which, of course, renders the patient morbidly conscious of his condition. **It is evident to me** that I must alter that environment and re-establish hope in my patient or the outlook is very grave. Do I send for a consultant? Not unless it is a baby less than two years old. **What I do is to look** every member of that family squarely in the face, and kindly but positively tell them, and also the patient, that he is going to get well. **I have frequently emphasized** that suggestion, and assured the patient that I had seen a hundred people ten times sicker than he with pneumonia, and the last one of them recovered.

Then getting close to him with my hand on his head, I quietly and calmly assure him that I have never treated a pneumonia patient above two years old who did not get well, with the single exception of one old man who had a bilateral pleuro-pneumonia, with an enormous effusion, **and I tell the truth.**

I leave that home with a newly created helpful environment as a therapeutic resource, and under such conditions my patient is enabled to relax and to proceed with a consciousness that gives rise to mental states favorable to his recovery.

Do I depend alone upon the psychologic factors thus set in operation? No, I give my patient the benefit of every other possible therapeutic adjunct, from the application of a brick, heated to a red heat and placed in boiling water and allowed to remain therein until all simmering ceases, wrapped in a woolen cloth, and the moist heat confined by a blanket to the diseased lung, or a corn-meal and mustard poultice, renewed and applied hot every hour or two, or an ice-bag in their stead, to the use of all other measures, medicinal, dietetic, and hygienic.

The hot brick, taken out of boiling water, has a weighty physiological significance, aside from being an excellent vehicle to retain heat and moisture, which it gradually liberates to the great comfort of the sufferer. **I do not hesitate** to tell both my patient and his family that this hot brick relieves the pain, relaxes the patient all over, and causes the blood to circulate more freely to the periphery, and thus relieves the lung of its congestion and inflammation, reduces his temperature, enables him to sleep and helps to make him a well man. **I tell him in perfect candor** and truthfulness, that I have never known a patient who has used the hot brick heated to a white heat and then taken out of boiling water and applied as indicated, to fail to recover.

Is the point clear? I am using that hot brick as a means of suggestion. Aside from the therapeutic value of heat and moisture, this harmless palliative resource is used to substitute sense impressions that are pleasant and comfortable in the place of existing ones that are distressing. **This enables my oral suggestion,** strongly and emphatically driven in upon his consciousness, to call myriads of living cells in his organism into helpful, useful and active service.

In a crisis like this the entire picture of the disease is changed by the personality of the physician.

CHAPTER XXI.

THE BRUTALITY OF FRANKNESS.

HONESTY IMPERATIVE.

A physician who fully appreciates the influence exerted by suggestion upon the mind and the influence exerted by the mind over the physiological processes of the body, will habitually give a more favorable prognosis than the one who does not appreciate the potency of such measures.

Every physician who has successfully practiced medicine for a few years has observed instances where the family of a sick member, upon becoming aware of the attending physician's grave prognosis, has insisted upon having a consultant, who, upon his advent in the sick room, has taken a more hopeful view of the patient's chances for recovery, and at once a marked improvement has begun, which has not abated until complete restoration to health has been secured.

A medical man in the West related this experience: He was once called to see an Indian chief, seriously ill with an acute double, lobar pneumonia, with high fever and severe pain. **After a careful examination,** he frankly and honestly made it known to the family of the sick warrior that in his opinion he could not get well and would have to die. **The brave old chief** did not so easily take his suggestion to die, and he refused to accept the physician's services, continuing to take a well-known Indian remedy, to render him less conscious of his suffering, and while surrounded by weird noises and dances and other savage ceremonies, the recuperative powers of the cells of his organism were allowed to assert themselves, and he made a safe recovery.

To this day that tribe of Indians refuse to accept the services of physicians, having had the strong conviction implanted that the white man's medicine is unreliable.

A gentleman of my acquaintance was sick for many months with chronic interstital nephritis, probably of alcoholic origin, and a competent pathologist found large quantities of tube casts in his urine, which bore a large percentage of albumin, and with his report gave his opinion that the prognosis was grave. **His attending physician** and also a consultant, gave him no encouragement. He was persuaded to take an infusion of some kind prepared by an illiterate farmer who was strongly convinced that this would effect a cure.

His physicians allowed the harmless experiment, to satisfy his patient, who was eager to try anything that offered a possibility of recovery. **With every dose** of the infusion, however, he became more influenced by the farmer's conviction of his recovery, and he began to improve from the time he commenced the remedy, till within a year was able to attend to business.

All cases of degenerative kidney disease are not necessarily fatal, but he was steadily growing weaker all the while until he began the farmer's prescription, which probably benefited him more through its psychic influence than otherwise.

I was called some years ago in consultation to see a little boy ten years of age, possibly infected with malaria at first, but he also had a sub-acute gastro-entero-colitis. He had been sick for nearly two weeks and was still having frequent, watery, mucous discharges from his bowels, and had, for thirty-six hours, vomited everything taken into his stomach. He had a pulse of 150, temperature 100.5°F., pale, weak and anaemic. **His physician** had given him the standard medicinal remedies, as recommended by our best authorities upon children's diseases, and the child was constantly growing weaker. **He had** **notified the family** that the outlook was grave, and was quite willing to adopt any suggestions that I might offer.

I endorsed all his measures, but suggested that they be discontinued, on the grounds that the results did not warrant their further use. **He was anxious** for me to share the responsibility of the situation and readily consented that 1-30 grain calomel only be given every hour while the patient was awake.

Sitting by the bedside, I dipped my fingers in a bowl of ice water and began gently to stroke the little sufferer's forehead. I was alone with him at the time while the attending physician was out of the room with his mother, giving orders for the day. **By the time they returned** to the sick room I had suggested the patient into a refreshing sleep, and had also given him other suggestions, appropriate to his condition. **That he should be** **asleep** was somewhat of a surprise to his mother, whose anxiety and nervousness had served to keep him from doing as well as he would possibly have done had she been more self-composed.

" **Will you do me the favor,** Mrs. Blank, to take that bowl away from the bedside, and remove all towels from the bed also?" I asked.

" Why, doctor, the child would vomit all over his bed and also on my floor," responded she.

" **Madam, take the bowl away** and cover your floor and his bed with newspapers, and if he vomits one time, put them back.   He will rest well to-day and sleep most of the time. You will have to awaken him to give the tablets, but that will quiet his stomach and keep him from vomiting again.   **Keep the room absolutely quiet,** allowing no conversation at all to disturb him.   Allow him to drink all the water he wishes when you give the tablet, to quiet his stomach and make him sleep. **He will want some chicken and barley broth** to-morrow, and if Doctor Blank says so, I think he will enjoy it."

The mother looked queer, but removed the bowl and towels.   I also requested her to tell him to go to sleep when she gave the tablets.

The little patient rested well that night, and when we returned again the next day, his face brightened and he smiled as he bade us good-morning.

" **Oh, he is so much better,**" exclaimed his mother, "and he is begging for something to eat."   He improved every day and went on to recovery in due time.

Every word spoken by me to that mother while the child was asleep was a suggestion, an indirect suggestion, which is always the most powerful kind.

Even a child four years old appreciates sense impressions, or suggestions made upon his brain cortex, far more than is realized by people and physicians in general.   **A little boy** of my knowledge, four years of age, was sick with an acute capillary bronchitis, and his father, who was a physician, felt much concerned about him.

His mother, as was her custom, at bedtime began to have him recite his infant's prayer, and after her the child repeated: " Now I lay me down to sleep, I pray the Lord my soul to keep, if I should—"—there he began to have a paroxysm of coughing, and when he could speak again, he said, **" Mamma, mamma, I don't want to say any dying prayer,** I want to say a living prayer, like that papa told you."

The substitute for the standard orthodox style of prayer had been learned from one of the current journals and went as follows:

." Now I lay me down to sleep,

I know the Lord my soul shall keep,

And I shall wake to see the light,

For God **is with me** all the night."

To satisfy the child and his mother, the father said, " Yes, my boy, we don't want a dying prayer, when we are sick at least," and he repeated the substitute, the child saying it after him, and then went quietly to sleep.

If an ignorant Indian chief, that child of the plains, and **a little four year old boy,** can appreciate a living prognosis and a living prayer, so are all men and women influenced by sense impressions or suggestions that a gloomy prognosis produces, with its weakening, paralyzing, inhibitory influence to all the nerve centers.

It is a physician's duty first, last, and all the time, to do that which will help the patient to get well.

There are many instances where, in a case of extreme illness, **the only help** that can be given a patient is to inspire him with hope, encouragement and optimism, allaying his fears, and bringing about those conditions necessary for the physiological processes ·to accomplish the work of restoring the patient to health.

By the influence exerted upon the mind, we encourage all the physiological processes, and thus, through them, convert potential energy into dynamic energy. We help the cells of the body to accomplish their work of fighting the etiological factors of disease, whether due to pathogenic germs or to other factors.

Physicians have frequently reminded me, in discussing this phase of our subject, that they have repeatedly witnessed a rapid lessening of the resistive powers and speedy death, as soon as they rendered an unfavorable prognosis, given frankly and honestly in response to the question, " Doctor, do you think I am going to get well ? "

If a patient who is extremely ill has important business matters in mind that are worrying him, let them be arranged to his satisfaction, upon the ground that it will help him to get well.

To such questions as " Am I going to die ? " you can evade a direct answer by giving one that will be perfectly satisfactory to your patient, and at the same time will create sense impressions that will set up a different line of thought.

I prefer so to impress my patient that such an idea will never come into his mind, and, also to engage the services of every member of his family to help me to accomplish this result, while on the outside I take them into my confidence and express my opinion to them honestly and frankly.

Even in a case of acute multiple neuritis with high fever, intense pain, hyperaesthesia and great tenderness, in which the disease reached its height in ten or twelve days, I was enabled to maintain a mental stoicism that was remarkable, and at the time of the patient's most distressing symptoms, he repeated back to me the suggestion that I had so often iterated to him. **I had so often** said to him, " You will get better," that he began to ask for the suggestion by saying, " I will get better, won't I, doctor? " **It was some months** before he was able to go about on crutches, but I never let him get away from the conviction of recovery.

At the time of the Galveston flood an unfortunate man was picked up perfectly helpless, in a half drowned, wounded condition, and for six months lay in bed wearing a plaster cast for a severe injury to his spine. **Two years later** he was hobbling on crutches, which he had been using for many months, but he was unable to get his hands to the floor and rise again without support. **He was in constant pain,** had numerous functional disturbances, insomnia, indigestion, frequent movements from his bowels, headaches, etc.

When I saw him I felt that possibly his nervous system was retaining impressions after the results of the physical injury which caused his pain, disturbances of locomotion, and other symptoms, had been removed; and, at the request of his physician, I gave him three suggestive treatments, using hypnotism as a means to secure the most effective results.

All his symptoms were relieved, including his indigestion and bowel complications, after three or four treatments; he put aside his crutches, and a week after the last treatment was comfortable and happy.

In all classes of practice the therapeutic value of suggestions, strongly put into the brain plasm of your patient, will help him to get well where recovery is impossible.

In some classes of work all that a physician can accomplish for the patient is to help him to endure his physical disabilities. This includes such cases as where the organic structure of the nerve cells is involved, atrophic changes have taken place in the spinal cord or any other parts of the motor nervous system, as well as inoperable pathological conditions, resulting from malignant disease, tuberculosis, and all such cases as are beyond the pale of recovery.

Even in these cases, however, we can use suggestive measures to enable the patient better to endure his sufferings, and do so, without the aid of hypnotism, much to the comfort of both the patient and his family.

In two cases of malignant disease—in one case, of the uterus, —in another, of the stomach—occuring in two people above the age of sixty, I kept them each so cheered by constantly holding before their attention a contemplation of their past lives which had been filled with usefulness, of duty done and successful achievement in their own humble way, and so pointed out the moral heroism that they were displaying and the value of such an example of cheerfulness and optimism, that they were enabled to meet **that sweetest and most welcome of all relievers of pain** and suffering under such existing conditions, death, with hardly a word of complaint.

If our patients have sufficient recuperative powers to give even the slightest hope of recovery, let us strengthen that hope and help them to get well.

If they are ill with incurable diseases, we should help them to endure their suffering, all the while working for their recovery even without the slightest ray of hope to encourage us. **Thousands and thousands** of such efforts have been rewarded by the recovery of apparently incurable patients.

A million years of advancement and progress will not have rendered our most expert diagnosticians sufficiently competent to prognosticate with infallibility, in all cases, against the determined and persistent effort of the truly alive physician who will stand up with all odds against him and fight for the recovery of his patient with every available therapeutic resource.

Absolute honesty and sincerity, under all circumstances are imperative to the self-respecting physician, but the weakening, paralyzing, discouraging frankness of the pessimist is brutal.

CHAPTER XXII.

PHYSICAL AND MENTAL HYGIENE.

The care and training of the body is the first step toward self-development. Other things being equal our most successful men in all professions are those of strong, vigorous physiques.

The sooner that every individual comes to realize that his physical anatomy is the most valuable piece of property that he will ever own, and that its proper care and preservation will, in a very large measure, determine his success and happiness in life, the better will he be prepared to guard against those abuses that dwarf its growth and development.

Children should be taught that the power and privilege is theirs to maintain and preserve the body as an instrument of health, strength and beauty. It is so often the case that the physical man or woman of the future is dwarfed and ruined by its misuse in childhood.

Morality itself is the result of environment and education, and many children and young people make blunders that maim them for life, weakening body and mind on account of the failure of the parents to instruct their children earnestly and seriously concerning the laws of procreation and reproduction. **In their ignorance** they are the easy victims of self-pollution and vice that leads to the consequences that fill hospitals, insane asylums and penitentiaries. Here also is the source of frequent suicide, **divorce,** murder, disease and death.

[22]

To send children to church and leave all moral guidance to its influence is not sufficient. **It may appear beautiful** to teach a boy to sing "There is sunshine in my soul today," but we who have seen the miserable mental depression and physical suffering resulting from gonorrhea and syphilis contracted by unthinking youths, know that it is far wiser to talk to them plainly about the sexual functions and to give them that knowledge that every boy is so eager to receive, and thus save him from the pitfalls that lurk in his path by an earnest appeal to his reasoning faculties.

Many people look with disapproval upon any effort to solve the question of social vice. They pride themselves in their ignorance and call this purity. **Violations of natural laws** in innocence and ignorance, however, are attended with the same penalty as other crimes of misconduct.

If suggestion is of value anywhere it is in such cases as these, upon the principle that an ounce of prevention is worth a pound of cure. **To teach children to pray** "Give us this day our daily bread" and not show them how to work for it is criminal neglect. **To have them sing** "We will walk in the light" and not forewarn them of the consequences of physical degradation and vice is mockery and deceit.

In early childhood is the time that we can plant sense impressions or suggestions upon the soft tablets of their brain plasm and so form habits of thought and action that will make them conquerors in life. **The evil consequences** of vice to the development of both mind and body should be explained to children and constantly iterated and repeated by those responsible for their care and training.

They should be made to feel that every part of their body was created for a purpose and that function should be carefully explained to them. **They should not be allowed** to become ashamed of their procreative organs, but should be taught to regard their care and preservation as a sacred trust, and that upon that care and preservation their future happiness will largely depend.

They should be taught the necessity of thorough cleanliness to prevent the consequences of irritating secretions that so frequently lead to masturbation.

To let a girl know that the passions that she experiences are the same that prompted the marriage of her own sweet mother and the act which culminated in her own birth, is to plant knowledge that is power that will be manifested in the production of character and pure womanhood.

Tell her that the passions that she experiences are given by the same animating power that causes the flowers to bloom in spring and the birds to sing in summer and let her know that these signs of awakening sexual life are Nature's call to her to be prepared for the responsibilities of motherhood.

Let her know that such passions are but an evidence of energy that seeks to find expression in her life and conduct, and that such energies can, by reason and will, be turned into intellectual and physical development.

The sexual impulse is in essence the same impulse that finds expression in music, poetry, literature and art.

It is the primal impulse that gives rise to the preservation of the species and creates the home, in which the little ones of earth are nurtured and protected.

It is the impulse that gives rise to educational institutions and to forms of government.

It finds expression in mechanical arts, invention and navigation.

It has manifested itself in the discovery of new countries, the clearing of the forests, the building of cities and the construction of railroads.

It is the impulse that gives rise to all the achievements of science and the birth of all philosophies and religions.

It is the instinctive impulse that has prompted human activity in all ages, which was formerly ascribed to an anthropo-morphic deity.

This awakening sexual life in boys and girls is an evidence of physical energy that can, by wise and judicious suggestion, be directed into deeds of usefulness as varied as the vocations of man.

It can be turned into channels of intellectual and physical development. **In wholesome employment,** in work of all kinds, in outdoor sports and exercises and **in mental and physical action;** in a thousand ways can this sexual energy, under the guidance of reason, find expression.

It is about the time of puberty that every healthy normal boy or girl feels an impulse to do something. This impulse can be expended in self-abuse or sexual intercourse or emotional religious worship to the great harm of both mind and body—in prostitution pure and simple.

But show a boy or girl how to convert or direct his or her energies that are seeking to manifest themselves, in useful and healthful lines of employment for the development of both mind and body, and the result is healthy, happy, self-reliant, virile men and capable women.

All strong characters of all ages are and have been strongly sexed. **A vigorous sexual nature** is the logical accompaniment of a great intellect and a strong healthy body.

What boys and girls, men and women, need is to know how to convert and direct their energies into useful channels of thought and conduct, and not to prostitute them in worry, emotion, passion, self-abuse, sexually as well as from whisky and tobacco, and in a hundred ways that lead to weakness, illiteracy, degeneracy, disease, poverty, crime, divorce, suicide and death.

Properly conserved and directed, however, the same sexual instinct produces men and women strong, capable and free in body and mind.

Many of our patients need to be taught how to direct their lives into natural and healthful channels of thought and action, as well as to have remedial measures that will help to correct the physical disability which has already been incurred on account of their own indiscretion.

Here is a young man who did not have the proper instructions upon the lines indicated. For several years he was a victim of self-pollution, and finally when he attempted to stop his disgusting habit, he was annoyed by nocturnal emissions. **It is**

the same old story. Quack literature fell into his hands, which unduly exaggerated his symptoms and suggested "loss of manhood," and planted fear into his mind. **He is unable to sleep,** all bodily functions are disturbed, his physical condition is below par, he is unable to concentrate his mind upon his studies or his business. **He feels a great sense of unworthiness** in the presence of the pure young woman that he would wed, but for his miserable psycho-neurotic condition, and this unduly aggravates his despondency and morbidness.

If he falls into the hands of an advertising quack who guarantees a cure, he is bled to the utmost of his financial ability. **But he comes to you.** Tactfully you draw him out upon every phase of his case. You assure him that every uninstructed boy was once the innocent victim of such habits and allay his fears of going insane. **You explain to him** that such practices are of themselves harmless, aside from the useless waste of energy that should have been directed into normal channels of physical and mental development and the loss of self-respect which it has caused him. **You advise a liberal, wholesome vegetable diet,** with meat but once a day, and plenty of water to encourage elimination, systematic physical exercise, deep breathing, etc., but above all, **by suggestion you drive back the morbid sense impressions** and substitute new ones in their stead by your own persuasiveness and encouraging optimism. **You appeal to the highest and best** that is in him, and show absolute confidence in the outcome, but insist upon a rigid conformity to your instructions.

You further advise him against testing his potency with a prostitute, and if he has taken such steps to prove the correctness of his own opinions as regards his impotency, you assure him that his failure to cohabit with such a creature only proves the highest type of manhood. **You see him often enough** to build up his physical and mental constitution and to establish wholesome habits of thought and action.

Such cases are attended with excellent results where the quality of brain plasm is such as to get a reaction from the sense impressions or suggestions made upon it.

Children should be so trained that their habits of thought and action during the first twenty-five years will produce strong bodies, clear minds and buoyant, happy spirits. **The best development** comes in the unconscious exercise of a child's faculties in wholesome endeavor and useful employment, such as will call both mind and body into action.

CHAPTER XXIII.

SUGGESTION IN EDUCATION.

The prime purpose of education is to equip the individual to make the struggle for existence.

More than ever before do we now realize that this necessitates the development of the body as well as the mind; that body, mind, and character, are all qualities of the one individual and that it is practically impossible to elevate one quality while the others are weak or degraded.

The problems of health concern all that contributes to the evolution of the individual, physically, mentally and morally.

The capacities and capabilities of the body should occupy more consideration in our educational system than is done at the present time. **When education or religion** interferes with the physical development of children, it strikes a weakening blow at the quality of brain plasm possessed by the child, and to obtain the best results in mental development, this should be kept at a high standard. **Moreover, any factor** that retards physical growth and development, while education is enforced, seriously jeopardizes the life of the individual, and our American cities have thousands of physically weak, neurasthenic boys and girls who have been maimed for life under the strain of the existing educational methods.

Everyone should be environed by those conditions that maintain the highest standard of protoplasmic energy during the period of childhood and adolescence. **The impressions that are**

made upon the brain through the senses from the cradle to the grave are the suggestions that constitute the education of an individual. **Here those that are useful** and good, or harmful and false, are alike recorded, to furnish foodstuff for the mind, which is manifested in thought and conduct.

School training, after all, consists only in furnishing an environment in which certain suggestions, ideas, mental pictures, concepts, or impressions, can be photographed on the rapidly developing cerebral cells. **Here consciousness itself is evolved,** habits are formed and a new world is opened to view as the child's perceptive powers are strengthened and individuality begins to assert itself.

While a certain quality of physical traits and habit tendencies is transmitted to the offspring, by far the most potent factors in making children what they are are the inherited environmental conditions which bring to bear upon the child their unconscious suggestive influences. **What we are** is largely the result of what we have experienced in life. **Habits of thought,** traits of character, religious beliefs, moral convictions, etc., are all directly the result of impressions that have been registered upon our cerebral cells. **Environment** contributes both to our physical and mental constitutions.

In the slums of one of our great American cities I noticed a little two-year-old child, without shoes and bare-headed and dirty, in ragged clothes that scarcely covered its poorly nourished body; **reared in filth and poverty,** with a drunken father to abuse its weak-faced mother who tolerated her pitiable state of existence because she did not know any better. **Had she been**

taught to work, and to think and do for herself, she could easily have extricated herself from this miserable role.

That a child born under such conditions should become a prostitute, contract disease, and die before she was scarcely out of her teens would be as natural as the law of gravitation.

A girl whose father at the time of her birth was occupying the position of president of a great college and who was reared in the lap of education and refinement, could have been nothing else than the mathematical resultant of the parallelogram of the forces that environed her.

A little child of my knowledge was taken at six months old by a couple of kind-hearted people who provided it with all the physical necessities of life. They saw in this little one latent possibilities and potentialities that could be developed and trained into active, useful service, and they enjoyed watching its growth. **They said she was beautiful** and the child smiled and cooed and grew more beautiful. They informed their friends that she was smart and every day reminded the little one of this belief in her, and, at an early age, she did all sorts of useful service. **They said that she was good and obedient,** and true to the law of suggestion, they moulded those very qualities in her. They loved to listen to **her merry prattle** and she early acquired a vocabulary of words to express her ideas.

Later, when she started to school, they believed that she would excel in her classes, and she led in every study. They encouraged her efforts to imitate her foster mother **in cooking,** and, though she soiled her clothing and wasted material, they were pleased, and she soon became an expert cook. **They appreci-**

ated her efforts at the piano, and she developed into a talented musician.

Still later in life she married, and was the pride and helper of her husband, and an honored woman in her community.

Such was the culminating force of suggestion in the home life in its influence upon the life and character of a motherless waif. **Who can dispute the saying** that " men and women make men and women " ?

" You are a bad boy, just as bad as you can be, and I will never let you come down town with me again," said a mother to her little six-year-old, who was the impersonation of the character that his mother had exhibited for him every day of his life.

Children are usually just what their parents make them.

A little four-year-old boy was playing on the floor with his fifteen-months-old baby sister, and he impulsively jerked some of his toys from her baby hands, and she in turn began to cry. **The mother,** who was quietly sewing nearby, witnessed the incident and looked up serenely, and in a subdued tone, called young America to her. **He sulked up to her** with a face that indicated that his rights were being transgressed, and he was not disposed to stand for it.

" Kiss me, my boy," said she, while she implanted a kiss upon his forehead. She then good naturedly placed her fingers under his chin, and with his face upturned to hers, quietly said to him, **" You are mamma's little man,** you are a good boy. **Yes, you are; you are a good boy,** and I know you are going to be just as sweet to your little sister as you can be. She is a little baby, but you **are a little man.** Now, I am going to see if you aren't."

In a few moments the mother looked up again and her little son had piled all the toys he could find around his sister, and now sat upon the floor, looking first at her and then at his mother, trying in vain to suppress his delight in his mother's approval which he seemed sure he would get. **" I told you so; come and kiss me again,"** said she, making a quick move as if to catch him while he dodged from the room with a joyous ha! ha!

The greatest factor in the education of a child, and the most important element in the development of character in children is the confidence that we show them; for the confidence reposed by others in us determines the estimate that we place upon ourselves. **To believe in a child** is to beget self-confidence in that child.

After we are older, and have more experience in the world, we are able to excuse ignorance and we only crave the confidence of the best people; **by this** we estimate ourselves, but in children the love and confidence and expressed appreciation of those nearest and most closely related, is the most powerful factor in the development and growth of all the latent elements of manhood and womanhood.

Children easily enter into sympathy with those with whom they are constantly associated, and the blighting influence of a home in which violent displays of temper are made or hysterical conduct in any form is exhibited, is harmful to both the mental and physical development of children. Here they unconsciously acquire habits that frequently last them through life.

In the use of suggestion upon children for the correction of vice and the cure of evil habits, moral perversions, etc., both with and without hypnotism, no rule can be given that will apply to all children alike. **One must know children** and deal with each one according to his or her own individuality, first securing their confidence. They are very suggestible without hypnotism, and easily come under any influence by those who have their confidence.

In one of our large cities a revival meeting was conducted by an advertising revivalist, under the auspices of several of the leading orthodox churches, and his text for seven days was " Hell, the kind of place it is and who is going there."

The physicians of that city were more than ordinarily busy during this period, on account of the psycho-neurotic condition induced by the fear that such preaching had implanted in the minds of unthinking men and women.

At one of their special services for children, held by the revivalist during the latter part of his stay in that city, only " workers " were invited, besides the children, thus securing such an environment and suggestive influence that hundreds of children, who were incapable of thinking and reasoning for themselves, were coerced into joining the church. **Under these circumstances children are unconsciously** moulded into a particular line of religious belief which but reflects the opinions of their parents or the makers of their church creed, and under this influence they are reared and educated. **The power of**

choice is denied them, and they grow into manhood and womanhood stamped as if they were so many bricks.

We might as well expect to make a race horse out of a colt
that had been imprisoned in a stable all his life, as to expect
children reared under such an environment to become broad-
minded, truth-loving men and women. As self conscious,
independent entities, they are not allowed to think for themselves, and failing to exercise their intellectual faculties their
minds become dwarfed and useless. How many people are
born and reared under such an enforced environment from
which they are never able to extricate themselves! They
acquire a one-sided way of seeing things, and such mental processes continuously indulged in, form habits, and such mental
habits form fixed anatomical grooves or channels in the brain
plasm to the extent that it becomes impossible for the individual
to think or believe any other way.

Mental faculties are mainly acquired and are the product
of environment and education. Chief among these are memory,
imagination, speech, knowledge, conception, judgment, will
and reason.

Reason is mankind's highest, truest, noblest faculty, but
it is only able to draw conclusions from the light of experience.

Many advanced thinkers believe that " the will is higher
than the mind, and that its rightful prerogative is to govern and
direct the mind just as it is the prerogative for the mind to
govern and direct the body." This seems to be true when we
see an individual using his entire mental equipment at a given
salary to promulgate a fixed religious dogma, or when " a

lawyer receives a retainer and commands his mind forthwith to busy itself with all its resources of reasoning and persuasion for the party who pays him. **Even his emotions from the extremes of pathos** to those of indignation may be pressed into the service as well."*

There are others who deny that there is such a faculty as " will " who take the position that mankind **is impelled to action by desire and held in restraint by fear,** and between desire and fear each human being stands.

Yet even will, desire and fear are only qualities of the individual body and mind and they conform to the general law of evolution, being the outcome of heredity, environment and education.

The logical conclusion, then, is that each human being is what he is, by the operation of the same infallible law that moves the earth around the sun, and that holds the stars in their places.

People mean to do well. They are seeking happiness **as best they know how,** according to their instinctive impulses inherent within the protoplasmic mechanism of the physical organism, modified or guided by knowledge and experience.

Some of the greatest, noblest, truest characters that exist in the world to-day are clergymen, who are so far in advance of the creed of the church under whose jurisdiction they are laboring, that they have become a law unto themselves. **They have been impelled by desire** to do that which is right, and

---

* Thompson: "Brain and Personality."

useful, and true, until they are found standing in orthodox pulpits, fearlessly doing all within their power to liberate men and women from the tyranny of creeds and dogmas, ignorance and superstition, through which all creeds have been evolved. **They are interpreting the problems of life** in the light of present-day knowledge and eagerly seeking the contributions shed upon the pathway of human endeavor and achievement by the light of science.

"**To live by science** requires intelligence and faith, **but not to live by it** is folly."

Men stand where they are in the world to-day held by the tyranny of fear and ignorance, unless liberated by knowledge and experience. **Frequently physicians,** who stand high in the medical profession, have said to me frankly and honestly that they felt the necessity of a more thorough knowledge of the theories and methods of using psycho-therapeutics, but they "were afraid their practices would be ruined if the people should find it out." **When such men are teachers** in our medical colleges, their pupils bear the stamp of moral weakness upon their professional characters. **They are the legitimate product** of weakness and fear as manifested in the personality of a physician.

On the other hand, the output of the majority of our medical schools **does not stand in the slavery of fear** because their faculties are constituted of men who were open minded and fearless.

A most valuable part of education is the incentives and intellectual ideals implanted through personal association.

CHAPTER XXIV.

MORAL STAMINA—A THERAPEUTIC POWER.

As we learn to discriminate between people of other classes presumably of like character and qualities, so do we also with physicians—there are among medical men some who, in the true sense of the word are not physicians at all. Here is a type of the latter class.

One day in speaking of the importance of the **psychological factor in therapeutics** with a physician, he said, "Well, there may be something in that; for not long since I had a patient who lay in bed a little over three months, and I could not find a thing the matter with her, but I never tried to exercise any influence over my patients in any way. **They expect medicine,** and I give it to them, and let them use their own minds to suit themselves. I am not in the profession for my health, and a man is liable to **lose out with his patients** by being too dictatorial."

"**How often** did you see her, doctor?"

"Twice a day."

"And you let her stay in bed **three months,** saw her twice a day, and did not even tell her that there was no reason for her staying in bed, and **advise** that she get up and move about, take exercise, get fresh air and take an interest in the affairs of life, both as a means of happiness and for her physical well-being?"

"No, she was a **very sensitive** woman, and I hated to hurt her feelings," he replied.

"**What was your bill** in that case, doctor?"

" Four hundred and eighty dollars."

" **And you are not afraid to hurt her feelings** with that sized bill?"

"Oh, no, she was **quite well satisfied** and paid it without a murmur."

" Why, doctor, if I saw no reason for that woman staying in bed and having me visit her **twice a day** I would as leave take money from off a dead man's eyes as receive pay for such work."

" That is **just the difference** between us," said he.

And it was. And this illustrates a type of men everywhere who call themselves physicians.

Some physicians are actually convinced that they have done their duty when they have been **kind, sympathetic, and attentive** to their patients and prescribed for them medicinally. **Since their patients are satisfied** they seem to feel that they have done their whole duty. **So long as there is money in the case,** the recovery of the patient does not seem to concern them.

The absolute lack of moral courage displayed by this class of doctors, who upon the surface give the appearance of being honest and conscientious professional gentlemen, is horrible to contemplate. **They use narcotics freely,** even when contra-indicated, inhibiting the normal physiological processes, **robbing their patients of self-reliance,** rendering them absolutely dependent upon the physician, lessening in every way their resistive powers, and actually retarding recovery. **We all have seen such men** who in the spirit of cold commercialism impress by word and conduct on their patients that they are very sick, when this attitude on the physician's part has proved to be a great causative factor in the case. Their patients, after a long illness, consider that their physician, in having impressed on them that such would be the case, has only displayed his knowledge and good judgment; whereas, in fact, this man in whom they have trusted has really been the greatest causative factor in the case.

Some physicians acquire a high reputation by giving a gloomy prognosis, thereby instilling fear into the minds of both patients and friends, bringing to bear upon them all the psychological conditions possible to depress them and hypnotize them into a long siege of illness. **The power and efficacy of suggestion,** in the cause and cure of disease, are but faintly appreciated by **one in a thousand of the people** of our time; hence their easy gullibility by such men. **The student of psychotherapeutics** can discern this class of physicians everywhere, who often stand high in the medical profession.

If I were to tell you that in a room I had a servant ever able and willing to obey my dictation or orders and execute them, in having everything in that house just as I wanted it, so could you form some idea about **the power of the great involuntary nervous system** in its control over the bodily functions. We influence this involuntary nervous system by the **sense impressions we make upon the brain plasm** of the patient whenever we come into his or her presence.

Fully nine-tenths of an individual's **psychic powers or protoplasmic energies** are subconscious; that is, he—the intellectual man—is unconscious of them. **These we can influence** for the good or harm of our patient. The physician who shakes his head, and gives a high-sounding name of the disease, often fastens the condition stronger upon his patient, **by adding a psycho-neurotic element** when there is no pathological basis for the condition named existing.

A lady of my acquaintance had been sick for several months and her physician took with him to see her a consultant who appreciated the psychic element in therapeutics. Together in the consulting room they discussed this case:

"**What is the matter** with her, doctor?

"Just weak and nervous, can't sleep, does not eat, discouraged, and getting worse every day."

The consulting physician quickly saw that the attending physician was the **most aggravating causative factor** in this case.

"Why does not she get better," said he to the consultant.

"**Because you don't talk and act right.**"

"What must I do and how should I talk?"

"Why, give her a sleeping capsule, and tell her that you are going to give her a good night's sleep. Then turn to the nurse and say, '**Give one of these sleeping capsules** at eight o'clock and if she is not sleeping soundly by nine, give her another, but **in no event** give her more than two, **she will sleep sound all night.**' **Say it as if you meant it.** Say it as if _you_ had not the slightest doubt about it. **Then, turning to the patient,** say 'You are going to sleep well to-night and will feel much better in the morning.'

"When you come to see her to-morrow, smile pleasantly as you walk into the room and, as you bid her good-morning, take her hand, and feeling her pulse affirm: '**You are better.**' Tell her she will improve every day now. Say to her, 'You will enjoy your food today and not be nervous and will feel much stronger; you are going to get well; **going right along to recovery.' Keep this up** as you see her at every visit.   **Getting in behind** a neurasthenic case like this with all the bodily functions perverted, you can stir latent energies and stimulate nervous centers into activity and be a factor for good."

The physician did so and his patient was soon well.

Too many physicians are nothing more than **slaves to their own desires.   They see** in their patient's illness a **chance to make money.**   They feel that they have done their duty when they have prescribed for them in **a perfunctory manner** and, putting their reliance solely in drugs, they overlook entirely the psychologic factor in therapeutics.   **They even tell their patients** that they are seriously sick, purely for personal aggrandizement.

The result is undue nervousness, over anxiety, sleeplessness, perverted functions and constant progress from bad to worse. These symptoms they attempt to relieve by narcotics.   They enter the sick room in this indifferent, half-hearted, **selfish manner** and their efforts are worse than useless.

Such physicians forget that man is a living organism, body, mind and spirit, and the ideal ego should be **the master,** not the the slave, of the body.

See in your patient potentialities that are susceptible to external stimuli, and regard something besides the physical manifestation of the individual.

Treat the man himself, the intelligent organized force—call this mind, soul or spirit—that has simply cast this physical cloak around him and stir him to renew, energize, vitalize and strengthen every part of his physical organism.

What do we stir? Call it what you will, let it be the "vis medicatrix naturae," the "resident energy within," "neuric energy," the "subconscious self," the "involuntary nervous system," the "psychic man," **"spirit," "mind,"** or **"soul," the name matters not. This fact is true.** Man has within him **reserve energy** that can be stirred into activity. **By suggestion the physiological processes** of the body can be influenced for his good. We can produce such impressions upon **his brain plasm** as will quiet nervousness, relieve pain, promote sleep, and acting thus, we can conserve his energy, resulting in a better appetite, better digestion, and improved nutrition. We thus re-establish all the **perverted physiological processes.** By this means you can get your patient well when drugs and other remedial agents absolutely fail.

If medicine or **surgery is indicated,** by all means use it.

The great trouble is that **many of the men** in our profession are ignorant of the potency of the psychologic factor as a therapeutic adjunct. **Some who have had a glimpse** of these latent possibilities lack the moral stamina boldly to take hold and do · their part. I know men who would **face a cannon absolutely devoid of physical fear,** yet too timid and half-hearted in the sick room to do more than give drugs, nine-tenths of which are worse than useless, in this class of **functional** and **neuropathic conditions.**

Many of these sick people need a good, sound, intellectual flogging. They need to be told that they alone are to blame for their condition.   Let them know that **health is a natural condition** and comes to every one who conforms to nature's laws, which they are continually violating every day of their lives.

Emerson has well said that "Man may boast that he can violate the laws of Nature and maintain health; the lie is on his lips, the conditions on his soul."

Let your patient know that to maintain health he must conform to the laws of health.   Get hold of him and put him in possession of himself.   **Urge him** to take into his system plenty of Nature's healthful beverage, pure water, to eliminate impurities from his system and to encourage all functional activity. A man should not drink less than four or five pints of water a day.   **Tell him or her to exercise freely** every muscle and hasten the blood to every part of his system to eliminate effete material as well as to build up, nourish and renew the life and strength of every cell in his body.   **Advise him against** becoming a slave to his appetites, over eating, sexual excess, etc.

Fully nine-tenths of the American people eat **too much meat** and keep their **nervous system overtaxed** to dispose of the amount of food in excess of what is actually necessary for nutrition.   Get such people, when nervous, to **learn to relax** and **to practice deep breathing** as a resource of healthfulness.   Impress upon them the **pleasure, beauty** and **glory** of **work** and useful endeavor and achievement, as a means to invigorate and strengthen both mind and body.   **Let them know** that we are born into this beautiful world surrounded by everything to make us happy and keep us well, but that **the world is ruled by law** and we must conform to laws of health, and that when we do that we shall be well and happy, which is our highest privilege, and not before.

It is often the case that our patients need education and encouragement, knowledge and guidance—other names for suggestion—**and not medicine or sympathy,** which only fixes them **deeper in the mire;** but there are some who are called physicians who **have not the courage** to attempt to make use of these therapeutic measures.

Why let Christian Scientists, osteopaths and other species of charlatanism thrive upon a large class of cases when, if we were but equipped in this higher art in therapeutics, we could day by day infuse health and happiness, joy and sunshine, into the lives of weak, erring, miserable children of this world who are crying to us for help. **Our patients are not merely chemical laboratories,** but human beings with intelligent faculties to comprehend our suggestions that **act upon every part of the body through** the nervous centers. If properly presented they will regulate all perverted functions **in perfect accord with the physiological processes of the body.**

Man is not a machine, but a living organism.

The unseen part of man, mind, spirit or soul, constitute the dynamics of this human organism and they constitute the greatest therapeutic factor at our command, ever present and ready for utilization.

CHAPTER XXV.

SELF-MASTERY AS A FINE ART.

"Man exists......not for what he can accomplish, but for what can be accomplished of him."—Goethe.

By suggestion we can add a dynamic quality to the mental equipment of an individual who is receptive. A new element is given to his personality by the impression made upon his brain plasm, which better equips him to meet the exigencies of life, and whereby he can be educated into the art of self mastery.

A little child, seven years old, was beginning her first day in school and appeared bewildered and confused as she anticipated the new experiences that the day had in store for her. As she started out of the home, her father, who was awaiting the arrival of the right psychological moment, called her to him.

"Papa, mamma says I must hurry or I shall be late," responded the child as she came up closer to find out what her father wanted.

"You have plenty of time, my daughter," said he. "I have a secret to tell you if you will promise not to give it away. Do you know there is **not a smarter child** in this town than you are?"

"No, papa, I did not know that."

"Well, there is not, and I will show you. Who can run faster than you among your little friends?"

"None of them," was her answer.

"Who rides a wheel or plays dolls better than you?"

"None," she answered.

"Well, here is our secret. They cannot learn faster in school than you can. They are all smart, but they don't know it. The girl that does what her teacher tells her is the one that learns the fastest. Now, that is our secret. **You go and find out what your lesson is** and come home and we will help you to study, and by the end of the term you will be at the head of your class."

The child's answer was, "**All right, papa, if you will help me, yes, I will.**"

"**Go to school now,** you have plenty of time, but don't give away our secret."

The child walked away with a new element added to her consciousness. She went with head erect, and a smile on her face that indicated that she was going out to conquer. **Of course,** this was followed by other similar suggestions, and during the **eight years since that time,** that little girl has stood with the head of her classes and found in her school work a genuine pleasure.

In another instance a child, thirteen years of age, was competing for a prize given in elocution. Her father had also offered her a reward and expressed a wish that she win that medal. **She had worked hard to succeed** and upon the morning of the contest the father called her into his den and handed her the promised reward for winning the contest.

"But," said she, "I haven't won it yet."

"See here, daughter," was his response, "**I know, and your teacher knows, that you render that selection aright.** Now, it matters not one bit what the judges or the audience think of it. Go, render your selection to **suit yourself and to do credit to your**

teacher, but forget all about the prize or the opinion of the judges."

She went away relieved of all apparent anxiety and shared the prize with an older contestant.

The question of self-mastery is one of education and self-development. **By suggestion we can plant ideas** that give rise to impulses or incentives within the individual to make effort at self-development, self-education, and self-control.

Every one should be made to feel that he is born to be of use in the world and should be taught how to exercise his capacity, for it is only through the self-reliance gained by our own activities that we can make a success in any vocation in life. **The individual** who can be of most help to others is the one who sees the greatest possibilities within them.

The problem of life for every individual is the one of self-mastery; how best to conserve and direct our energies into useful, wholesome lines of thought and action. **To be of help to others** one must at least in some degree have become master of one's self.

It has been a matter of observation to see a physician so utterly lacking in self-control that he was incapacitated to use efficacious suggestion upon an individual, even after the latter had assumed an attitude of voluntary receptivity. In him **the self-conscious ego** had not been evolved sufficiently to give him force of character to be of influence.

It is for each one of us to decide whether we shall control and govern ourselves in the light of reason, education and experience, or be held by the opinions of others. **To do our best in life** we must be independent, strong, capable and free.

The leaders of all professions in all ages have been men who have overleaped the limitations of environment, of ignorance and superstition, and have dared to stand up for what they believed to be right.

To have achieved self-mastery is to be guided by reason, impelled by truth, and freed from the tyranny of fear, selfishness and ignorance. It denotes courage, humble service, magnanimity, sympathy, friendliness and a tenacious stand for the right. To reach this high ideal of moral attainment human evolution must go on forever. We are as yet in the *amoeba* and *moneron* stage of our appreciation of this higher conception of ourselves and our relation to others.

> "With this poor life, with this mean world
> I'd fain complete what in me lies;
> I strive to perfect this—my me;
> My sole ambition's to be wise."

Fear is the natural consequence of weakness and ignorance.

To be masters of our bodies does not mean that the physical basis of existence is to be ignored. **Far from it. On the other hand,** to maintain a strong, healthy body is the first essential to development. **Will power and determination** are natural accompaniments of a healthy organism.

There is a peculiar psychic quality that is the heritage of some individuals. They are content to drift with the crowd and have not the courage to dare to use their own reasoning faculties. **The problem of education** is to deliver these individuals from such tendencies and thus to prevent them from lapsing into physical weaklings, mental nonentities, or moral cowards.

It is the inalienable birthright of every human being to manifest the highest expression of individuality and selfhood; to give the world **the very best** that he can make of himself according to the limitations of **heredity, environment** and **education.** Fear and selfishness are the greatest barriers to the progress of aspiring humanity.

The "thou shalt" and "thou shalt not" of an irresponsible hierarchy no longer fetters the spirit of the man who has obtained sufficient self-mastery to live up to the light and knowledge of the present age.

But not for ourselves alone must we live. We gain in strength by helping others, by assuming responsibility, by work and useful achievement.

A great deal of the hysteria and neurasthenia and despondency and weakness of men and women is due to their failure to exercise sufficient self-mastery, to use the powers and capabilities inherent within the cells of their organism. Such people we can wonderfully benefit by suggestion.

Medicine will ever have a place in our therapeutic armamentarium, **but its use** to relieve nervousness and psychoneurotic and functional disturbances, by lulling and inhibiting the normal physiological processes, **where the individual should be taught** the art of self-mastery, self-control, self-activity and conformity to such physiological methods of development as breathing, relaxation, dietetics, water drinking, exercise and work, with sunshine, fresh air and cheerfulness, **is a crime.**

The use of suggestion in therapeutics is nothing more or less than getting an individual to exercise self-mastery and self-control.

Here I am reminded of a stalwart man, six feet two inches high, weighing one hundred and ninety-eight pounds, who had a wife and two children in another portion of his State, while he was being supported by his brother, and all the while nursing and encouraging a psycho-neurotic condition. **His physician informed me of this element** of sloth and laziness that was a great factor in his case, besides his morbid self-consciousness, and sought my aid to arouse him from such psychic incumbrances and put him in possession of himself.

He came into the office walking upon a cane, and besides his symptoms of indigestion and insomnia, he complained of a constantly painful and weak back.

Our treatment was to give such suggestions as to drive back his morbid existing sense impressions. To substitute a new consciousness he was placed with head on one chair and heels on another and made to sustain my weight of 200 pounds upon his body. **Then, looking him in the face,** after he was awakened, I imformed him frankly and honestly of the test we had made and assured him that a stronger man did not exist in his State, that all he needed was exercise, and that the right thing for him to do **was to go to work. I met him upon his own plane,** that of a physical laborer, and used such methods as would most convince him that he was a man, **and he appreciated it.** He did go to work and had no farther trouble.

Such harsh treatment is not applicable in private practice, but when I see people whining and complaining and morbidly self-conscious of their own life's battles, I can but wish that they could be aroused in some way and be made to see the pleasure and beauty and glory of work.

Upon the exercise of our own self-activity does the welfare of the future race depend.

The intellectual world brings life's greatest pleasures, but as we now understand it, the head and hands must be educated together. Mental and physical development must go hand in hand.

When wealth causes the individual to depend upon the physical and mental efforts of others to do for him what he should do for himself. it is a means of degeneration and weakness.

It is all a question of mental attitude. We must ever press onward for the acquirement of more knowledge, the discovery of new truths, and for facts revealed by new experiences. We must never be willing to accept as a finality the imperfection of present attainments.

To be glad to live for life's own sake, to love and to help others for the pleasure it gives us, and in our own humble way to crown our lives with useful endeavor and achievement. leaves no excuse for the question, Is life worth while?

It never becomes stale, flat and unprofitable, save as it reflects our own stupidity.

INDEX

THE
DIAGNOSIS AND TREATMENT
OF DISEASES OF
WOMEN

By H. S. CROSSEN, M. D.

Clinical Professor of Gynecology, Medical Department,
Washington University, St. Louis.

816 Pages.   700 Illustrations.   Price, cloth, $6.00; morocco, $7.50.

Sent anywhere prepaid upon receipt of price.

NEW YORK MEDICAL JOURNAL: "This is one of the best works on Gynaecology that we have ever seen. It owes its excellence chiefly, we think, to the fact that its author is able to think of something besides operative measures, showing no contempt for pessaries, but giving indeed a true exposition of their modus operandi and a reasonable rating of their value. The book is strong, however, even in the matter of operations, as is shown in the masterly statements concerning the numerous operations for retroversion of the uterus. Another feature which makes the book of immense value to the general practitioner and to the comparatively inexperienced specialist in Gynaecology is the amount of attention given to diagnosis, to which 308 pages are devoted."

PROVIDENCE MEDICAL JOURNAL: "It is most emphatically the helpmeet of the intelligent General Practitioner, and serves to place before him in a compact and forceful manner the main facts of diagnostic value and to point out the proper therapeutic indications. The manner of exhibiting the remedies applicable to a given condition is carefully set forth and the reason for this usefulness explained. The section on pessaries is of particular value and will be warmly welcomed by the profession, which has long labored under a hazy impression of the proper indication for the use of pessaries, and the principles involved in their selection and application. The author's discussion of retrodisplacements of the uterus is also worthy of particular mention, as setting forth in a simple yet striking manner the cause and treatment, non-operative and operative, of this frequent and badly treated condition. The 700 illustrations scattered throughout the volume are excellent in character and very materially enhance its value."

HOWARD A. KELLY: "It will surely meet the needs of the general practitioner and student, as well as specialist. You have taken such pains to be explicit in so many details of our art."

TODD GILLIAM: "After a careful and much interested examination of your work on gynecology, I want to congratulate you on the text, illustration, arrangement and mechanical make-up of the book. It is unique in its way, and has a field of its own."

DR. ROBERT L. DICKINSON: "You are simple, and practical, and clear That is what men want."

C. V. MOSBY MEDICAL BOOK AND PUBLISHING CO.,
ST. LOUIS, MO.

Golden Rules of Dietetics

By A. L. Benedict, A. M., M. D., Buffalo, N. Y.

416 PAGES **OCTAVO** **PRICE $3.00**

Circular Sent Upon Request.

CONTENTS.
Part I.

Part II.

C. V. MOSBY MEDICAL BOOK AND PUBLISHING CO.
ST. LOUIS, MO.

Golden Rules of Pediatrics

By JOHN ZAHORSKY, A. B., M. D.,

Clinical Professor of Pediatrics, Medical Department,
Washington University, St. Louis, Mo.

362 Pages   Circular sent upon request.   Price, $3.00

CONTENTS

PART I.

General Rules of Diagnosis

General Rules
Loss in Weight.   Appetite
Convulsions
Physical Examination
Head and Neck
Some Deformities
Teeth and Gums.   Dentition
The Enanthemata
Vomiting.   Hematemesis
Diarrhea
Distended Abdomen
Abdominal Pain
Abdominal Swellings
The Nose and Nasopharynx
The Larynx
Anomalies of Breathing, Cough
The Lungs
The Heart and Circulation
The Urine.   The Eruptions
The Nervous System
Paralysis

Tremor, Choreiform Movements.
   Headache, etc.
Changes about the Eyes
Changes about the Ear
Clinical Syndromes
Fever.   Chronic Fever
Status Gastricus
The Typhoid State
Infantile Atrophy
Gastroenteric Infection, Diarrhea
Chronic Indigestion in Older Children
Chronic Constipation
Peritoneal Irritation
Severe Anemia.   Edema
Ascites.   The Adenoid Face
Acute Pneumonic Consolidation
Intestinal Obstruction
Nervous State.   Scrofula
Tuberculosis
Impending Heart Failure

The Syndrome or Cerebral Irritation

Golden Rules of Prognosis

PART II.

Golden Rules of Hygiene and Infant Feeding

The Nursing Mother
The Wet Nurse

Artificial Feeding
Feeding the Sick

Golden Rules of Treatment

General Therapeutics
The Newly Born
Diseases of the Mouth
The Neck and Scalp
The Throat
The Respiratory Organs
Gastroenteric Diseases
Rickets and Scurvy
Heart and Circulation
The Blood
The Genitourinary Organs

The Nervous System
Specific Infectious Diseases
Malaria.   Cerebrospinal Fever
Diphtheria.   Intubation
Tuberculosis.   Pertussis
Mumps.   Septicemia
Rheumatism and Endocarditis
Syphilis.   The Exanthemata
The Severe Infectious Fevers
The Skin
FORMULARY

C. V. MOSBY MEDICAL BOOK AND PUBLISHING CO.
ST. LOUIS, MO.

Diseases of the Skin

...BY...

A. H. OHMANN-DUMESNIL, A. M., M. E., M. D., Ph. D., etc.

Formerly Professor of Dermatology and Syphilology in the St. Louis College for Medical Practitioners; the St. Louis College of Physicians and Surgeons; the Marion-Sims College of Medicine; Member of the St. Louis Medical Society, of the Missouri State Medical Association, of the American Medical Association, of the 1st, 2d, 3d, 4th, 5th and 6th International Dermatological Congress, etc.

THIRD EDITION

THOROUGHLY REVISED AND ENLARGED
150 ORIGINAL ILLUSTRATIONS
600 PAGES. PRICE: CLOTH, $4.00. MOROCCO, $5.50.

PREFACE

This book is not a treatise. The intention has been to make of it a practical guide to the easy recognition of skin diseases, as well as to their successful treatment. The remedies which have been recommended are such as may be found in every practitian's armamentarium medicinorum. No attempt has been made to write an elaborate work, but rather to furnish, in a clear, concise manner, just that information most desired by medical students and general practitioners.

TABLE OF CONTENTS.

C. V. MOSBY MEDICAL BOOK AND PUBLISHING CO.
ST. LOUIS, MO.

Examination of the Ear

By SELDEN SPENCER, A. B., M. D.,

Instructor in Otology, Medical Department, Washington University,
St. Louis, Mo., with an introduction by H. N. Spencer, M. D.,
Professor of Otology, Medical Department, Wash-
ington University, St. Louis, Mo.

65 PAGES - 5 FULL-PAGE PLATES - 12 OTHER ILLUSTRATIONS
PRICE, $1.00

CONTENTS

CHAPTER I.—Methods of Procedure (General consideration).
CHAPTER II.—The External Ear.
CHAPTER III.—Diseases of the Canal.
CHAPTER IV.—The Middle Ear.
CHAPTER V.—The Middle Ear Continued, Non-Suppurative Conditions.
CHAPTER VI.—The Middle Ear Continued, Post-Suppurative Condi-
tions.
CHAPTER VII.—The Middle Ear Continued, Suppurative Conditions.
CHAPTER VIII.—The Middle Ear Continued, Purulent Otitis Media.
CHAPTER IX.—The Middle Ear Continued, Purulent Otitis Media.
CHAPTER X.—The Middle Ear Continued, Operations in Chronic Pur-
ulent Otitis Media.
CHAPTER XI.—The Internal Ear.
CHAPTER XII.—Hearing Tests.
CHAPTER XIII.—Intra-Cranial Complications.
CHAPTER XIV.—Exercises in the Surgical Anatomy of the Temporal
Bone.

Golden Rules of Surgery

By the late A. C. Bernays, A. M., M. D., F. R. C. S.
(England), St. Louis, Mo.

232 PAGES   Portrait circular sent upon request.   Price, $2.50

Contents

The Education of a Surgeon.   Science and Surgery.
About Fees.   Off With the Cloak of Superstition.
On Scientific Communications to the Literature of Medicine and Surgery.
Inflammation and the Confusion it has caused.

Asepsis,	Burns,	Gangrene,	Oesophagus,
Anesthesia,	Breast,	Hand and Foot,	Pelvis,
Abscesses,	Genito-Urinary,	Moist Dressing,	Rectum,
Abdomen,	Operations,	Mouth,	Spine,
Appendicitis,	Joints,	Nose,	Throat,
Aneurysm,	Ear,	Goitre,	Veins,
Artery Bleeding,	Erysipelas,	Shock,	

Can Minor Surgical Operations be done in office.
Death following Minor Surgical Operations,
Fractures and Dislocations,   Therapeutic Hints,
Irrigation Drainage of Abdominal Cavity,
Minor Surgical Operations,   Stomach and Intestines.

C. V. MOSBY MEDICAL BOOK AND PUBLISHING CO.
ST. LOUIS, MO.

A VERY YOUNG OVUM IN SITU

BY

G. LEOPOLD, Dresden, Germany,

AND

W. H. VOGT, A. M., M. D.,

Obstetrician and Gynecologist to the Lutheran
Hospital, St. Louis, Mo.

100 Pages. 35 Lithographic Plates. Price, $3.50.

OFFICE TREATMENT OF RECTAL DISEASES

BY

R. D. MASON, M. D.

Professor of Diseases of the Rectum, Creighton Medical College,
Omaha, Neb.

4th Edition, greatly enlarged, completely reset, many new illustrations.

Price, $2.50.

CHRONIC CONSTIPATION

AETIOLOGY, PATHOLOGY AND TREATMENT

BY

J. A. MacMILLAN, M. D.,

Professor of Therapeutics in the Detroit College of Medicine,
Detroit, Mich.

250 Pages. Price, $2.00

Circular sent upon request.

**C. V. MOSBY MEDICAL BOOK AND PUBLISHING CO.
ST. LOUIS, MO.**

ARTERIOSCLEROSIS

BY

L. M. WARFIELD, A. M., M. D.

Assistant in Medicine, Medical Department, Washington University,
St. Louis, Mo.

With an Introductory Chapter by Dr. W. S. Thayer,
of the Johns Hopkins University.

204 Pages. Price, $2.00.

GONORRHEA IN WOMEN

BY

PALMER FINDLEY, A. M., M. D.

Professor of Genecology, Creighton University,
Omaha, Nebraska.

120 Pages. Royal Octavo. Price $2.00.

TUBERCULOSIS OF THE NOSE AND THROAT

BY

L. B. LOCKARD

Consulting Laryngologist to Agnes Memorial Hospital
Denver, Colorado.

85 Plates; 64 of which are colored.—350 Pages.—Price $5.00.

C. V. MOSBY MEDICAL BOOK AND PUBLISHING CO.
ST. LOUIS, MO.

Printed in the United Kingdom
by Lightning Source UK Ltd.
114959UKS00001B/243